D0346991

Evaluation for Crime Prevention

Nick Tilley
Editor

Crime Prevention Studies
Volume 14

Criminal Justice Press
Monsey, NY

Willan Publishing
Devon, UK

2002

CRIME PREVENTION STUDIES

Ronald V. Clarke, Series Editor

Crime Prevention Studies is an international book series dedicated to research on situational crime prevention and other initiatives to reduce opportunities for crime. Most volumes center on particular topics chosen by expert guest editors. The editors of each volume, in consultation with the series editor, commission the papers to be published and select peer reviewers.

22219668

ISSN (series): 1065-7029
ISBN: 1-881798-35-6 (cloth)
ISBN: 1-881798-36-4 (paper)

TABLE OF CONTENTS

INTRODUCTION: EVALUATION FOR CRIME PREVENTION

by

Nick Tilley
Nottingham Trent University

Evaluation in crime prevention is almost universally called for. It is widely required by funding bodies, and, as a result, it is almost as widely attempted. It is technically very tricky both in relation to specific initiatives (Ekblom, 1990) and in relation to the sorts of partnership approach that are now widely promoted (Rosenbaum, this volume). Critics are agreed that standards are generally very low (Sherman et al., 1997, Ekblom and Pease, 1995; HMIC, 2000; Scott, 2001). There are some fundamental debates about how evaluation should be construed and conducted (Pawson and Tilley, 1997). There are also diverse stakeholders in evaluation, and a range of uses to which evaluations can be put.

The papers in this volume are concerned primarily with the design and conduct of evaluations that are intended to help improve crime prevention policy and practice. Other possible purposes — for example to justify programs, to account for public expenditure, to celebrate achievement, or to encourage greater participation in crime prevention — are not much at issue here.

Much literature on crime prevention has stressed the importance of evaluation for program improvement. The preventive process described by Ekblom (1988), the action research approach advocated by Clarke (1997), and the SARA (scanning, analysis, response, assessment) steps developed by Eck and Spelman (1987) to help operationalise Goldstein's (1979) problem-oriented policing all include evaluation as a key element. The purpose of evaluation in all cases is to provide feedback that will generate corrections to and refinements in crime prevention theory, policy and practice. The University of Maryland report to the United States Congress on evaluations in crime prevention (Sherman et al., 1997) and the British Home Office report on findings of evaluation studies (Goldblatt and Lewis, 1998) were both designed to inform improvements in what was done in an effort to reduce crime. Likewise, the emerging international Campbell Collaboration has a strong criminal justice stream, which promises systematic reviews of crime prevention with the aim of improving the choice of interventions (Farrington and Petrosino, 2001).

The bottom line in evaluation for crime prevention, is of course, crucial. Evaluation results should allow us more effectively and efficiently to lessen crime and its effects, and we need to measure outcomes in these terms. A number of tricky technical challenges confront the measurement of outcome effectiveness. These include, for example, discounting regression-to-the-mean effects, establishing a secure counterfactual, attributing responsibility for observed changes to the measures introduced, identifying active ingredients in packages of measures, identifying short and long-term effects, identifying significant side-effects, and attaching figures to costs and benefits of interventions. Though these technical challenges need to be met adequately if evaluations are to be useful, that is not sufficient. Evaluations need, preferably at the same time, to produce results that can be generalised.

Science, Theory and External Validity

If evaluation findings are to be useful beyond the program to which they relate, they need to enjoy external validity, and traditional "gold standard" methods may not best deliver this. History, crime investigation and auditing are all activities that require rigour but do not require external validity. In history we need to know how particular events of the past unfolded. In crime investigation, we need to know who committed a particular crime or series of crimes. In auditing we need to know what happened to the turnover, profits and losses of a particular enterprise over a particular period. Both history and crime investigation may from time to time use science, where it is helpful. Auditing aspires to be rigorous in its standards and techniques, but has no pretensions to being a science. Science is concerned with making general statements about regularities and about where and how they are produced. It develops theories and rigorously tests hypotheses better to understand how the natural or social world works. Where theories have been sufficiently tested then they can be applied.

To be most useful — to have external validity — evaluations need to go beyond mere technical rigour. They need to be scientific. This means they need to be driven by theories about how and where changes are produced. Moreover these theories need to be tested.

Decisions about the extension, continuation, alteration or cancellation of a program all depend on findings being applicable beyond the particulars of past events in particular places.

There are some corollaries of adopting a scientific approach, which will be very challenging. Science deals in unobservable causal powers (for example natural selection, gravity), that may challenge common sense (Bhaskar, 1974). It does not always use the categories available to common sense. Instead it looks to regularities and causal processes that lie beneath the surface, and on this basis reconstitutes how we classify. Just as post-Darwinian classifications of animals and plants go beyond mere resemblance to look to real distinctions by origins, so too the classification of crime prevention measures will change with a better grasp of how they work. Clarke's classification of crime prevention measures by the ways in which they are deemed to operate is a case in point (Clarke, 1997). It is rooted in a theory of how patterns of crime generation are altered. The policy and practitioner communities, working alongside evaluators, need to learn not to ask crass questions, for example, about whether or not, for example, Neighbourhood Watch or Block Watch "works." The diverse activities that may or may not be involved in what is done in its name, and the multifarious ways in which those activities may impact on crime, make Neighbourhood Watch a convenient common-sense peg, but an inappropriate class for the purposes of science (see Laycock and Tilley, 1995). At least that would be the implication of adopting a scientific approach. Science is often slow, while policy and practice will not wait. Science stresses the uncertain, whilst the rhetoric of policy-making asserts confidently and trades on shared understandings with practitioners and the public.

It is worth remembering that the active ingredients in programs are frequently not self-evident. In the case of street lighting upgrades, for example, the alterations in community confidence triggered by them appear to have been capable of effecting changes in crime, rather than the lighting per se (Painter, 1995). In property marking, the publicity showing resident burglars that crime risks were being increased appeared to be the active ingredient in a South Wales experiment, rather than the property marking per se (Laycock, 1985, 1997). In the case of CCTV, the transmitted pictures appear to be but one of a series of mechanisms through which changes in crime levels can be brought about (Phillips, 1999). In the case of mandatory arrest for domestic violence, the changes effected varied according to contrasting mechanisms that were context-dependent. Mixed findings have been reported for the effects in different cities (see Sherman, 1992). These may be explained by variations in reactions to arrest by those living in different social conditions. Arrest is liable to trigger anger amongst some and shame amongst others. Anger is more likely for those who are unemployed and not attached to stable communities, and shame amongst employed members of stable communities. Anger may precipitate repeat violence and shame inhibit it. Smith et al. (2002) show that many crime prevention initiatives begin to have their effects before they are implemented; the active ingredient is clearly not or not just what is actually put in place. The discovery of diffusion of benefits raises questions about the means by which effects are apparently frequently felt beyond the immediate operational range of measures. Sherman (1990) again furnishes an example in his demonstration of the enduring effects of crackdowns, apparently disrupting crime beyond the time when they are being applied. Each of these examples suggests that surface, lay and policy maker definitions of what comprise key elements in programs can be inadequate and misleading.

The simple association of rate change with a particular measure will be a poor guide to what might usefully be learned and transferred. It is the salient underlying mechanisms triggering the change that are critical: e.g., community confidence, offender uncertainty, heightened perceived risk among offenders, shame, anger and so on. And these more fundamental mechanisms may be triggered in multiple ways by diverse interventions according to context. Evaluations need to tease out the underlying processes to derive practice and policy-relevant lessons. A fixation on surface measures, which may be the overt interest of policy makers, introduces a counterproductive bias overestimating the significance of measures and potentially blinding evaluation studies to the more significant underlying mechanisms. In medicine, the concern with placebos describes a basic effort to sort out physical mechanisms (often tentatively suggested by laboratory and clinical work) from psychological ones. Surface evaluation that simply associates measures with outcomes fails even to make this basic discrimination. We need only to go back to the telephone relay assembly experiments at General Electric's Hawthorne factory to appreciate the difference between direct and indirect mechanisms in producing change (Mayo, 1933; cf., also Smith et al., 2002). There, readers will remember, productivity went up when lighting was increased, but also went up when almost all other changes were introduced. The active ingredient was not the lighting intensity increase per se but the cooperative, self-motivating group brought about by the fact of experimentation. The misleading conclusions that could be drawn for policy without making this distinction are all too obvious. The Hawthorne studies have uncanny echoes in the literature on lighting upgrades and crime (Pease, 1999; Painter, 1995).

Whilst better policy-making and practice may need evaluations that adopt a scientific approach, this will not necessarily initially be popular amongst the policy makers and practitioners we address. Getting good answers entails asking good questions. Good questions are not necessarily the self-evident ones. Colluding with bad questions may win friends in some policy circles. It will not, though, best serve crime prevention and the scientific foundations needed for its improvement.

AN OVERVIEW OF THE FOLLOWING PAPERS

Each of the following papers addresses an important issue in evaluation for crime prevention. They all highlight the potential of well-conducted evaluations to contribute to improvements in policy and practice. They demonstrate the importance of theory both for practice and for evaluation. In particular, they indicate the importance of attending to mechanisms that may produce change or inhibit it. Moreover, they show too a need to be sensitive to the contexts in which crime prevention strategies are developed and measures are put in place. They show that practitioners and policy makers are theory users, and that they can become more effective with better theories and with their better application. They also show how evaluation can help bring theories to the surface, test them and feed findings back either during the lifetime of a project or for future programs. In these ways, the papers published here all constitute efforts to show how scientific evaluation can be conducted in the interest of policy and practice improvement.

Niall Hamilton-Smith takes the knotty issues of displacement of crime and diffusion of crime prevention benefits as unintended consequences of the introduction of crime prevention measures. (Displacement is the relocation of crime from the prevention program project area to neighboring districts. Diffusion occurs when the benefits of a crime prevention program spill over from the project area to neighboring districts.) He treats these as both measurement problems for the evaluator and as practical issues to be addressed by those trying to prevent crime. He shows that the research literature is helpful in shaping our expectations about likely patterns of displacement and diffusion. He also shows that local thinking can usefully be drawn upon in applying this knowledge in specific settings. The implication of his arguments is that in different contexts different patterns of displacement and diffusion of benefits should be expected. Members of the research community therefore need to develop informed hypotheses about potential displacement and diffusion of benefits following the introduction of preventive interventions, and to adopt bespoke measurements to test the hypotheses. Practitioners need to develop their preventive strategies to minimize unwanted but predictable displacement, and to maximize potential diffusion of benefits. Hamilton-Smith highlights the importance of theory in both practice and evaluation. He shows that the theory needs to focus both on the mechanisms through which displacement and diffusion of benefits are brought about and the particular contexts in which these mechanisms work.

John Roman and Graham Farrell address the relatively underdeveloped but important field of cost-benefit analysis in crime prevention evaluation. They make a trenchant defence of its use in informing policy. They highlight the ubiquity of cost-benefit estimates in decision making over resource allocation at both individual and societal levels, even though these are often implicit or ill-informed. Roman and Farrell show how cost-benefit analysis might usefully be applied broadly to inform crime policy, for example in relation to programs, products, designs and routine practices, both when these do and when they do not have overt crime-related objectives. They show how the demand and supply of criminal opportunities can be modeled, and how to derive the costs and benefits of changes in such opportunities. Roman and Farrell address the tricky issues of non-monetary costs and the means of their estimation, highlighting the problems that follow from excluding such costs. They discuss the possibility of tax-adjustments in respect to the crime-generating activities of manufacturers whose products supply crime opportunities. As with the preceding chapter, Roman and Farrell highlight the importance of attention to mechanisms producing patterns and changes in them, the importance of attention to unintended consequences as well as intended ones, and the use of appropriate methods in the formulation of policy as well as its post-hoc assessment.

John Eck challenges a contemporary methodological shibboleth: that experimental, random controlled trials that are designed to maximize internal validity are always the appropriate "gold standard" (best method) in the evaluation of crime prevention interventions. He highlights the importance of context sensitivity, which is: "the variation in effectiveness caused by implementing the same measure in different social, temporal and physical settings." "The greater the variation," he says, "the greater is the context sensitivity." Eck contrasts small-scale, small-claim interventions with large-scale, large-claim ones, where experimental evaluation may be appropriate. The sorts of place-based, small-scale, small-claim interventions developed in problem-oriented policing are, he suggests, particularly unsuited to classic, technically rigorous experimental methods. What is important in much local small-scale work is analysis of the particularities of the presenting problem in its context in the light of well established theory — notably that from situational crime prevention and routine activities — and the formulation of a tailored, informed strategy. Orthodox, rigorous, experimental methods aiming to maximize internal validity, he argues, do not make sense here. Instead, simple evaluations examining whether change has occurred and attempting to eliminate obvious alternative factors make more sense. These can help practitioners learn and adapt their interventions. Like other contributors, Eck again stresses the importance of understanding contexts and causal mechanisms in effecting change, and the usefulness of this not only in post-hoc evaluation but also in planning interventions. Eck shows what it is to bring the general findings of science to particular situations for practice, and to learn from the experience of doing so.

Brian English, Rick Cummings and Ralph Straton highlight the different purposes for, types of, approaches to and methods used in evaluations of community crime prevention programs. In particular, action-oriented evaluation is aimed at program development, whilst research-oriented evaluation is aimed at enhancing knowledge. Different time scales and different appropriate methodological standards apply in each case. Methods need to be chosen in the light of purposes. None, they argue, is intrinsically superior. What is actually done will involve trade-offs in the light of the conditions in which the evaluation is conducted. Like Eck, they suggest that attributes of programs themselves are also important in evaluation design. Moreover, as with other contributors, they stress the importance of theory, mechanisms and program contexts in making sense of programs and making decisions about evaluation designs. English et al. sample community crime prevention program evaluations and conclude that there is scope for use of a wider range of approaches. Currently, for example, they find that goal-based evaluations dominate. There is relatively little rich analysis of the ways in which the program is experienced by participants, staff and others implicated in it. This kind of analysis, they suggest, could be helpful in making judgments about how a program is working and ways in which it could usefully be modified.

Dennis Rosenbaum considers the evaluation of multi-agency anti-crime partnerships, which have widely come to be seen as essential for effective crime prevention. He reviews and synthesises a substantial literature from health promotion and drug prevention, as well as crime prevention, to inform the conceptualisation and evaluation of partnerships. The rationale for partnership has to do with the complexity and multidimensionality of the problems they are supposed to address. Partnerships, in theory, promise a way better to define problems, develop creative solutions, deliver multiple interventions, address problems at multiple levels, and trigger multiple mechanisms that may operate synergistically. Key partnership mechanisms that may deliver these benefits include putting heads together to stimulate new ideas, aligning resources to increase intervention dosage and co-ordination to improve service delivery. Partnerships will vary in what they do and their underlying working theories, informing their "domains of influence," "causal mechanisms," "intervention targets," and "partnership services." Effectiveness may turn on combinations of and interactions between these, but in ways yet to be tested. Rosenbaum provides a range of suggestions for measuring input and context variables, processes involved in planning, program development and implementation, and outcomes. He remains a strong adherent of traditional experimental methods as the gold standard in outcome measurement – as a way of establishing the counterfactual, which is crucial. Rosenbaum also emphasises the benefits of other approaches, however, including case studies, theories of change, time series analysis, qualitative methods, and the use of multiple methods. As with the other contributors to this volume, he strongly emphasises throughout the importance of theory as a guide to measurement and method.

Address correspondence to: Nick Tilley, Department of Social Sciences, Nottingham Trent University, Burton Street, Nottingham NG1 4BU. E-mail: <tilley@home-office.swinternet.co.uk>.

REFERENCES

Bhaskar, R. (1975). *A Realist Theory of Science*. Brighton, UK: Harvester.

Clarke, R. (1997). "Introduction." In: R. Clarke (ed.), *Situational Crime Prevention: Successful Case Studies*. Guilderland, NY: Harrow and Heston.

Eck, J. and W. Spelman (1987). *Solving Problems: Problem-Oriented Policing in Newport News*. Washington, DC: Police Executive Research Forum.

Ekblom, P. (1990). "Evaluating Crime Prevention: The Management of Uncertainty." In: C. Kemp (ed.), *Current Issues in Criminological Research*. Bristol, UK: Bristol Centre for Criminal Justice.

—— (1988). *Getting the Best out of Crime Analysis.* (Crime Prevention Unit Series, Paper No. 10.) London, UK: Home Office.

—— and K. Pease (1995). "Evaluating Crime Prevention." In: M. Tonry and D. Farrington (eds.), *Building a Safer Society: Strategic Approaches to Crime Prevention.* (Crime and Justice series, vol. 19.) Chicago, IL: University of Chicago Press.

Farrington, D. and A. Petrosino (2001). "The Campbell Collaboration Crime and Justice Group." *Annals of the American Academy of Political and Social Science* 578:5-49.

Goldblatt, P. and C. Lewis (1998). *Reducing Offending: An Assessment of Research Evidence on Ways of Dealing with Offending Behaviour.* (Home Office Research Study No.187.) London, UK: Home Office.

Goldstein, H. (1979). "Improving Policing: A Problem-Oriented Approach." *Crime & Delinquency* 25:236-258.

Laycock, G. (1997). "Operation Identification, or the Power of Publicity?" In: R. Clarke (ed.) *Situational Crime Prevention: Successful Case Studies.* Guilderland, NY: Harrow and Heston.

—— (1985). *Property Marking: A Deterrent to Domestic Burglary?* (Crime Prevention Unit Series, Paper No. 3.) London, UK: Home Office.

—— and N. Tilley (1995). *Policing and Neighbourhood Watch: Strategic Issues.* (Crime Detection and Prevention Series, Paper No. 60.) London, UK: Home Office.

Mayo, E. (1933). *The Human Problems of Industrial Civilisation.* New York, NY: MacMillan.

Painter, K. (1995) "An Evaluation of the Impact of Street Lighting on Crime, Fear of Crime and Quality of Life." Unpublished Ph.D. thesis, Cambridge University.

Pawson, R. and N. Tilley (1997). *Realistic Evaluation.* London, UK: Sage.

Pease, K. (1999). "A Review of Street Lighting Evaluations: Crime Reduction Effects." In: K. Painter and N. Tilley (eds.), *Surveillance of Public Space: CCTV, Street Lighting and Crime Prevention.* (Crime Prevention Studies, vol. 10.) Monsey, NY: Criminal Justice Press.

Phillips, C. (1999). "A Review of CCTV Evaluations: Crime Reduction Effects and Attitudes Towards Its Use." In: K. Painter and N. Tilley (eds.) *Surveillance of Public Space: CCTV, Street Lighting and Crime Prevention.* (Crime Prevention Studies, vol. 10.) Monsey, NY: Criminal Justice Press.

Scott, M. (2001). *Problem-Oriented Policing: Reflections on the First 20 Years.* Washington, DC: U.S. Department of Justice, Community Oriented Policing Services.

Sherman, L. (1992). *Policing Domestic Violence.* New York, NY: Free Press.

—— (1990). "Police Crackdowns: Initial and Residual Deterrence." In: M. Tonry and N. Morris (eds.), *Crime and Justice: A Review of Research*, vol. 12. Chicago, IL: University of Chicago Press.

—— D. Gottfredson, D. Mackenzie, J. Eck, P. Reuter and S. Bushway (1997). *Preventing Crime: What Works, What Doesn't and What's Promising. A Report to the United States Congress*. Washington, DC: U.S. Department of Justice.

Smith, M., R. Clarke and K. Pease (2002). "Pre-igniting Crime Prevention." In: N. Tilley (ed.), *Analysis for Crime Prevention*. (Crime Prevention Studies, vol. 13.) Monsey, NY: Criminal Justice Press.

U.K. Her Majesty's Inspectorate of Constabulary (HMIC), (2000). *Calling Time on Crime*. London, UK: author.

ANTICIPATED CONSEQUENCES: DEVELOPING A STRATEGY FOR THE TARGETED MEASUREMENT OF DISPLACEMENT AND DIFFUSION OF BENEFITS

by

Niall Hamilton-Smith

Policing and Reducing Crime Unit, U.K. Home Office

Abstract: *This paper examines how displacement and diffusion of benefits can be measured within the context of crime reduction project evaluations. Attempts to monitor the impact of Reducing Burglary Initiative (RBI) projects in the United Kingdom highlighted an existing lack of measurement strategies in this area. This paper seeks to make a start at addressing this problem through a three-stage approach. First, this paper examines existing empirical and theoretical literature on displacement and diffusion of benefits and highlights some of the established difficulties associated with their measurement. It is argued that many of these difficulties relate to the lack of a systematic basis for targeting measurement. Second, the paper reviews some of the key literature on offender decision making, motivation and mobility to see if there is any empirical basis for anticipating the direction and form of any displacement/diffusion of benefits. Third, this paper goes on to explore how one might, within the context of typical project evaluation research, model offending characteristics with the aim of anticipating any possible offender adaptation to the impact(s) of project work. This is illustrated with the example of the "buffer zone selection model," which was developed to select areas to test for spatial displacement/diffusion of benefits from RBI project areas. The discussion then turns to examining how one might interpret changes in crime levels in project and buffer areas, and a number of possible confirmatory tests are outlined that could be utilised to validate any resulting hypotheses.*

Crime Prevention Studies, volume 14, pp.11-52.

Finally, the paper attempts to frame this discussion within a practical consideration of how the measurement of displacement/diffusion of benefits should be tied into the ongoing tasks of problem analysis, project development, and the strategic review of local crime pattern/level changes.

INTRODUCTION

The fundamental aim of this chapter is to advance the discussion as to how displacement can be measured by researchers and crime reduction practitioners undertaking project evaluations. The origins of this work lie in efforts to monitor the performance of over 160 crime reduction projects funded under the second phase of the U.K. government's Reducing Burglary Initiative (RBI). The structure of the RBI mirrors an established tradition of funding crime reduction work through the central provision of short-term grant funding to projects that have been predominantly based around local, multi-agency partnerships operating at the district or city level. These partnerships, in turn, have usually focused their work upon one discrete local geographic area or "community."

Central to attempts at monitoring the performance of these projects has been not only assessing whether they have reduced burglary in the project areas, but also whether project work has led to either the "displacement of crime" or to a "diffusion of benefits." (These terms are defined in the next two sections.) However, at the outset of this task it became clear that prior research studies offered minimal assistance in providing a systematic methodology for predicting and measuring displacement. Whilst the theoretical foundations of displacement have been well developed, it seemed that there had been a limited application of this theory to the development of theoretically-informed measurement strategies.

Typically in project evaluations, displacement/diffusion of benefits has been measured through the simple comparison of project area crime figures with neighbouring geographic units. These units have either been chosen on the basis of rigidly applied geographical criteria or on the basis of unspecified, or loosely reasoned, principles. This unfocused approach to measuring displacement has contributed to the general pessimism that Barr and Pease (1990) have rightly identified as being a common affliction of crime reduction practitioners and academics. Pessimism about the possibility of measuring and thereby *discounting* the occurrence of displacement contributes to a wider pessimism that crime reduction activity simply results in crimes being displaced.

The purpose of this chapter is therefore threefold. First, this chapter seeks to provide a basic review of the various forms of displacement/diffusion of benefits, together with a brief discussion of some of the traditional problems that are encountered when attempting to measure them. Second, the chapter examines the available empirical evidence and theory which can potentially assist in developing a more systematic measurement strategy. Finally, the chapter presents and develops the strategy that was used to target the measurement of spatial displacement under the RBI monitoring exercise. Though the discussion in this chapter is framed in terms of measuring displacement/diffusion of benefits resulting from burglary reduction work, much of what is covered should be widely applicable to measuring displacement from other types of crime reduction activities.

Displacement of Crime

A perennial question that must be faced when attempting to assess the impact of crime reduction projects is: "Was crime displaced as a result of the project's activities?" The key literature covering displacement is comparatively well known so this section will only recap the most salient points.

Displacement of crime refers to the phenomena where offenders adapt to a restriction in criminal opportunities with the result that the established pattern and/or level of crime changes. Typically a crime reduction practitioner would hope that offenders would adapt to the introduction of crime prevention activity in one location by desisting from their offending activity altogether or at least for an appreciable period of time. Conversely a practitioner might fear that offenders might alternatively adapt to this activity by switching to another location to commit their offences or to a different type of offence. The now standard displacement typology (see Reppetto, 1976; Hakim and Rengert, 1981; Barr and Pease, 1990), refers to six main forms of displacement. These are:

- Temporal displacement: committing the same intended offence but at a different time.
- Spatial displacement: committing the same intended offence against the same type of target but in a different location.
- Tactical displacement: committing the same intended offence but using a different method.

- Target displacement: committing the same intended offence but against a different type of target.

- Crime type/functional/offence displacement: committing a different type of offence.

- Perpetrator displacement: after the removal of one offender, the same offence is committed, but by a new offender (the notion being that some criminal opportunities are so lucrative that the incapacitation of one offender will simply result in a new offender taking his or her place: see Barr and Pease, 1990).

Clearly, one can have several forms of displacement at work at the same time. For instance, if offenders are put off offending in one area owing to recently installed street lights, they may not only move to a new area to offend (spatial displacement), but they may also tailor their method of offending to suit the opportunities and characteristics of this new area (tactical displacement).

Pessimism regarding the inevitability of displacement centres around notions about the fallibility and etiological superficiality of situational crime prevention techniques. The argument goes that if one blocks an offending opportunity through some physical impediment or some design modification, the net result will be that, at best, the offender will be displaced from that crime target at that specific point in time. This is because the temporary blockage of opportunity will in no way alter the offender's determination and *motivation* to offend, and plenty of alternative criminal opportunities will always be available. This raises the theoretical possibility of "total displacement": namely, where crime will not go down at all but instead offenders will simply amend their behaviour to circumvent any blockage/removal of opportunities.

Situational crime prevention, by contrast, has been developed on the basis of a less deterministic view of offender behaviour. Mayhew et al. (1976) have argued that offender behaviour is not always strongly motivated and, indeed, is often restricted to an exploitation of a readily available opportunity. Empirical research into offending careers largely bears out this less deterministic and more restrictive view of offending behaviour. Offending careers are generally short[1] and offenders predominantly do not conceive of themselves as purely "criminals"; rather, their illegal activities are often fluidly intermingled with the pursuit of legitimate activities and the fostering of conventional socio-economic aspirations (see, for instance, Hobbs, 1998). In their development of "rational choice theory," Cornish and Clarke (1986; Clarke and Cornish, 1985) have taken this conception of offenders forward, arguing that an offender, in carrying out a criminal act, makes a rational decision that the benefits of carrying out that act outweigh any associated costs. If the costs of exploiting an opportunity are therefore perceived as being too high, or if an opportunity is reduced or removed altogether, then at least a temporary desistance by the offender is just as plausible as some form of displacement.

Empirical research partially affirms this portrayal of offenders as rational and as capable of suppressing their offending behaviour. Bennett and Wright (1984) and Cromwell et al. (1991) both found that burglary offenders employed some degree of rational decision making in their offending behaviour. They also concluded that offender motivation was not so strong an impetus that it was incapable of being suppressed (even amongst drug-using offenders). More generally, research into displacement has not been able to find any evidence contrary to the fears of "displacement pessimists" — that crime prevention measures ever result in a total displacement of crime. For instance, Hesseling (1994) reviewed over 55 studies of displacement and found that in 40% of cases there was no evidence that displacement had occurred at all.

Even where displacement does occur, its existence does not automatically equate with a reduction in the success attributed to a project. As Barr and Pease (1990) have argued, displacement need not be negative (or malign), it can in fact sometimes be positive (benign). Crimes can be displaced away from more serious crimes to less serious crimes, or away from more vulnerable populations to less vulnerable populations. For instance, an evaluation of a burglary reduction project in Burnley hypothesised that the increase in incidents of criminal damage during the project period was in part a consequence of burglars failing to gain entry to the increasingly secure pool of domestic households (Hamilton-Smith, 1999). Therefore, far from detracting from the achievements of the project, the increase in this offence category could be seen as an indicator of the project's success.

Diffusion of Benefits

It has been demonstrated that crime reduction projects can also result in the reverse of displacement: i.e., crime reduction gains can "spill out" beyond the property or people that have been targeted by the project. For instance, Poyner (1991) found that when a closed-circuit television (CCTV) system was introduced to cover three car parks at the University of Surrey, a reduction in crime was observed not only in the three targeted car parks but also in a fourth car park that was not covered by the camera system. Poyner hypothesised that offenders, having observed that a CCTV system had been installed, had assumed that the system covered all four car parks; they therefore desisted from offending in all four car parks. Miethe (1991) has termed this "the free rider effect," where neighbours (or neighbouring targets) benefit vicariously from crime prevention activity. Clarke and Weisburd (1994), in turn, have argued for the adoption of the term "diffusion of benefits," as crime reduction gains can spill over not only to non-targeted property or people but also to other time periods, to other places and indeed to other crime types.

An example of the broader spin-offs that can derive from crime reduction activity is provided by Sherman (1990), who found that intensive police operations targeted against specific crime problems or problem areas (termed "crackdowns") could have beneficial effects beyond the period of the crackdown itself.[2] Sherman, in turn, hypothesised that the benefits of police crackdowns could be further enhanced if such operations were implemented and rotated at different times and places on a randomised basis. Such a strategy would leave offenders uncertain as to the extent of police activity and liable, in turn, to overestimate the risks of offending at any given location or point in time.

Difficulties of Measurement

Though the preceding discussion may provide reassurance that displacement is not inevitable, and indeed that a diffusion of benefits is a possible alternative outcome of crime reduction work, it moves us no further forward in terms of measurement. Accurately measuring displacement/diffusion of benefits is particularly difficult because attributing the occurrence or non-occurrence of one crime to the prevention of another is ostensibly a somewhat speculative pastime! There are, in particular, five related problems that initially confront us:

(1) If offenders do employ rational decision making when offending, and if they operate in an environment that provides a bountiful quantity of criminal opportunities, then predicting what form any possible displacement might take will be problematic.

(2) This uncertainty is compounded by the fact that studies of offenders have generally shown (see Tarling, 1993) that most offenders are not specialists (i.e., they do not concentrate solely on specialising in one type of crime), but can in fact range across a range of different criminal activities. Offenders are versatile in that they amend their criminal behaviour to take advantage of changing criminal opportunities.

(3) Theories of modernity emphasise the increasing mobility of the general population in terms of their movement across time and space (Urry, 1991). This increased mobility extends to both potential offenders and victims (Felson, 1994). Thus, offenders may be seen as both versatile and mobile, again impeding attempts to predict the direction and form of any possible displacement activity.

(4) If the focus of any crime reduction evaluation work involves crimes that are thinly spread across time and space[3] — or if to compensate for the uncertainty of offender mobility/versatility an evaluator looks for displacement across a wide range of offence categories and/or a wide geographic area — then any possible displacement effect will be difficult to distinguish from the natural fluctuations of the background crime rates (Barr and Pease, 1990).

(5) Finally, even if we feel confident that we can distinguish some effect over and above natural crime rate fluctuations, then we will still be confronted with the difficulty of attributing any possible displacement/diffusion of benefits to the impact of the project under study. Other external or extraneous activities or events in the study area(s) may account for any crime. The larger the area in which we search for displacement, the more complex this "background noise" is liable to be.

Clearly if we wish to be able to have a realistic chance of gauging the presence and approximate extent of displacement then we need to avoid the measurement problems covered in points four and five above. Our search for displacement needs to be targeted (Clarke and Weisburd, 1994). However, points one to three in turn, if true, deprive us of any systematic bases on which we could build a targeting strategy! Fortunately, however empirical research into criminal decision making and behaviour does not fully bear out the fluid and unpredictable portrait of offending outlined above.

The Reasoning Criminal

Cornish and Clarke (1986) acknowledge that while offenders do make rational choices when committing a criminal act, they act nevertheless with only limited rationality. This is borne out by empirical work that shows that burglars do not usually select targets on the basis of elaborate pre-offence planning (Wright and Decker, 1994); more typically they exploit criminal opportunities that they spot "by chance" or "in passing" (Wiles and Costello, 2000). Moreover, evidence would suggest that this rather casual opportunism is as true for displacement as it is for target selection, with offenders tending to displace on a fairly immediately basis, if at all (Bennett and Wright, 1984).

This characterisation of displacement is supported in Hesseling's (1994:219) review of the displacement literature and the most frequently reoccurring forms of displacement observed. The ranking across 55 studies was as follows:

Temporal displacement	=	100%
Spatial displacement	=	53%
Target displacement	=	48%
Tactical displacement	=	38%
Offence displacement	=	35%

It should be noted that this ranking allows for multiple forms of displacement (hence, temporal displacement was predictably a feature of every incident of observed displacement). What is striking about this ranking is that offenders, in displacing from blocked opportunities, are clearly more likely to be displaced along the line "of least resistance" — namely, offenders commit the same type of crime using the same method. This is congruent with our portrait above of offenders exploiting criminal opportunities on a fairly immediate basis. These patterns of displacement however do not support any contention that the other dominant influence on offender behaviour is irrational or chaotic decision making. Offenders sensibly displace, first and foremost, to the same or similar opportunities.

What underpins and links this mix of opportunistic behaviour and rational decision making is the fact that offenders base many of their judgements and actions not on conscious decision making but on the employment of pre-defined and readily available "rules of thumb" (Cromwell et al., 1991; Cornish, 1994). Both Cromwell and Cornish have developed multi-stage models of how offenders assess and exploit criminal opportunities. Whilst the full structure and assumptions underlying these models may be contentious within the field of psychology, a consistent point that both models convey (and which is also conveyed in Giddens' [1984] more general conception of "practical consciousness") is that offender decision making and behaviour is partially *routinised*. These routines derive from an individual's personal repository of practical knowledge, accumulated experience, and reinforced behaviours relating to the commission of a particular type of offence. These assist the offender in the offence process by helping him or her to recognise a suitable criminal opportunity, to assess risks related to that opportunity (in particular immediate situational factors), and to accomplish the task of exploiting that opportunity. In short, at each stage of the crime commission process the employment of routines mitigates against the need consciously to think through each and every stage and circumstance relating to the commission of a specific offence. This employment of routines inserts an element of predictability into offender behaviour (including target selection *and* displacement).

The Motivated Offender

Hesseling's ranking of displacement types, while it may support our portrait of opportunistic offenders pursuing favoured types of criminal activity, still highlights a significant number of cases where tactical or offence displacement occurs. As discussed earlier, most offenders do not specialise in one exclusive type of criminal activity. Thus, if one type of opportunity is blocked (and, in particular, is persistently or permanently blocked) an offender may choose to exploit another opportunity that involves the utilisation of a different method of offending or a different type of offence altogether.

One key factor in determining whether or not this type of adaptation and displacement takes place will be the strength and nature of offender motivation. Farrington (1987) has previously noted that offenders who have longer and more serious criminal careers are more likely to displace, and also to display more flexibility in their displacement patterns. The nature of motivation is also important because it is likely to significantly determine the direction of any displacement, in particular offence displacement. For instance, the primary motivation for most burglary offenders is instrumental gain, principally the acquisition of money (Maguire, 1982; Bennett and Wright, 1984; Rengert and Wasilchick, 1985; Cromwell et al., 1991). Clearly, if material gain is the principal motivation behind an offence, then the most likely direction for offence displacement to take is to another type of crime that provides similar rewards. Tarling (1993) provides some evidence for this in his study of offender careers. He found that burglary offenders — if they were going to commit another offence aside from burglary — were more likely to commit some other type of acquisitive crime.

Felson and Clarke (1998) provide further evidence of the importance of motivation. In their discussion of research into the theft of motor vehicles, they argue that the direction of displacement away from any particular model of car will depend on the particular motivation behind the original theft. Joyriders prefer different models of cars from thieves who are looking to steal a car for its parts; in turn, the preferences of thieves who are stealing cars "to order" are different again. Thus, if a joyrider car model is "target hardened," one would expect displacement towards another one of the other car models favoured by joyriders.

Choice-structuring Properties

The reader may at this point think that the preceding discussion promises the possibility of developing typologies that will allow us to predict displacement fairly accurately. Offender behaviour is not simply based upon rational decision making. Rather, the pure cost-benefit calculus suggested by rational choice theory is circumscribed by routinised behaviours and the motivation of offenders. It might therefore seem that we have a strong basis for making generalisable displacement/diffusion of benefit predictions for certain types of offenders.

Unfortunately, matters are more complicated than this. First, though there may be, for instance, similarities in the underlying motivation and the types of routines and decision making employed by burglary offenders, there are also likely to be significant individual and sub-group differences. Offenders differ both because they possess different personal attributes and also because offenders operate in varying social and physical environments. For instance, Cromwell et al. (1991) found that, while for most burglars the dominant motivation was acquisitive gain, for many younger burglars the main motivation was in fact excitement (which if we are trying to predict offence type displacement is a very significant difference). Equally, the skills and decision making of a burglar operating in an environment where opportunities are to be found in breaking into high-rise flats may be very different from those of a burglar operating in an area where no high-rise building is present.

Cornish and Clarke (1987) have gone some way to modelling this complexity with their concept of "choice-structuring properties." No one operates on the basis of unlimited choices, rather we make choices on the basis of available options, or our *perceptions* of what options are available. These options will vary between different individuals because the choices available to us will be based on the particular social and physical environments that we inhabit, as well as our own individual attributes. Thus, offender motivation and decision making cannot be divorced from the social, physical, and individual "properties" which determine the choices available to a given offender. "Choice-structuring properties" provide a framework for modelling what choices are available to offenders. Though Cornish and Clarke do not draw up a list of properties specifically for burglary offenders, we might broadly summarise here some generic properties that would be pertinent to burglary under the headings "individual properties," "social properties," "physical properties" and "opportunity properties."

Individual Properties

Offenders need to be aware of offending opportunities and/or have the skills for identifying opportunities. Offenders need to have the relevant expertise/knowledge of crime commission methods as well as methods of disposing of stolen goods. They need to be available to commit the offence at the appropriate time and they need to have the time generally to plan and commit the offence. They need to be motivated to commit the offence (including the fact that they must have decided that the benefits of commission outweigh any cost). They also need to have the relevant physical, affective, and cognitive aptitudes required to commit the offence.

Social Properties

The offender may be dependent upon the availability of associates (in some cases with particular skills). Offenders also need fences who are interested in purchasing the sort of goods that they steal. If offenders wish to adapt or develop their offending behaviour, they also need to be able to draw on locally available knowledge of offending opportunities and offending methods. The admiration, approval or support of social peers may be essential to an offender's motivation.

Physical Properties

The offender may require specific tools/materials for the commission of the crime or the subsequent disposal of property. Transport may be required. Safe sites for the storage of stolen property may also be needed.

Opportunity Properties

Suitable opportunities need to be available to the offender. Clarke (1999) has developed an acronym — "CRAVED" — to capture the properties that a product or item needs to possess to make it "suitable" for stealing. An item needs to be "concealable" (so it can be safely removed with limited risk), "removable" (some items are harder to remove owing to protective measures), and "available" (the items are available locally and they are visible to offenders). Items also need to be "valuable" (whether in monetary or other terms), "enjoyable" (this is related to an item's value, as the value of items is sometimes found in the enjoyment or status they provide) and "disposable" (the stolen items are easy to sell).

These choice-structuring properties form the background to an offender's decision making and routine behaviours. These properties not only enable offenders to commit certain types of offences, but they also define the boundaries of an offender's options (and hence they define the boundaries of any possible displacement). The fact that the choices available to offenders are ultimately unique to each offender should not disguise the fact that generalisations can be made about types or groups of offenders. However, the limitations and scope of such generalisations clearly need to be recognised. The level at which generalisations can be made will also vary by offence. In the case of burglary, most offenders operate at a geographically local level, exploiting locally available opportunities and working with local offending resources. Any generalisations that are employed to model potential displacement away from residential burglary therefore need to be checked against the particularities of local offending. Cornish and Clarke's "choice-structuring properties" provide a conceptual framework that can assist us with this task.

However, before we move on to examine how we can practically utilise this knowledge there is one further issue that needs to be considered. While our discussion to date has focussed upon offender decision making and motivation, and the properties that shape these attributes, one final aspect of offender behaviour that has not been considered is offender mobility. The characteristics of the social and physical environment may well fundamentally inform and limit the choices available to a given offender, but these environments vary from place to place. If offenders move freely through "space," then our ability to make any predictions about their likely offending choices becomes severely compromised! The question is, therefore, are offenders freely mobile, and, if not, is there any basis on which we can predict their restricted movements?

Offenders in Space

A productive development in criminology has been the gradual convergence of rational choice theory with "routine activities theory" (Bottoms and Wiles, 1997). While the former, as we have seen, helps us examine how offenders assess a criminal opportunity, routine activities theory addresses the issue of how offenders come across criminal opportunities in the first place. Central to this theory is the notion that criminal offences occur in circumstances where motivated offenders come across suitable opportunities in the absence of a capable guardian (Cohen and Felson, 1979). Routine activities theory therefore examines the movement, distribution and conjunction of offenders, victims, capable guardians and opportunities.

The grounds for convergence have been based around the increasing importance being attributed to "routines" both in rational choice theory and routine activities theory. As we have seen in our discussion of offender decision making, the majority of offenders do not engage in elaborate pre-offence planning or target selection searches. Rather, targets predominantly consist of opportunities that are identified and acted upon as an offender moves "routinely" through space. This raises the question of how one can characterise — and whether one can predict — these routine movements of offenders.

Clearly, the literal and metaphorical point of departure for any discussion of offender mobility must be the offender's residence. Offender residences are important because any limitations in their mobility can be best measured from their home residence. Wiles and Costello (2000) examined changes in offender mobility in the city of Sheffield, comparing police data from 1966 and 1995. Whilst they did find evidence that offender mobility had increased in so far as the distance travelled to a burglary scene had increased, they still found that over 40% of offenders travelled less than one mile from their place of residence to their chosen crime site. In 1995 the average journey to a burglary offence was 1.88 miles. So is there therefore any basis upon which we can predict these limited travel patterns? Fortunately there is a well-evidenced and developed set of work in environmental criminology that enables us to make such predictions. Brantingham and Brantingham (1981, 1984) are the most well known exponents of a model of human mobility that emphasises the routinised aspects of travel.

People (including offenders) do not travel around a city in a random manner (Lenz, 1986), nor are any of us usually familiar with more than a part of any given city or town. Rather, our movements display a directional bias based around certain key "anchor points" or "nodes" (Rengert, 1992) . A central anchor for all of us is usually our place of residence, followed in turn by those locations were we engage in work and leisure activities. What Brantingham and Brantingham argue is that our travel movements are largely determined by these anchor points and our knowledge/consciousness of our surroundings are centred upon these points and the corridors of travel that lead from one point to another. Thus it is predominantly along these "paths of consciousness" and around these anchor points that offenders will be aware of the criminal opportunities on offer. This hypotheses that offenders commit offences in areas with which they are routinely familiar has a strong evidential base in empirical studies (Carter and Hill, 1979; Rengert and Wasilchick, 1985; Beavon et al., 1994; Wiles and Costello, 2000).

While Brantingham and Brantingham's modelling of offender movements stands up well against the empirical evidence, the portrayal of travel routes and zones of consciousness being based around the three anchor points of home, leisure and work holds up less well within a contemporary setting. Rengert and Wasilchick (1989) have argued that for many offenders an important anchor point in terms of their daily routines is their drug sale or consumption locations. Wiles and Costello (2000) observed that a large percentage of the offenders that they studied were either unemployed or economically active only on a sporadic basis. They also found that for many offenders the residence of friends or girlfriend formed an important anchor point around which they offended. In their study, they found that the key anchor point for offenders were (in order of priority):

- areas of current residence;

- areas previously lived in; and

- areas well known.

Unsurprisingly, offenders generally lived in areas characterised as socially and economically deprived. Wiles and Costello found that of the 23 neighbourhoods that their study covered in Sheffield, 68% of offenders had lived in six or less of these neighbourhoods, and these neighbourhoods were all characterised by their unpopular social housing. Thus, offenders — at least when it comes to movements and anchor points that are related to their individual residence or the residence of their friends and family — are likely to offend in deprived neighbourhoods. Consistent with previous studies, the authors found that offenders in Sheffield were least likely to know middle class areas and, consequently, they were less likely to offend in these areas.

Another complicating aspect of offender mobility is that some offenders have an itinerant lifestyle with frequent moves between short-term addresses. Wiles and Costello found that their sample of offenders was clearly dichotomised between those offenders who had a stable residential address and those that didn't. Generally, however, they found (2000:44) that most offenders were not that mobile, a conclusion that they found unsurprising.

> Long range travel, like much other human activity, requires knowledge, confidence, skills and resources. However, the risk factors associated with offending are either the lack of such skills or are closely correlated with them.

The implications of this body of environmental research are that offender movements, with the general exception of movements in and out of the city centres, are disproportionately centred around deprived and more disadvantaged residential areas. This concentration accords well with routine activities theory. Not only are offenders more likely to travel in or be familiar with more deprived neighbourhoods, but this very familiarity is also likely to ensure that offenders have a better knowledge of suitable opportunities in these areas. Moreover, these areas frequently play host to vulnerable populations who are more prone to personal victimisation (Kershaw et al., 2000), while the generally lower levels of physical security in these areas (Budd, 1999) make access to property easier. Finally, it is precisely these types of areas that are characterised as frequently exhibiting higher levels of social disorder and lower levels of informal social control, with the implication being that levels of capable guardianship will also be lower (Skogan, 1986).

MEASUREMENT STRATEGIES

What the preceding sections tell us is that the problems of measurement that we identified in relation to offender motivation, rationality and mobility are not as severe an impediment to the measurement of displacement as we first thought. Offender motivation is not fluid or inexhaustibly flexible, nor is offender behaviour solely based around pure rational decision making. Furthermore offenders do not range freely through time and space. In short, the importance of routines in informing offender movements and decision making, and the limitations placed on offender behaviour by the choice-structuring properties available to a given offender, provide us with a critical element of predictability. This predictability allows us to target our search for displacement.

This final section therefore deals with the practical task of converting our discussion to date into a practical measurement strategy that can be used either in practitioner-driven or independent research. Such research is typically conducted within fairly tight resource constraints. This is problematic because — as we have seen — it is not possible to pre-specify universally applicable typologies of offenders and their likely displacement choices. Nor, is it practical with limited resources, to undertake for each piece of research a full and systematic analysis of all the choice-structuring properties identified by Cornish and Clarke. However, while we may not be able fully to characterise all the pertinent aspects of the offences and offenders that we are studying — and consequently we may not be able to predict every possible permutation in offender behaviour when faced with a blocked criminal opportunity — what we *can* do is at least narrow down the possibilities.

A Time and a Place for Measurement?

This leads to the question of how and when should one fit in the task of predicting displacement or diffusion of benefits into the typical setting of project-based work? The simple answer is that this task should ideally be built into the task of general problem analysis at the very outset of a given project. A project analysis of any quality will normally provide at least some information on offenders, victims and offence locations, in the project area. This information is increasingly analysed through following the precepts of the "problem analysis triangle" (PAT; see Hough and Tilley, 1998) in that analysts endeavour to elicit those salient aspects of offenders, victims and locations that lead to the generation of a criminal event. This sort of analysis can also be re-utilised to help us predict displacement/diffusion of benefits.

In predicting displacement or diffusion of benefits essentially what one is doing is modelling patterns of offending and considering how they might be affected by the introduction of a given crime reduction measure(s). This is of course exactly the sort of analytical work that is required in developing a crime reduction project in the first place. As we develop a theory of our problem and a theory about how our project interventions will impact on this problem, we are in effect modelling the interaction between each intervention and the offender (this interaction is often referred to as the "mechanism" through which the intervention impacts on the problem — see Pawson and Tilley, 1997). However, a common shortcoming of many project analyses is that this mapping of project impact stops at the point of modelling how an intervention impacts on the offender *in one particular way,* and it does not consider how an offender might subsequently react. Typically, many crime reduction interventions work by blocking the offenders' access to a suitable criminal opportunity. What is too often not considered in project design is how the offender might respond or adapt to this blockage.

Heal and Laycock (1988) have previously noted that displacement is more likely to occur if the design of any crime reduction measure is weak in terms of anticipating how the offender might attempt to circumvent or counter the measure. For instance, one might fit improved door locks to households in an area because forcing existing locks has been a dominant method for burglars to gain entry. Such a measure, however, is of limited value if the same houses offer easy alternative design weaknesses that will allow the offender to gain entry by other means (for instance, through forcing open windows). Thus, anticipating displacement and offender adaptation is an essential part of project design.

However, project design should not only be refined with a view to minimising displacement, it should also be harnessed to maximise the benefits of the project (Clarke and Weisburd, 1994). This may sometimes involve addressing the problem from several angles to ensure a more lasting preventative effect, or a diffusion of benefits beyond the targeted crime type or target area. Enhancing project impact, as we have seen, may also move beyond simply blocking or removing opportunities or apprehending offenders to the more subtle art of affecting offender *perceptions* of opportunities and risks through publicity and disinformation strategies.[4]

Information on Offenders, Victims and Locations

In bringing together this information to consider potential displacement or diffusion of benefits information, we need in essence imaginatively to reconstruct the criminal event to try and understand how the combination of these elements equates with an attractive and viable criminal opportunity. In short, we need, in Ekblom's (1997) words, to put ourselves in the place of the offender and to "think thief." Information on victims, on offences, and offence locations tells us much indirectly about the skills and motivation of offenders. But how do we move, in turn, from information on current offender behaviour and decision making to predicting alternative offender behaviours and decisions? Given what we know about offending behaviour from our discussions above, we need to examine how the project interventions are intended to impact on the targeted offending behaviours and then consider how offenders might in turn respond by changing their patterns of offending, as follows:

Temporal, Spatial and Target Changes

Where and when are crime reduction measures being introduced? Do they cover all of the identified high crime area and do they cover all the attractive targets in that area (incident records will provide an indication of the characteristics and location of attractive opportunities)? If the measures have a temporal aspect to them, are the same criminal opportunities available at non-targeted times? (Offenders for instance might be at school or capable guardians might be at home.) Are there alternative areas within easy reach of offenders that offer similar opportunities? (Offender records may give some indication of the geographical "range" of those offenders who are operating in the project area.) Equally, even if the measures do not cover all of the targeted opportunities in the project area all of the time, is there nevertheless a likelihood that they might *appear to offenders* to have a wider coverage (even possibly beyond the project area)?

Tactical Changes

Looking at the common *modus operandi* of offenders in the project area, and considering which skills or tactics employed by offenders are *not* covered by crime reduction measures, are there alternative opportunities available that can be exploited using existing skills?

Crime Type/Offence Changes

Are opportunities available to commit other offences in the project area or an accessible alternative area? These opportunities need to accord with the skills and tactics of known offenders together with the offenders' motivation and "portfolio" of offending experience: i.e., what other offences of a similar type have they committed in the past? Equally, looking at the *modus operandi* of other crime types, is it possible that the reduction measures might block non-targeted criminal opportunities as well?

In short, an examination of not only dominant patterns of offending, but also the wider range of related offending behaviours, together with a consideration of the likely impact of any crime reduction measures, can provide critical pointers as to possible forms of displacement/diffusion of benefits.

So what sort of information is typically available at the project level to inform this modelling of offending? In an ideal, resource-rich, research environment official data on offending would be supplemented by more probing sources, such as interviews with offenders and victim surveys. However, in most project analysis work, the resources are not available to exploit such methods. Nevertheless, official data sources can still provide considerable information. The two main sources of data are, of course, police offender records and police crime incident records. Between them, these records can generate information on the age, gender, race, residential location, *modus operandi*, and the "breadth" and length of the *detected* criminal careers of offenders. Incident records provide information on the age, gender, race and sometimes occupation of victims. They also provide an account of the modus operandi behind an offence (including, in case of acquisitive crime, what goods were stolen), the spatial and temporal location of an offence, and some of the characteristics of the offence location. Under the RBI, a good analysis of these records frequently generated distinct patterns of offending that allowed practitioners to build up actionable portraits of offenders and their preferred offending locations and opportunities.

There are however, well-identified problems associated with utilising official data on offending (see, for instance, Bottomley and Coleman, 1995; Burrows et al., 2000; U.K. Her Majesty's Inspectorate of Constabulary, 2000). In particular, the ostensible volume and content of certain offending records are often more a reflection of the targeting of enforcement activity or reporting and recording decisions, and less a reflection of the actual levels of a given criminal activity (this is particularly true of drug offence records). However, for the majority of high-volume crimes, comparisons of recorded crime data and crime survey data have shown that recorded data does provide a reliable indicator of crime trends, if not of overall volume (U.K. Home Office 2000). There are, though, three further problems with offending data, which are of particular relevance here:

(1)   Electronic offence and offender records are often oversimplified versions of the original paper incident and intelligence reports. This is often due to limitations of database design, with, for instance, the full paper accounts of offence *modus operandi* being summarised and squeezed into a few standardised categories and tick boxes. The fact that this conversion of paper records into digital ones is often undertaken not by the attending officer but by a third party, simply adds to the potential for distortion and for critical detail to be lost.

(2)   One way round this problem is of course to go back to the original paper records. For instance, Mativat and Tremblay (1997), in their study of credit card counterfeiters, used police investigative files to "put flesh" onto computerised offender records. Such files provide more detail on the attributes of offenders and on their methods of offending, and in doing so can illuminate many of the choice-structuring properties that underpin their offending. Mativat and Tremblay, for instance, were able to model the sort of personal affective attributes — together with the sort of resources (including associates) — required to commit different types of credit card offences. They then used this model to attempt to predict likely routes of offender adaptation and/or displacement. However, the quality and reliability of intelligence records can vary hugely from formal records systematically compiled in the course of dealing directly with offenders, through to third-party intelligence and hearsay. The difficulty in assessing the reliability of such intelligence is that

information of markedly different quality can often be found mixed together, though this information is sometimes rated for reliability by "host" agencies.

(3)   A final consideration is that official data on offenders are relatively scant in that detection rates for many crimes in many areas can be very low (typically for burglary as low as 10%, though the national average for burglary in England and Wales in 2000/1 was 14.2% — Povey et al., 2001). Thus, any profile of offenders that one derived from such data would arguably be biased. Compensating for a low detection rate through including retrospective records on offending over several years is of dubious legitimacy in view of the brevity of most criminal careers and the tendency for offenders to change their patterns of offending over time. However, a 10% clear-up rate in a high crime area can actually produce a reasonable sample of offenders for high volume crimes, such as burglary, even if only one or two years' worth of data are examined. Moreover, data on offenders are biased for our purposes in a wholly constructive way. As Farrington (1989) found in his comparative study of self-report and official data on offenders, police records tend to pick out the more persistent and prolific offenders. As these are the very offenders that we would anticipate to be most likely to continue offending in the face of any introduced crime reduction measures (i.e., to be displaced), this bias should assist us in our modeling of potential displacement.

THE RBI APPROACH: PRACTITIONER ACCOUNTS

Under the RBI, limitations in police data on offending were often ameliorated by the availability of data held by other agencies. For instance, probation records, as well as providing further general information on the characteristics of offenders, were also often more reliably accurate about certain details (notably the residential addresses of offenders and their drug-using status). However, such records are not always available to researchers or project analysts, and, even when they are, these combined official sources still often omit critical information. There may, for instance, not be enough data to illuminate what sort of alternative criminal opportunities might be available in the project or adjacent areas, nor may these records be sensitive enough to identify emerging crime trends. Records on individual offenders may also not indicate sufficiently the associations and dynamics existing *between* offenders.

An approach that was therefore adopted under the RBI was to triangulate this formal data with a more qualitative practitioner-informed account of crime in the given project area. This entailed assembling relevant local multi-agency representatives, *at the project planning stage,*[5] to discuss and consider both the existing formal sources of data and their own "on the job"-based knowledge of offenders, victims and locations. Representatives were invited from all the agencies that were contributing to a given project. Where possible, agency representatives included not only those agency staff who had a knowledge of the strengths and weaknesses of their agencies' formal data on offending, but also "ground level" representatives who had an active and qualitative working knowledge of the problem area.

Critically, this approach added finer local detail to a consideration of displacement/diffusion of benefits. Utilising a skilled facilitator, these sessions also offered the opportunity to triangulate formal data on offending with local "folk knowledge."[6] An additional benefit of this approach in some instances, was that it compensated for situations where agencies were not willing to share individual-level data, but were willing to discuss in general terms the salient characteristics of their data. Finally, these sessions had an important subsidiary function in that they also provided the opportunity for project participants to analyse the likely impact of their project and, in doing so, to identify points of weakness or limitations in their existing approach. This, in turn, often led to a consideration of ways in which project impact could be enhanced or widened.

This was an extensively employed approach when selecting suitable areas to test for spatial displacement from round two RBI project areas. The resources were not available to select, collect and analyse individualised offence categories for each project, nor were we able to collect disaggregated data to examine temporal, tactical or target-based crime shifts. Rather, a standard batch of acquisitive crime categories were selected to test for functional/offence displacement/diffusion of benefits, while a "buffer zone" was selected to test for spatial displacement/diffusion of benefits. It was only in relation to this last type of crime shift that we were able to develop and utilise a more systematic, theory- and data-informed method of testing for displacement. In this next section, we examine the development of a measurement strategy to test for spatial displacement/diffusion of benefits.

The Buffer Zone Selection Model

Within the context of the RBI, efforts to predict displacement focussed around the selection of a buffer zone to test for spatial displacement. The majority of RBI projects were focussed upon reducing burglary within a single geographic area. In looking to test for spatial displacement from a project in such an area, one selects another area which is commonly termed a "buffer area" or "buffer zone." A buffer zone is an area one would expect to be the most likely site for displacement from the project area. In this section the discussion will predominantly refer to "displacement" rather than "diffusion of benefits." However, as we shall see, the characteristics of an area that recommend it as a site for any possible displacement would also *generally* recommend it as a site for any possible diffusion of benefits as well.[7]

Figure 1: Buffer Zones

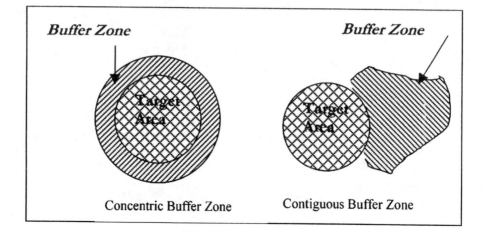

Conventionally, buffer areas fall into one of two types, concentric buffer zones and contiguous buffer zones. These two types are illustrated in Figure 1.

Concentric buffer zones are defined by taking an area that fully surrounds the project area. Usually these zones are defined in such a way that at all points the boundary of the buffer zone is at a set distance from the boundary of the project area. The simple assumption behind concentric buffer zones is that if offenders are displaced from the project area criminological theory would suggest that they are unlikely to displace far. By taking a "strip" around the project area, one can gauge whether or not offenders are displaced to the immediate surrounding area. The advantage of such an approach is that one can test for displacement regardless of the direction in which offenders move out of the project area. The disadvantage of such an approach is that defining and extracting data for concentric buffer zones can be complex (and typically requires the use of a geographic information system). A further disadvantage of the concentric approach is that it is based upon one criminological idea, and fails to take advantage of other predictable aspects of offender movement that provide the possibility of making a more refined selection.

In monitoring the Reducing Burglary Initiative, the decision was taken to opt for something akin to contiguous buffer zones instead. A contiguous buffer zone refers to a neighbouring area that borders onto the project area, but, unlike a concentric buffer zone, does not usually completely surround it. An advantage of contiguous buffer zones is that they are invariably based around geographic areas that are pre-defined in terms of administrative units. This makes the task of obtaining crime data for these areas less problematic. However, while the buffer zones used under the RBI were usually contiguous to the target area, they were not exclusively so. The aim was to select buffer zones that provided as robust a test of displacement as possible. These zones were therefore selected not simply on the criteria of direct proximity to a target area and/or being based around conven ient administrative units. Rather, the empirical literature on offender mobility and target selection was utilised to make a more theoretically informed selection. The type of buffer zones developed under the RBI might therefore best be called "theory-driven" rather than "contiguous."

A model was developed for helping RBI project participants to select a buffer zone(s) for their project. This model initially grew out of a "beat selection model" developed for the RBI by Johnson et al. (2000) at Liverpool University. Utilising pooled information on offenders, victims and locations, project participants in collaboration with a facilitator followed three key stages in selecting a buffer zone for their project.

(1) *Select a buffer zone(s) that is contiguous to the target area boundary (unless a non-contiguous area is strongly recommended under 2).*

In view of generally short "travel to crime" distances, practitioners were encouraged initially to consider contiguous areas as possible sites for displacement. There were, however, a number of cases where non-contiguous areas were seen to be preferable to contiguous ones. Typically, these exceptions occurred for one of two reasons. First, in some urban areas there are often strong social and familial links between non-contiguous areas. In one East Midlands town, for instance, the project area consisted of local authority flats that predominantly housed young single adults. This group was believed to provide the main supply of offenders. These young adults, however, had in turn generally grown up in another council housing area on the other side of town. Allocation procedures therefore created a social link between these two areas, with young adults from the project area frequently travelling between the two areas visiting friends and family. It was therefore considered that displacement was more likely to this non-contiguous "anchor point" than to any of the contiguous areas.

A second common reason for choosing a non-contiguous buffer zone was that a number of project areas hosted a very specialised form of offending that was not transferable to any of the contiguous areas owing to a lack of similar opportunities. For instance, choosing a contiguous buffer zone for a project based around distraction burglary offences (or "burglary artifice" offences as they are commonly known) against the elderly is only appropriate if there is a reasonably large elderly population living in a contiguous area.[8] Given what we know about distraction burglars — namely that they are specialised offenders who are generally quite mobile (Choli, U., forthcoming) — it would be theoretically more likely that such offenders would transfer their particular skills to another suitable area rather than displace a short distance to commit a more conventional type of burglary or another offence type altogether.

(2) *In selecting a buffer zone, review the socio/demographic and physical characteristics of the project and potential buffer zone areas.* Key characteristics to consider in making this selection should include:

(a) *Offender Residence and Characteristics.* It is helpful to know the location of offender residences (as in those offenders offending within the project area) and the basic demographic characteristics of those offenders. Clearly if offenders live outside the target area then this will affect one's consideration of likely spatial displacement routes. Conversely, if the majority of offenders are known to be relatively young and to reside within the project area, then one may choose to limit one's search for spatial displacement to the fairly immediate surrounding area. If direct data on offenders is lacking, then crime incidence data may well provide invaluable clues. For instance, the modus operandi behind offences may reveal that in a given project area the dominant style of offending is based around the rather amateurish theft of small, low value goods that can be easily removed (and concealed) from the property by an offender on foot, and which are easy to dispose of (cash, cigarettes, alcohol, etc.). In several RBI projects, the presence of these offence characteristics *suggested* that offenders were both fairly local and young and were not therefore liable to be displaced far (if, of course, they were displaced at all). In contrast, if the dominant modus operandi indicates that offenders are highly skilled and organised, then the scope for displacement (both spatially and otherwise) is likely to be much broader.

(b) Anchor Points/Offender Knowledge of Other Areas. As we saw in our review of research into offender movement, a critical consideration in assessing likely routes and sites for displacement is assessing offenders' frequenting/familiarity/knowledge of other areas. If specific intelligence on the offending sites of project area offenders is lacking, then such an assessment is frequently made on the basis of considering the general mobility of the broader socio-demographic group or community to which the offenders belong. Under the RBI, commonly identified anchor points included socially-linked housing areas, schools which included young offending populations within their catchment area, and contiguous areas that fell between the project area and the nearest commercial/leisure centre (i.e., which fell along a major route of travel, as well as commercial/leisure centres themselves). Practitioners often brought a considerable amount of local knowledge to this sort of assessment. For instance, in two cases buffer zones were centred around residential areas that included hospitals that served the main offender residence areas. In one of these cases, police intelligence was available to show that drug using offenders offended along the foot route to the hospital (where a needle exchange scheme operated). Generally practitioners not only had a practical knowledge of common transport corridors (and the quality of transport links), but also frequently knew the social and *symbolic* significance of different locations within the locality.[9]

One final factor in predicting offender movement was basic physical access. Offenders frequently had limited access to transport, while in many cases certain contiguous areas were physically separated from the project area by distinct barriers. Typically, these barriers consisted of motorways, railways and rivers. However, even here practitioner knowledge was important in assessing the extent to which these ostensible barriers acted effectively as a block on offender movement. For instance, whereas in one West Midlands project the presence of motorway was considered to be a distinct barrier to offender movement across to a contiguous area, in a project in the North West a railway line was not judged to impede access owing to the presence of a footbridge linking the target area with the contiguous area. Moreover, police intelligence already pointed to offenders using the footbridge to transport stolen goods out of the contiguous area.[10] Finally, a railway line in the East Midlands that superficially looked on a map like a physical barrier to offender displacement, in fact proved to be a semi-derelict line and a well-known offender "rat run." Offenders used this informal travel corridor both to transport stolen goods (with minimal risk of detection) and to access properties that adjoined the line.

(c) Opportunities in Other Areas. Having considered the impact of offender residence and routine movement in shaping any possible displacement, the final consideration relates to the availability of opportunities in other areas. Offenders may well be familiar with a particular contiguous area, but this area may not offer the same opportunities. A critical issue to consider is "can the offence style be easily transferred to a contiguous area"? Neighbouring housing areas may not display the same vulnerabilities and may not therefore provide the same offending opportunities. For instance, a common reason for deciding that a buffer zone *was* a good test of displacement was that the housing design was similar. On this basis, one could presume that unless the buffer area limited opportunities in other ways (either because the houses did not contain the same desirable goods, or because the area exhibited better capable guardianship), then the similarity in housing design would allow burglars to easily transfer their offending.

An example of restricted opportunities is provided by an RBI project in the North West. The contiguous area to the north of the project area was ruled out on the grounds that the housing stock was newly built and conformed to "secure by design" standards. The contiguous area to the south was also ruled out on the grounds that as part of another recent crime reduction project, alleygates had been extensively installed throughout the area. This example, of course, points to the fact that opportunities may not only be restricted as a result of longstanding area attributes, but they might also be temporarily restricted as a result of activities being undertaken by other agencies/projects in the area in question.

(3) *Select a buffer zone(s) for which the population (or in the case of burglary the number of households) is comparable to the project area or, if possible, no more than two times that of the project area.* One easy way to select a buffer zone of a similar size to the project area is to define the buffer zone using the same administrative unit used to define the project area (for instance, typically a police beat or a local authority ward). The advantage in having a buffer zone that is of a similar size to the project area is that it makes it easier to identify possible displacement effects. Buffer zones that are too large or too small in relation to the project area suffer from what can be termed either the "drowning" or "amplifying" of any effect.

For instance, if we take the example given in Table 1 below, where the buffer zone is ten times the size of the project area, we can see that a significant percentage drop in burglary in the project area amounts to no more than a small percentage rise in the chosen buffer zone. The difficulty is that burglary has risen by the same number of incidents in our buffer zone as it has fallen by in the project area, which might suggest that displacement has taken place. However, the size of the buffer zone means that this rise represents a small percentage change relative to the size of the zone and therefore we cannot discount the possibility that this rise is simply a product of random fluctuation. Moreover, the size of the zone also might introduce the difficulty that a large number of other alternative explanatory factors could account for this rise. For instance, a buffer zone of this size may contain, or be contiguous to, separate offending populations that are not active in the project area. In short, a larger buffer zone introduces a greater degree of what can be termed "background noise" that will impede our ability to judge whether or not displacement (or a diffusion of benefits) has occurred. If we have project and buffer areas of a similar size, a rise or fall in one area of a certain magnitude will be easier to compare to similar changes in the other area.

Table 1: First Hypothetical Case

	Project Area	Buffer Area
Number of Households	2000	20,000
No. of Burglary Incidents Year −1	200	1,800
No. of Burglary Incidents Year +1	150	1,850
Change in number of incidents	−50	+50
% change in number of incidents	−25%	+3%

Alternatives to Geographic Buffer Zones

It should be noted that there might be instances where — having followed the buffer zone selection model — it is concluded that there is no appropriate geographical buffer zone. There are circumstances where spatial displacement can be dismissed as practically and/or theoretically implausible. One RBI project, which focussed on targeting multiple-dwelling properties in a city centre area where both offenders and their victims resided, did not have a buffer zone set. The rationale in this case was not that there was a lack of contiguous residential areas (there were). Rather, offenders were markedly unfamiliar with these neighbouring areas (which contrasted with the densely populated town centre of this seaside report, consisting as they did of more sparsely laid out areas of suburban bungalows and detached dwellings). The contiguous areas lacked the sort of facilities that might provide offenders with a reason for passing through them, while offenders lacked the personnel transport easily to access these areas (and public transport was limited). Finally, offenders had ample alternative opportunities for functional/crime type displacement in the city centre areas.

In other cases, it may be determined that displacement is less likely to occur in a specific geographic area but may rather occur amongst a specific population group or other target type. For example, if again we have a project that is focussed on targeting distraction burglaries against the elderly within a specific area — it may be felt that there is no one alternative geographic concentration of elderly residents that can be identified as a suitable buffer zone. An alternative might be to create a buffer zone consisting of all residents aged 60 or over living within the wider police division or local authority area.

Interpreting Trends in Buffer Zones and in Other Crime Categories

After one has selected a buffer zone to test for displacement, and decided on which crimes to monitor to test for any displacement to other crime types, it is worth considering how one subsequently interprets the crime figures that are collected. This discussion cannot encompass all the usual technical and conceptual issues that accompany the general interpretation of crime figures (for that see, for instance, Ekblom, 1988; and Ekblom and Pease, 1995). An assumption will therefore be made that we have arrived at a set of crime change figures for the target and buffer area, and that issues such as seasonal variations, regression to the mean, pre-project trends, comparative performance against wider background trends, etc., have already been taken account of. We will also presume that any estimates have also been balanced against the impact of other possible non-project events or activities in the target *and* buffer area (a convenient presumption in view of the conceptual difficulties associated with this task!).

In producing estimates of changes in crime levels over one or more time periods, one will often end up not with a single estimate of change but an "estimate range." In view of the difficulties involved in accurately attributing either displacement or diffusion of benefits to the work of a project, a prudent strategy might be ultimately to select a single estimate for each crime based on the most conservative end of any estimate range (unless, of course, the characteristics of the data already recommend one estimate over another). The "most conservative" estimate should be taken to mean here the estimate that provides the lowest figure for displacement or diffusion of benefits. For simplicity's sake we will base our example here on monitoring only one other crime "heading"[11] — namely vehicle crime.

Table 2 below provides figures for a hypothetical burglary reduction project with a buffer zone of a similar size to the project area. The estimates given tell us how much crime has risen above or below the levels expected (after one year of the project) based on the most conservative projection.

Table 2: Second Hypothetical Case

	Burglary Dwelling		Vehicle Crime	
	N	(%)	N	(%)
Project Area	-93	(-25%)	+9	(+4%)
Buffer Zone	-15	(-7%)	+6	(+1%)

From these estimates it could be hypothesised that whilst burglary has declined in the project area by 25% more than expected, there has also been a decline in burglaries in the buffer zone. This positive picture is tempered by the small amount of potential displacement within the project and buffer areas away from burglary and into vehicle crime. Attributing the drop in burglary in the buffer zone to the impact of the burglary project would be inappropriate unless it was theoretically plausible that the project work could have had an impact on this offence in this area. If the project, for instance, involved widely disseminated publicity or entailed the apprehension of offenders who may have operated in both areas, then it could be claimed that the project work has resulted in a diffusion of benefits. Conversely, this need for plausibility applies equally to the rise in vehicle crime being attributed to displacement of offenders away from burglary.

Obviously, if our search for displacement has been well informed and systematic then the plausibility of any findings will be greater. But are there other steps we can take to test or strengthen the findings that we have? Moreover, how can we interpret the significance of other shifts in crime patterns (from, say, one time period to another or from one method of offending to another)? Though the RBI monitoring exercise has not yet been able fully to explore this question, prior research might suggest that the following strategies could provide helpful corroborative evidence to support any hypotheses as to the occurrence of displacement and/or diffusion of benefits.

- One can examine differences in modus operandi/offence characteristics between the original target offence and any other offences that may rise or decline in the buffer or project area. One may wish, for example, to examine whether a decline in a non-targeted offence type could plausibly be attributed to a diffusion of benefits. If the dominant characteristics of this additional crime type were similar to the characteristics of the targeted offences (in particular if the motivation, rewards, required skills and resources were similar) — then this would suggest that diffusion of benefits is at least theoretically plausible. Even if the characteristics of these offences are different, if the *mechanism(s)* by which the reduction measures impacted on the targeted offences could also plausibly have an effect on the modus operandi of these extra saved offences, then an argument for diffusion of benefits can be made. For instance, to use a simple example, a project might install street lighting in an area to deter burglary offenders. However, this lighting might also plausibly impact on a number of other offending behaviours present in the area on the basis that they all partly rely on the low levels of lighting (for instance street violence and car theft).[12]

- If the dominant modus operandi of the target offence changes, it may be worth asking the question whether the new modus operandi is consistent with the offending style, skills, aptitudes and resources of offenders observed at the outset of the project. For instance, Clarke et al. (1994) found that measures that dramatically reduced ticket machine fraud on the London underground were soon followed by a change in the modus operandi of offenders. However, the new patterns of offending were wholly inconsistent with offending in the pre-project period, with the offending process being organised along different spatial lines and with a considerable increase in the sophistication of the offending method and the resources required. The authors therefore concluded that a new offending group was responsible for the continuing levels of fraud and that there was no evidence of displacement by the original offenders.

• If one is looking at relatively large numbers of crimes over several years, one could examine offender records in the project and buffer area on a "before and after" basis. Taking, say, four years of data (two years pre-project and two years during/post-project), one might establish an offending "base" in terms of the number of offenders detected for the targeted offence[13] in the project area. One could then examine how many of these offenders from this four-year base were detected in the project and buffer areas, respectively, during the two pre-project years. One could then produce a percentage figure for each area (i.e., what percentage of all these detections in the pre-project period occurred in the buffer zone?) Repeating these calculations for the two post-project years, one could finally compare the percentage of project area offenders operating in the buffer zone in the pre-project period with the percentage operating in the buffer zone in the post-project period. If the number of project area offenders being detected in the buffer zone rises in the post-project period, this would suggest that some spatial displacement may have occurred. Clearly such a method would only be valid if there was a relatively high detection rate in both the project and buffer areas. Biases in the data may also need to be confronted (for instance, detection rates may change significantly over time in either one or both areas). This method could also be used to examine temporal, tactical, target and functional/offence displacement (as well, indeed, as any hypothesised diffusion of benefits).

• An alternative method which has been utilised for a different purpose before would be to undertake exactly the same matching process but using forensic data (and, in particular, DNA data) instead of offender records. For offences where there is a comparatively high rate of forensic evidence gathered (of which burglary is one), this method has the advantage that it will identify more unique offenders than detection records. A disadvantage of this approach, as its developers have readily identified (Wiles and Costello, 2000), is that forensic records held in Britain by the Forensic Science Service can only be easily traced back to the police station from which they originated (and even then the relevant crime incident may have occurred outside of that station's official operational boundaries).

- Finally, if crime trends in the project and buffer zones show marked linearity in the pre-project period then this might suggest that many of the active offenders are common to both areas (and conversely non-linearity might suggest the opposite). If, for instance, one then observes a significant move away from linearity with crime, say, falling in the target area but rising in the buffer zone, then this would provide some evidence for the possibility of displacement to the buffer zone.

Such tests cannot provide firm answers but they do provide confirmatory evidence for any hypotheses. Assuming that we *do* decide that the figures presented in Table 2 *are,* respectively, indicators of diffusion of benefits and displacement — this leaves us with the question — how do we adjust any original estimate of project impact? If one has no alternative explanation for the additional falls in burglary then one might wish — not so much to adjust one's estimate of project impact up — but to create an estimate range based on the addition of these "saved" crimes (e.g., presenting the project as having saved somewhere between 93 and 108 burglaries). In relation to the rise in vehicle crime, it would not be appropriate numerically to deduct one type of offence from another (e.g., the rise in vehicle crime from the burglary savings). Rather, one can simply qualify any presentation of impact with the possibility that there *may* have been some marginal displacement to vehicle crime. What is more important than coming up with a neat single estimate of impact is presenting a clear range of facts and figures together with an account of the underlying assumptions on which these figures are based.

CONCLUDING REMARKS

The purpose of this chapter has been to examine the existing empirical evidence on offenders and offending behaviour to see if one can use this evidence to construct a more systematic strategy for measuring displacement. But even if we can demonstrate that displacement can be measured (albeit roughly!) and is not an inevitable phenomena, the attitude of many practitioners may still be that the effort involved in such a measurement exercise is not worth the investment of time. What this chapter has sought to argue is that this disinclination to measure can be reduced if measurement is placed within the broader context of project development. Predicting displacement offers the opportunity not only to prevent displacement but also to widen the impact of crime reduction work.

A strong case can be made for the need not only to open up the discussion beyond measuring displacement to maximising and measuring a diffusion of benefits, but also to move the discussion onto the wider plane of modelling, maximising and measuring the consequences and impact of crime reduction projects. The concentration of researchers and practitioners on measuring crime outcomes often comes at the expense of ignoring the wider consequences of project work. A recent example of this was evident during an HMIC inspection of a police division where a major undercover operation had been conducted in one of the area's main (and long-standing) "problem estates." The police view of the project was that while several arrests had been made as a result of the operation, these results were not of a sufficient magnitude to justify the considerable investment of resources. The view of the local council housing department, however, was far more positive. Though, only a few convictions had been secured, evidence gathered by the police had assisted the department to evict several key problem families from the estate through civil proceedings. The consequences of these evictions had been dramatic. The level of void properties on the estate declined significantly, as did the level of incivilities. Moreover, the confidence of the residents in their estate and in the police had — reportedly — improved markedly. The revenue savings for the housing department were estimated to far outweigh the operational costs incurred by the police. Moreover, these non-crime outcomes almost certainly would, if they were sustained, also impact on crime levels and patterns in the area.

Even concentrating more narrowly on crime levels there are important issues that extend beyond the simple question of whether crime has been displaced or reduction benefits diffused as a result of crime reduction work. *How and to whom or what* crime has been displaced or benefits of diffusion enjoyed is equally critical and can often have long-term strategic implications. For instance, in this author's research into a burglary reduction scheme in Burnley (Hamilton-Smith, 1999), crime levels fell with limited evidence of displacement either within or outside the target area. However, there was strong evidence that even though crime fell within the target area it fell in such a way that the patterns and concentration of crime altered in certain critical ways. Notably, an area that had previously been characterised by a burglary problem that was driven by a very high rate of burglary *prevalence* and an unusually low rate of repeat victimisation, came to enjoy significantly lower rates of prevalence but at the expense of increased rates of repeat victimisation. Moreover, within the target area the spatial distribution of burglary altered, with offences "retreating" into two notorious council estate areas and increasing in concentration in private residential areas.

The immediate implications of these changes for ongoing crime reduction was obvious (a need to refocus their strategy on repeat victims). However, there were also long-term implications of a broader sort in the movement of offending into private residential areas. This movement coincided with a general upsurge in private renting within these areas, as tenants who had previously lived in council housing areas took advantage of the far cheaper rents and housing available in private residential areas. Council moves to tighten up conditions of tenancy in order to rid themselves of problem tenants also threatened to add to this trend through driving problem tenants into private residential areas. These trends, driven as they were by a mix of housing allocation policies, imbalances in the wider regional housing market structure, and individual resident decisions,[14] had serious implications both for crime reduction practice and also for neighbourhood-based regeneration strategies. Thus, wider social trends, and the consequences of wider social policies, interact with changing trends and patterns in crime. This interaction can often be complex and can produce unforeseen or unintended consequences.

Finally, even if crime reduction measures do not lead to displacement or diffusion of benefits in the short term, the monitoring of crime patterns and trends may reveal more long term adaptations by offenders to blocked opportunities, or more generally may illuminate the exploitation of new opportunities. As Ekblom (1997) has vividly illustrated, offending behaviour evolves, with offenders adapting their offending technique to circumvent blockages, acquiring new skills, resources and associates to exploit alternative targets, and "innovating" to exploit new opportunities. The latter are frequently associated with the development of new high-tech consumer goods or with the emergence of certain social trends.) The proactive identification of new criminal behaviours or new crime patterns clearly allows for an early operational response. An example of this is provided by Hope and Foster (1992) who in examining the impact of regeneration measures on an estate in Hull found that crime within the project area had been displaced internally to one particular part of the estate. However, this picture of short-term displacement was buttressed by a potentially altogether more significant observation: namely, that the regeneration measures had seemingly fostered new connections between older established criminals on the estate and new potential/active criminals who had been allocated accommodation in the area. If true, the long-term implications of these developments would be worrying.

An exclusive preoccupation with displacement is therefore an unhealthy condition. It is symptomatic of the practitioner or academic who conceptualises his or her work as one of reducing the quantity of crime in the short-term (or measuring that reduction). This is not to say that crime cannot or should not be reduced, but rather that this focus needs to broadened to include both the short and long-term *impacts of crime.* In this respect any assessment of displacement and diffusion of benefits needs to be combined with an ongoing assessment of what Barr and Pease (1992) have termed "crime placement." As we have seen, crime levels even if they do not go up or down can nevertheless be redistributed in ways that are either more or less socially harmful. Crime placement raises difficult issues of social justice and equity. The excessive concentration of crime in pockets of deprivation and amongst the most vulnerable members of society *arguably* exacerbates the social harm resulting from crime (whether that be in terms of material loss, personnel injury, or emotional impact), whilst also generating more crime (as criminal opportunities are easier to exploit).

Thus, the way to "sell" the measurement of displacement is to not only link this exercise into the key task of project development (by focussing on maximising the benefits of project work), but also to tie it to the more strategic task of routinely monitoring crime *and social* trends and patterns generally. Positioning the monitoring of displacement and diffusion of benefits in this broader strategic setting adds value to the exercise. Thus placed, such monitoring can inform the ongoing consideration of crime and social trends and the formulation and evaluation of policies, and provide a perspective on the long-term consequences (anticipated or otherwise) of both.

Acknowledgments: With thanks to Peter Homel, Paul Ekblom, Liz Curtin and Nick Tilley for comments upon a draft of this paper. I am particularly indebted to Shane Johnson, Kate Bowers, Alex Hirschfield and Chris Young for their assistance in the development of a buffer zone selection model as part of the RBI monitoring exercise.

Address correspondence to: Niall Hamilton-Smith, Senior Research Officer, Policing and Reducing Crime Unit, Research, Development and Statistics Directorate, U.K. Home Office, Rm. 413/4, Clive House, Petty France, London, SW1H 9HD. E-mail: <Niall.Hamilton-Smith@homeoffice.gsi.gov.uk>.

REFERENCES

Barr, R. and K. Pease (1992). "A Place for Every Crime and Every Crime in Its Place: An Alternative Perspective on Crime Displacement." In: D.J. Evans, N.R. Fyfe and D.T. Herbert (eds.), *Crime, Policing and Place*. London, UK: Routledge.

—— and K. Pease (1990). "Crime Placement, Displacement and Deflection." In: N. Norris and M. Tonry (eds.), *Crime and Justice: A Review of Research*, vol. 12. Chicago, IL: University of Chicago Press.

Beavon, D.J.K., Brantingham, P.J. and P.L. Brantingham (1994). "The Influence of Street Networks on the Patterning of Property Offences." In: R.V. Clarke (ed.), *Crime Prevention Studies*, vol. 2. Monsey, NY: Criminal Justice Press.

Bennett, T. (1986). "Situational Crime Prevention from the Offender's Perspective." In: K. Heal and G.K. Laycock (eds.), *Situational Crime Prevention from Theory into Practice*. London, UK: Her Majesty's Stationery Office.

—— and R. Wright (1984). *Burglars on Burglary: Prevention and the Offender*. Farnborough, UK: Gower.

Bottomley, K. and C. Coleman (1995). "The Police." In: M.A. Walker (ed.), *Interpreting Crime Statistics*. (Royal Statistical Society Lecture Note, Series 1.) Oxford, UK: Clarendon Press.

Bottoms, A.E. (1993). "Recent Criminological and Social Theory: The Problem of Intergrating Knowledge about Individual Criminal Acts and Careers and Areal Dimensions of Crime." In: D.P. Farrington, R.J. Simpson and P-O Wikstrom (eds.), *Intergrating Individual and Ecological Aspects of Crime*. Stockholm, SWE: National Council for Crime Prevention.

—— and P. Wiles (1986). "Housing Tenure and Residential Community Crime Careers in Britain." In: A.J. Reiss and M. Tonry, (eds.), *Communities and Crime*. Chicago, IL: University of Chicago Press.

—— and P. Wiles (1992). "Explanations of Crime and Place." In: D.J. Evans, N.R. Fyfe and D.T. Herbert (eds.), *Crime, Policing and Place: Essays in Environmental Criminology*. London, UK: Routledge.

—— and P. Wiles (1997). "Environmental Criminology." In: M. Maguire, R. Morgan and R. Reiner (eds.), *Oxford Handbook of Criminology* (2nd ed.). Oxford, UK: Clarendon.

Brantingham P.J. and P.L. Brantingham (1981). *Environmental Criminology.* Beverly Hills, CA: Sage.

—— (1984). *Patterns in Crime.* New York, NY: Macmillan.

Budd, T. (1999). *Burglary of Domestic Dwellings: Findings from the British Crime Survey.* (Research, Development and Statistics Directorate Statistical Bulletin, Issue 4/99.) London, UK: Home Office.

Burrows, J. R. Tarling, A. Mackie, R. Lewis and G. Taylor (2000). *Review of Police Force's Crime Recording Practices.* (Home Office Research Study No. 204.) London, UK: Home Office.

Carter R.L. and K.Q. Hill (1979). *The Criminal's Image of the City.* New York, NY: Pergammon Press.

Choli, U. (ed.) (forthcoming). *Distraction Burglary Good Practice Guide.* London, UK: Home Office.

Clarke, R.V. (1999). *Hot Products: Understanding, Anticipating and Reducing Demand for Stolen Goods.* (Police Research Series Paper No. 112.) London, UK: Home Office.

—— and D. Cornish (1985). "Modelling Offenders' Decisions. A Framework for Policy and Research." In: N. Norris and M. Tonry (eds.), *Crime and Justice: A Review of Research,* vol. 6. Chicago, IL: University of Chicago Press.

—— R. Cody and M. Natarajan (1994). "Subway Slugs: Tracking Displacement on the London Underground." *British Journal of Criminology* 34:122-138.

—— and D. Weisburd (1994). "Diffusion of Crime Control Benefits: Observations on the Reverse of Displacement." In: R.V. Clarke (ed.), *Crime Prevention Studies,* vol. 2. Monsey, NY: Criminal Justice Press.

Cohen, L.E. and M. Felson (1979). "Social Change and Crime Rate Trends: A Routine Activity Approach." *American Sociological Review* 44:588-608.

Cornish, D.B. (1994). "The Procedural Analysis of Offending and Its Relevance for Situational Prevention." In: R.V. Clarke (ed.), *Crime Prevention Studies,* vol. 3. Monsey, NY: Criminal Justice Press.

—— and R.V. Clarke (1987). "Understanding Crime Displacement: An Application of Rational Choice Theory." *Criminology* 7:933-47.

—— and R.V. Clarke (eds.) (1986). *The Reasoning Criminal: Rational Choice Perspectives on Offending.* New York, NY: Springer-Verlag.

Cromwell, P.F., J.N. Olson and D.W. Avery (1991). *Breaking and Entering: An Ethnographic Analysis of Burglary.* Newbury Park, CA: Sage.

Ekblom, P. (1997). "Gearing up against Crime: A Dynamic Framework to Help Designers Keep up with the Adaptive Criminal in a Changing World." *International Journal of Risk, Security and Crime Prevention* 214:249-265.

—— (1988). *Getting the Best out of Crime Analysis.* (Crime Prevention Unit Paper No. 10.) London, UK: Home Office.

—— (1987). *Preventing Robberies at Sub-Post Offices: An Evaluation of a Security Initiative.* (Home Office Crime Prevention Unit Paper No. 10.) London, UK: Home Office.

—— and K. Pease (1995). "Evaluating Crime Prevention." In: M. Tonry and N. Norris (eds.), *Crime and Justice; A Review of Research,* vol. 19. Chicago, IL: University of Chicago Press.

Farrington, D.P. (1989). "Self-reported and Official Offending from Adolescence to Adulthood." In: M.W. Klein (ed.), *Cross-national Research in Self-reported Crime and Delinquency.* Dordrecht, NETH: Kluwer.

—— (1987). "Predicting Individual Crime Rates." In: D.M. Gottfredson and M. Tonry (eds.), *Prediction and Classification: Criminal Justice Decision Making.* Chicago, IL: University of Chicago Press.

Felson, M. (1994). *Crime and Everyday Life: Insights and Implications for Society.* Thousand Oaks, CA: Pine Forge Press.

—— and R.V. Clarke (1998). *Opportunity Makes the Thief: Practical Theory for Crime Prevention.* (Police Research Series Paper No. 98.) London, UK: Home Office.

Giddens, A. (1984). *The Constitution of Society.* Cambridge: Polity Press.

Hakim, S. and G.F. Rengert (1981). *Crime Spillover.* Beverly Hills, CA: Sage.

Hamilton-Smith, L.N. (1999). "Safer Cities? A Contextual Analysis of a Multi-agency Crime Prevention Programme." Nottingham, UK: PhD. thesis, Nottingham-Trent University (unpublished).

Heal, K. and G.K. Laycock (1988). "The Development of Crime Prevention: Issues and Limitations." In: T. Hope and M. Shaw (eds.), *Communities and Crime Reduction.* London, UK: Her Majesty's Stationery Office.

Hesseling, R.B.P. (1994). "Displacement: A Review of the Empirical Literature." In: R.V. Clarke (ed.), *Crime Prevention Studies,* vol. 3. Monsey, NY: Criminal Justice Press.

Hobbs, D. (1988). *Doing the Business: Entrepreneurship, Detectives and the Working Class in the East End of London.* Oxford, UK: Clarendon Press.

Hope, T. and J. Foster (1992). "Conflicting Forces: Changing the Dynamics of Crime and Community on a 'Problem' Estate." *British Journal of Criminology* 32:488-504.

Hough M. and N. Tilley (1998). *Getting the Grease to the Squeak: Research Lessons for Crime Prevention.* (Crime Detection and Prevention Series Paper No. 85.) London, UK: Home Office.

Johnson, S.D., K.J. Bowers, A.F.G. Hirschfield and C.A. Young (2000). Measuring the displacement of crime. Presentation to NACRO and Crime Concern, Regional Government Office for the North West, Manchester, UK, May.

Kershaw, C., T. Budd, G. Kinshott, J. Mattinson, P. Mayhew and A. Myhill (2000). *The 2000 British Crime Survey: England and Wales.* (Home Office Statistical Bulletin 18/00.) London, UK: Home Office.

Laycock, G. (1992). "Operation Identification, or the Power of Publicity." In: R. Clarke (ed.), *Situational Crime Prevention: Successful Case Studies.* New York, NY: Harrow and Heston.

Lenz, R. (1986). "Geographical and Temporal Changes among Robberies in Milwaukee." In: R. Figlio, S. Hakim and G. Rengert (eds.), *Metropolitan Crime Patterns.* Monsey, NY: Criminal Justice Press.

Maguire, M. (1982). *Burglary in a Dwelling.* London, UK: Heinemann Educational Books.

Mativat, F. and P. Tremblay (1997). "Counterfeiting Credit Cards: Displacement Effects, Suitable Opportunities and Crime Wave Patterns." *British Journal of Criminology* 37:165-183.

Mayhew, P.M., R.V. Clarke, A. Sturman and M.J. Hough (1976). *Crime as Opportunity.* (Home Office Research Study No. 34.) London, UK: Her Majesty's Stationery Office.

Miethe, T.D. (1991). "Citizen-based Crime Control Activity and Victimization Risks: An Examination of Displacement and Free-rider Effects." *Criminology* 29:419-439.

Painter, K.A. and D.P. Farrington (1999). "Street Lighting and Crime: Diffusion of Benefits in the Stoke-on-Trent Project." In: K.A. Painter and N. Tilley (eds.), *Surveillance of Public Space: CCTV, Street Lighting and Crime Prevention.* (Crime Prevention Studies, vol. 10.) Monsey, NY: Criminal Justice Press.

Pawson, R. and N. Tilley (1997). *Realistic Evaluation.* London, UK: Sage.

Pease, K. (1997). "Crime Prevention." In: M. Maguire et al., *Oxford Handbook of Criminology* (2nd ed.). Oxford, UK: Clarendon.

Povey, D. et al. (2001). *Recorded Crime.* (Home Office Statistical Bulletin 12/01.) London, UK: Home Office.

Poyner, B. (1991). "Video Cameras and Bus Vandalism." *Journal of Security Administration* 11:44-51.

Rengert, G. (1992). "The Journey to Crime: Conceptual Foundations and Policy Implications." In: D.J. Evans, N.R. Fyfe and D.T. Herbert (eds.), *Crime, Policing and Place.* London, UK: Routledge.

—— and J. Wasilchick (1985). *Suburban Burglary.* Springfield, IL: Charles C Thomas.

Reppetto, T.A. (1976). "Crime Prevention and the Displacement Phenomenon." *Crime & Delinquency* 22:166-177.

Sherman, L.W. (1990). "Police Crackdowns: Initial and Residual Deterrence." In: M. Tonry and N. Morris (eds.), *Crime and Justice; A Review of Research,* vol. 12. Chicago, IL: University of Chicago Press.

Skogan, W.G. (1986). "Fear of Crime and Neighbourhood Change." In: A.J. Reiss and M. Tonry, (eds.), *Communities and Crime.* Chicago, IL: University of Chicago Press.

Tarling, R. (1993). *Analysing Offending: Data Models and Interpretation.* London, UK: Her Majesty's Stationery Office.

Taub, R. D.G. Taylor and J.D. Dunham (1984). *Paths of Neighbourhood Change.* Chicago, IL: University of Chicago Press.

U.K. Her Majesty's Inspectorate of Constabulary (2000). *On the Record: Thematic Inspection Report on Police Crime Recording, the Police National Computer and Phoenix Intelligence System Data Quality.* London, UK: Home Office.

U.K. Home Office (2000). *A Review of Crime Statistics.* London, UK: Home Office.

Urry, J. (1991). "Time and Space in Giddens' Social Theory." In: C.G.A. Bryant and D. Jary (eds.), *Giddens' Theory of Structuration: A Critical Appreciation.* London, UK: Routledge.

Wiles, P. and A. Costello (2000). *The 'Road to Nowhere': The Evidence for Travelling Criminals.* (Home Office Research Study No. 207.) London, UK: Home Office.

Wright, R. and S. Decker (1994). *Burglars on the Job: Street Life and Residential Break-ins.* Boston, MA: Northeastern University Press.

NOTES

1. Tarling (1993), for instance, found that the average length of an offending career for nearly 60% of men and nearly 80% of women was less than one year.

2. See also Laycock (1992) for an example of a similar effect achieved in a different operational setting.

3. For an example of the difficulties experienced in measuring displacement from thinly dispersed low-volume crime, see Ekblom's (1987) study of post office robberies.

4. As an extension of Sherman's (1990) crackdown approach, Ken Pease has recently advocated the systematic development of disinformation strategies that would seek to "trick" offenders into believing that their risk of apprehension, and/or the restriction in opportunities, is more severe than it in fact is.

5. A post-project version of this process would be methodologically dubious as it would invite participants to make sense of pre-project patterns on the basis of post-project results.

6. A problem observed in the RBI monitoring exercise was that while practitioners frequently had a rich repository of knowledge on local offending, they did not always critically scrutinise the use they made of it. For instance, one common tendency has been for practitioners to choose offence types as potential routes for likely displacement, not on the basis of theoretical plausibility, but on the basis of the offence being one of a number about which they are routinely preoccupied. For instance, invariably practitioners nominate "robbery" as a possible route of displacement from "burglary" in spite of the fact that in many cases their own local knowledge demonstrates that this is theoretically implausible.

7. The most likely site for spatial displacement may not always be the same as the most logical site for any spatial diffusion of benefits. To use a hypothetical example, a project area may be bordered by two other areas with which project area offenders are familiar and where alternative criminal opportunities are available. The project may result in a diffusion of benefits to one of these adjacent areas owing to offenders perceiving that project work is restricting opportunities in this area. However, offenders may still feel that opportunities are available in the second adjacent area and may consequently displace in this direction. Thus, displacement and diffusion of benefits could occur simultaneously in two different areas (and of course could equally occur simultaneously within one area!).

8. "Distraction burglary" (or "burglary artifice") refers to burglary offences where the offender gains entry to a property through means of a trick such as, commonly, posing as an official.

9. Bottoms (1993) has previously commented on the importance of understanding the symbolic significance of locations to offenders. A reliance purely on formal data will not provide access to many of the more subtle social dynamics and meanings attendant on specific locations. However, these more qualitative perspectives are important because an offender's offending decisions will not simply be based on a mechanistic assessment of social space but will also take into account these symbolic attachments.

10. This is a good instance of a project where the consideration of possible displacement should be linked to the refinement of the project's reduction strategy. As evidence already existed of offenders offending in both areas, with the footbridge providing the sole point of access for foot-based offenders, the project should ideally have broadened its work to include perhaps some form of increased surveillance on the footbridge to deter or detect offenders using it as a transport corridor for stolen goods. Through such a strategy potential displacement could be transformed into a diffusion of project benefits.

11. The term "heading" is used here because the single figure that is being taken is in fact the sum of the four Home Office vehicle crime notifiable offence categories. It may sometimes be appropriate and more clear cut *initially* to aggregate offence categories like this to produce one total that covers a distinct and coherent family of offences.

12. See Painter and Farrington (1999) for a recent study that has demonstrated the generalised crime reduction effect that can follow the introduction of street lighting.

13. If one has produced a "portfolio" of all the similar types of offences that one would theoretically expect that this group of offenders could displace to, then one could examine this full portfolio rather than just the target offence.

14. For more detailed coverage of how housing market and allocation dynamics can impact on neighbourhoods (and in particular on patterns of crime) see Bottoms and Wiles (1986, 1992) and Taub et al. (1984).

COST-BENEFIT ANALYSIS FOR CRIME PREVENTION:
Opportunity Costs, Routine Savings and Crime Externalities[1]

by

John Roman
The Urban Institute

and

Graham Farrell
University of Cincinnati and
Jill Dando Institute of Crime Science

Abstract: *Research on cost-benefit analysis of situational crime prevention is examined and found wanting. The few existing studies do not accurately represent the likely benefits of the situational approach. While measures of non-monetary crime costs are improving, at least four other key areas warrant more attention: First, "routine savings" derive from routine precautions. Second, models of victim (producer) and offender (consumer) surplus are underdeveloped in this field. Third, crime externalities occur when entities (such as manufacturers, premises managers, some persons and environments) produce targets and situations that provide criminal opportunities. These entities "externalize" or do not bear the crime costs to society that they produce. We propose the concept of "crime as pollution" for the study of crime externalities, and outline the potential of policies adapted from environmental economics. Fourth, the intentional absence of crime prevention has an opportunity cost that might be examined as a form of negligent omission.*

I. INTRODUCTION

It is a truth universally acknowledged that a policy maker in possession of a large pending decision must be in want of a cost-benefit analysis. However little known the feelings or views of the policy maker, this truth is so well fixed in the minds of the surrounding advisors, that the decision is considered the rightful property of someone or other of their economists.[2]

There is a relative dearth of extant cost-benefit analyses of crime prevention. The most useful and comprehensive review is that of Welsh and Farrington (1999), who identify only 13 studies, and note that they are of widely varying quality. It is also the case that not all of the 13 studies included cost-benefit analyses: the 1999 article notes that they had to construct some of the cost-benefit analyses where the relevant information was available. Yet, despite this seemingly poor present state of affairs, this emerging cost-benefit literature is an implicit acknowledgement that crime prevention research is making progress. In fact, the argument can be made that cost-benefit analysis is a second-generation evaluation tool for crime prevention, since it moves beyond the questions 'Can crime be prevented?' and onto the more advanced questions 'Where and when is crime prevention most efficient?', or, rather, 'What factors allow crime prevention to maximize the net social benefit that it can produce?'. We argue here that expanding both the conceptualization and use of cost–benefit analysis is a critical next step in developing effective crime prevention policy and programming, and we offer some potential approaches to initiating these efforts.

It can be argued that, from a policy perspective, cost-benefit analysis has always been present in the study of crime prevention. Like it or not, cost-benefit analysis (hereafter CBA) is implicit to almost all crime prevention effort, in the same way it is implicit in most evaluation and assessment. When a prevention program is demonstrably shown to yield positive outcomes, it is normally assumed, at least in policy circles, that the overall benefit is greater than the overall cost, even when this is not empirically demonstrated. There are three main reasons why empirical CBAs are so few in number. First, crime prevention is an emerging area of research. Second, many programs, decision makers (and researchers) adhere to the notion that, where there are positive programmatic outcomes, logic dictates that the benefits truly outweigh the costs (and you just know it). Third, it is sometimes difficult and expensive, in relative terms, to do a comprehensive CBA of crime prevention that includes quantification of the whole range of costs and benefits (see Cohen, 2000; Greenwood et al., 1996; Miller et al., 1996; Gramlich, 1981). Fourth, even the most sophisticated analyses of costs and benefits can often be picked apart as and when necessary by the critic, so that many programs are reticent about undergoing a CBA.

A general implication of this discussion is that either the standard of CBA as applied to crime prevention needs to improve, or else there needs to be a formal delineation of its potential and limits as it applies to this field. For the most part, the key problems relating to implementing quality cost-benefit analyses are not related to its theoretical appropriateness, but rather lie within its application. However, it is also proposed below that the cost-benefit analysis of crime prevention might benefit from expanding its focus. As with most emerging areas of study, there are a range of areas that remain to be explored. One aim of this essay is to begin to chart some of those areas.

In what follows, the role of cost-benefit analysis in evaluation in general, and its application to (situational) crime prevention in particular, are described. This is followed by a discussion of cost-benefit methodology, which, it is proposed, has been rather misunderstood in its current application. The subsequent section examines some of the more controversial aspects of measurement relating to cost-benefit analysis, and offers suggestions for progress. Finally, we suggest three areas for exploration using cost-benefit analysis. It is proposed that the opportunity cost of the absence of crime prevention should be assessed using CBA. It is also proposed that many crimes can be viewed as a form of "externality" or "pollution," or the unwanted byproduct that is caused by manufacturers making products that create criminal opportunities. Following these two analyses, it is proposed that there is a need for a policy alternative in response to manufacturing processes and designs that create criminal opportunities.

Assumptions of and Definitions for This Essay

Some familiarity of the reader with the crime prevention literature is assumed. More specifically, the first given is that situational crime prevention can work, and that crime can be prevented (see the previous volumes of the *Crime Prevention Studies* series, the *Security Journal,* or the series of over 100 studies produced by the Policing and Reducing Crime Unit of the U.K. Home Office). The second given is that not all prevented crime is displaced (see Eck, 1993; Hesseling, 1994). Often no prevented crime is displaced (committed at or by a different time, place, crime type, modus operandi, or offender), and when some is displaced it is typically less than 100%, so that a net social benefit generally still results. Further, crime displacement might be preferably viewed as crime deflection and used as a policy tool to deliberately shape crime patterns so as to minimize their over-all social cost (Barr and Pease, 1990). The third given is that crime prevention can sometimes result in a diffusion of benefits. The term 'diffusion of crime prevention benefits' refers to the notion that effective crime prevention in one location can produce reductions in crime in neighboring areas or in relation to other types of crime (see Clarke and Weisburd [1994] for the definitive statement). Fourth, it is assumed that individuals who are, or own, potential targets, are risk-averse, and that risk-aversion does not vary with levels of crime. We refer to 'situational' crime prevention (Clarke, 1980, 1995, 1998) as crime prevention.[3]

For simplicity, the key definitions relating to cost-benefit analysis that are stated by Dhiri and Brand (1999) are used throughout and are reproduced as Appendix 1. The one modification for present purposes is the acknowledgement that monetary units of measurement for cost-benefit analysis are merely a commonly accepted reference point for marginal utility units (i.e., welfare gain or loss). While many commentators are generally content that most costs and benefits can be converted to a consistent unit of analysis — i.e., can be monetized — some find this notion abhorrent, perhaps misunderstanding the rationale. The key aspects of the rationale are that utility units are the real issue, but that money is used as a more readily comprehendible proxy, and that while measurement is often imperfect, a far worse option is to exclude such cost items altogether. Social costs and benefits as referred to here can include both monetized and non-monetized components. Finally, since 'costs' and 'benefits' are the same thing viewed from the opposite side of the riverbank (costs are negative benefits, benefits are negative costs, and together they result in changes in net social welfare), they are sometimes referred to simply as costs. These issues are not discussed further.

II. WHY COST-BENEFIT ANALYSIS?

The analysis of the costs and benefits of crime prevention is necessary since, even though crime may be prevented (one of the 'givens,' above), it is certainly plausible that the cost of prevention could outweigh the benefits. In such a case, allowing the present situation to continue is a preferable policy solution, presumably while seeking a less costly form of crime prevention. Cost-effectiveness analysis — a variation of CBA to allow comparison of the outcomes of policy options with comparable costs — is also worth pursuing to allow for selection among a menu of prevention programs, given scarce public and private resources for all things.

Cost-benefit analysis as it has evolved in applied social research is a form of evaluation. In theory it is arguably the most sophisticated form of evaluation currently available. However, the absence of relevant information in many instances, the research expenses incurred in collecting the requisite data for small projects, traditional impediments to creating well-conceived comparison groups, as well as the sometimes disputed nature and definitions of the assumptions (and sometimes even the variables) involved, often distinguish the practice from the theory.

The main aim of CBA, like all forms of evaluation, is to provide information of utility to policy makers. The information might be used to assess and refine current policy, or to develop new policies. CBA can be focused on different levels, from the evaluation of philosophies and perspectives, to assessment of strategies, policies, tactics, specific activities, or the manner in which combinations of these are applied in specific circumstances. However, since crime prevention efforts typically need to be tailored to specific crime types and contexts, the theoretical spectrum of applications of crime prevention, and hence of the CBAs required, could be infinite. Hence for the purposes of informing crime control policy, evaluation via cost benefit analysis might usefully inform broad areas of knowledge. This may be related to the fact that cost-benefit analysis developed as an economic instrument for the assessment of macro level social policies, whereas its application in relation to crime prevention has been primarily at the micro- or project level. However, unlike many interventions typically studied using a CBA framework, crime prevention has clear macro- and micro-policy effects. Therefore, CBA seems especially well suited for its study.

Implicit Cost-Benefit Analysis

Individuals and society have already made many implicit cost-benefit decisions and continue to do so on an ongoing basis. Some people may choose to spend money on vacation rather than invest in a burglar alarm. Governments may have chosen to invest in education, health, education and crime control instead of transportation infrastructure. In each case, the decision between competing priorities is one of resource allocation: money is allocated to each up to the point where the perceived marginal costs and benefits are equal, i.e., where an extra dollar spent on more of it — the marginal cost — would give less extra or marginal benefit than spending the dollar on an alternative option, within their given resource constraints. In their implicit cost-benefit calculations, governments incorporate the estimated costs of going against the will of the public and various pressure groups, which may reflect imperfect knowledge or beliefs about crime. Governments at all levels make similar decisions in resource allocation between competing social policy priorities, including crime prevention.

It is clear that many informal, implicit, and possibly ill-informed cost-benefit analyses take place on an ongoing basis, influencing decisions varying from those of the individual to those of social policy. Each decision relates in some way, often indirectly, to spending on crime prevention. As such, each decision can be viewed as embodying a cost-benefit analysis of crime prevention in all its varieties. An aim of formal cost-benefit analysis in the field of crime prevention, therefore, might be to reduce the inaccuracy of current implicit cost-benefit decisions. Reducing inaccuracy may be a more modest and realistic goal, perhaps preferable to a holy grail of CBA informed by perfect information. Such a shift in emphasis is potentially important, however, for crime prevention research and how it relates to policy. It suggests that easily-obtained broad-brush cost-benefit parameters, with reasonable confidence intervals, may be a more realistic and more useful aim than one of conducting a perfect cost-benefit analysis that accounts for all of the minutiae. For crime policy purposes, "rough 'n ready" may be preferable to "perfect but never completed," since a benchmark with known limitations is better than none.

Break-even Analysis

Ekblom and Pease (1995), among others, suggest that evaluators should, prior to implementation of an intervention, identify the mechanisms by which a crime prevention intervention is expected to work. That is to say, it is not enough to know that a program produces a desirable outcome: Evaluators should endeavor to determine *a priori* why it is expected to work. An analogous suggestion could be made in relation to cost-benefit analysis. It should be possible for evaluators to produce broad parameter estimates of a break-even point for interventions, prior to implementation. For example, assuming some knowledge of the costs of the crime (from previous studies), and some estimate of the fixed and variable costs of the intervention, it would be possible to produce an estimate of the reduction in crime that would be required to reach a break-even point. It could then be determined whether the required prevention level is realistic. Examples using limiting cases will clarify the issue and its potential utility: If a crime is minor and the proposed intervention is expensive, it might require a 95% reduction in crime to break even. Absent a particularly strong preventive mechanism, that required prevention level is unlikely to be attained. However, if the crime being targeted is very costly to society, and the intervention is very cheap, then a 2% reduction in crime might be the break-even point. A proposed project is risky if it has a high break-even point and uses an untried prevention measure in a context where the preventive mechanism is uncertain. A proposed project is far less risky if it has a low break-even point where only a small percentage drop in crime required to produce a net gain. This latter scenario might be the case where, for example, a project replicates the application of a successful intervention, but puts it in a different context that is also thought to be conducive to a sound preventive mechanism being triggered.

Towards Standard Cost Estimates

The pioneering work of Miller et al. (1996) produced estimates of the tangible and intangible costs of crime for a range of crime types. Though their estimation method of victim-compensation has been questioned (and is discussed later,) it is nevertheless a landmark in the study of the costs of crime. The Miller et al. estimates were brilliantly adapted by Painter and Farrington (1999) in their cost-benefit analysis of improved street lighting. Painter and Farrington applied the Miller et al. estimates of the costs of crime to their own crime prevention scenario. In fact, Painter and Farrington may light the way towards methodological standardization of cost-benefit analysis for crime prevention. Assuming that estimates such as those of Miller are continually updated (and that any critics of the methodology can present improved or competing estimates rather than simply throwing mud), the field of cost-benefit analysis of crime prevention should improve markedly and be able to achieve some degree of methodological standardization. Such an element of standardization could result since, even if local project cost estimates vary widely from national estimates (Miller et al., [1996] use the U.S. National Crime Victimization Survey), they could be compared via the common metric of the standardized national estimates. Spatial variation in cost estimates will simply produce different lenses through which interventions can be compared. Local, regional, national or international mean estimates of the costs of crime are all simply different means or standards that allow different levels and types of comparability.

The following section examines the underlying economic model for measuring the costs and benefits of crime prevention. The section after that uses this model to inform cost-benefit models of crime prevention that look at prevention outcomes that typically have not been explained by conventional CBA applications.

III. DEVELOPING A COST-BENEFIT MODEL

This section examines the key components of the CBA model. The fundamental of this approach to evaluation might be thus summarized: Analysis of marginal costs and benefits, appropriately discounting for future events, can inform researchers and policy makers about changes in 'net social welfare' resulting from crime prevention initiatives.

Traditional Types of CBA

CBA was developed as a straightforward application of standard macroeconomic techniques in cases where a third-party intervened in the free market, leading to changes in consumer and/or producer behavior (Gramlich, 1991, 1998). Three types of intervention dominate the cost-benefit literature:

(1) *Product viability*: The first 'traditional' application of CBA is to determine whether a product is viable in the market. An example would be a judgment, an evaluation, relating to the production of a new drug. The CBA would compare the expected efficacy to the potential lethality, subject to information constraints, since both effectiveness and lethality of a new drug are unknown. This is the category into which most crime prevention research to date would fit — determining whether the crime prevention benefits of an intervention outweigh the costs. The programmatic cost-benefit evaluations, such as those conducted within the Safer Cities programmes (Ekblom et al., 1996) and the ongoing ambitious cost-benefit and cost-effectiveness assessments which will be produced within the U.K.'s Crime Reduction Programme (see Dhiri and Brand, 1999; Legg and Powell, 2000), would fit within this category, as akin to an evaluation of a portfolio of products. However, it is also the case that this category of cost-benefit analysis has far broader applications in the crime prevention sphere. For example, CBA would be applicable to the testing of new consumer products in determining the extent to which they might encourage or facilitate crime. The crime 'Foresight' program being developed in the U.K. (U.K. Department of Trade and Industry, 2000) is currently tackling such issues. The program may find that proposing a CBA approach will accelerate the implementation and broader adoption of the assessment of the criminogenic potential of new consumer products.

(2) *Government intervention in a monopoly market*: The most common example of CBA evaluations are those of a govern-

mental intervention in a monopoly market. The intervention typically takes the form of a tax or regulation, when it is assumed that social welfare is less than would be the case were there multiple suppliers. Such could be the case for an electricity monopoly where prices and output levels may be tightly regulated. This is arguably the relevant category for the analysis of aspects of government intervention to tackle the absence of crime prevention in many situations of market failure that, inadvertently or otherwise, promote crime (if absence can be viewed as a monopoly that needs breaking). Other crime-related examples would be the debates relating to the overall social cost or benefit of introducing privatization and competition to policing and prisons.

(3) *Taxation*: The third traditional application of CBA relates to the application of a tax. The basic question to be answered is 'Does a tax produce a net social benefit?' Increased social welfare is the aim of taxation: the question is, do societal benefits outweigh the costs, where such notions as freedom, justice and equity are included in the cost-benefit calculus, in addition to resource transfers. The correct level of general taxation, such as that on income is, of course, hotly contended, but the principle remains the same. Typically, cost-benefit analysis is applied to a situation where it is found, for example, that use of a product creates negative externalities. An example would be where, in relation to emissions from automobiles, the government imposes a tax to both change consumer and producer behavior. The tax reduces driving by consumers because of the higher cost, while the extra funds provided *could* be used to reimburse those harmed by emissions. In other instances, a fine or other punishment could also be imposed upon producers, such as manufacturers causing pollution. The punishment would encourage manufacturers to reduce the externalities, that is, to cut pollution, or to compensate society for the pollution costs imposed. Paul Ekblom suggested that "where crime problems are 'externalized' (i.e., where those who create the opportunity are not those who suffer the consequential crime) sanctions could be introduced to encourage closing the loophole" (Ekblom, 1998:29).

This third main category of CBA can be applied to crime policy in various ways. Fines and imprisonment are a tax imposed upon offenders for the cost they impose by their offending, and part of the aim is to change consumer behavior (to deter offenders). Victim compensation has a precise parallel with the funds used to compensate those harmed by emissions into the environment (crimes). Perhaps most importantly for crime prevention, however, is the possibility that CBA might be used to encourage reductions in criminogenic products and environments. For many years, car makers produced cars without necessarily building in the socially optimal level of crime prevention to car designs. Whether inadvertent or not, the manufacturers saved on costs at the expense of the public. The result has been millions of car crimes of various sorts. It is certainly plausible to suggest that auto manufacturers could be encouraged to build in crime prevention to their products that would produce a significant reduction in crime and a major reduction in cost experienced by society as a whole.[4] A cost-benefit analysis would tease out the specifics and propose a level of taxation, fines or other regulation, that might encourage manufacturers (and/or designers of products, buildings and environments) to reduce the level of criminal opportunity supplied by their products, while accounting for the costs of doing so (such as increased consumer prices and/or reductions in profit from automobile production) from changes in the supply of automobiles). If it is argued that the creation of criminal opportunities also causes criminality by encouraging offenders to commit crime and to accelerate a criminal career, then the social cost is even greater. Many examples of crime externalities exist, and the argument could be made that some types of crime (but not all — it would be difficult to categorize domestic violence as such) should be viewed as forms of pollution (Farrell, 2000). This application of CBA may have potentially significant implications for the cost-benefit analysis of crime prevention and for crime policy as a whole. The issue is returned to later in this essay.

Limitations of CBA

Formal CBA has four implicit restrictions. First is that the goal of a cost-benefit analysis is to compare the current state of affairs to one where the market is expected to behave *more* efficiently. Programs that sacrifice efficiency for effectiveness (specialized courts such as drug courts tend to fall into this category) are much more difficult to evaluate. Second is the fact that the effects being studied have to include a change in the behavior of either the consumer of the good or the producer of the good or both. In the absence of a behavioral change, cost-benefit analysis is unnecessary: it is simply an exercise in accounting. Third, cost-benefit analysis is often performed in situations where information is imperfect: therefore the analyst must perform the analysis with caution and prudence, but preferably without pride and prejudice. Fourth, it is assumed that producers and consumers will act rationally, at least according to the economic definition of rationality (maximization of utility). This last point can sometimes raise the hackles of readers unfamiliar with the territory. The most likely explanation for this is misunderstanding over the use of a range assumptions. Such assumptions are made to add clarity and manageability to a complex subject, and can be modified and adapted as necessary to fit different scenarios and conditions.

CBA and the Market for Crime

Economic models of crime are typically models of punishment, and equate risk with price, at least since the time of Becker (1968). The present model is of crime prevention rather than punishment, however. The next short section outlines how the relationship of risk and price differs in the crime prevention market model from its role in the traditional economic punishment model, since this is central to an understanding of what follows in relation to cost-benefit analysis.

Redefining Risk

As with the economic model of crime and punishment, price equates to risk in our economic model of crime prevention. However, in this model, risk explicitly incorporates elements of the time and effort required by an offender to commit an offence. Hence risk can be manipulated via a crime prevention intervention that increases the time and effort required to commit an offence. In the traditional punishment model of crime, variation in punishment was the principal means by which public policy could influence risk. In the present analysis, risk levels and the supply of criminal opportunities can be manipulated via policies and practices that influence the actual and perceived time and effort required to commit an offence. Other punishment variables are assumed constant in order that key influences upon risk, namely the supply and demand for criminal opportunities, can be perceived. While the emphasis here is upon crime prevention, a combined model that integrates prevention and punishment influences upon risk can also be envisaged.

Victim Surplus and Offender Surplus

CBA is a tool that is fundamentally concerned with measuring changes in surplus. In traditional analysis of social policy, there are two types of surplus: producer surplus and consumer surplus. With respect to the market for crime we adopt the terms 'victim surplus' and 'offender surplus,' respectively. A simple translation is to think (as proposed by van Dijk, 1992) of victims as the *unwilling* producers of a supply of criminal opportunities, and of offenders as the consumers who produce a demand for criminal opportunities. Hence victims are producers, and offenders are consumers in what follows.

A victim surplus is incurred since, at a given market level of risk required to commit an offense, some members of society would (unwillingly) supply criminal opportunities at a lower level of risk. That is, some targets would have provided some easier criminal opportunities. These potential targets decline in number as risk levels decline, down to a very small number who take virtually no anti-crime measures. These persons are society's free-riders, who have purchased less than the market level of protection (perhaps less guardianship or less security), so that the victim surplus is not a good thing for society.

An offender surplus is also incurred since, at any given risk level, some offenders would have committed crimes at a higher risk level. However, society loses since these higher-risk crimes are not committed. Therefore, if offenders are not allowed to stockpile reduced risk (i.e., offenders are made to commit riskier crimes closer to their highest level of risk tolerance), then society benefits from a reduction in offender surplus. Note that, contrary to what might be expected, society gains in the crime market from both a reduction in victim surplus and in offender surplus. This is precisely the inverse of a traditional market, where both consumer and producer surpluses are positive. Due to the manner in which these social costs operate, it is arguable that they might preferably be termed victim deficit and offender deficit rather than surpluses, but we retain the traditional terminology for simplicity in the present instance. In the market for crime therefore, the key is to realize that a reduction in victim surplus, or a reduction in offender surplus, is a good thing for society even though it initially sounds counterintuitive.

How does a crime prevention intervention produce a net social benefit? Society experiences a net social benefit if an intervention yields a net reduction in victim surplus, a net reduction in offender surplus, or a combination of increases and reductions where there is a net reduction in overall surplus. This can be illustrated. Figure 1 shows an equilibrium in a market for crime where curve S_1 represents the supply of criminal opportunities by unwilling victims, and the curve D_1 the demand for crime by offenders.[5] The market has a level of risk shown by p_1 and a quantity of crime committed of q_1. The victim surplus is described by the area 'A' and offender surplus by the area 'B.' Aside from the changes in terminology, this representation is, so far, essentially the same as that of a traditional commodity market. For present illustrative purposes we discuss a crime market for theft of new automobiles. Into this scenario, a government intervention is introduced that encourages manufacturers to improve the level of security on new cars as they are produced. Such an intervention was described by Barry Webb (Webb, 1993) when government legislation made car steering wheel locks mandatory.[6, 7] Due to the intervention, the level of risk that offenders incur to commit a car theft has increased in the aggregate. This is shown in Figure 2 as an inward shift in the supply curve, representing a reduction in the supply of criminal opportunities, from S_1 to S_2, and an increase in risk from p_1 to p_2. As a result, the number of crimes committed falls from q_1 to $q2$.

The government intervention to reduce the supply of criminal opportunities for a given level of risk has clearly reduced crime. The net social gain however, is shown by the changes in surplus. Victims have lost the surplus described by the shaded area 'C' in Figure 2, which represents a benefit to society (less low-security potential targets since all new cars are now safer). Victims have gained, and offenders lost, the surplus described by area 'D.' Area 'D' is a transfer and represents no change in net social welfare. Offender surplus is reduced by the checkered area 'E,' also representing a benefit to society. In this simple model, whether society gains or loses in the aggregate as a result of the intervention is dependent upon the relative sizes of the cost and benefit components shown as areas C (social benefit), D (transfer) and E (benefit). In Figure 2, a net social benefit is produced since the additional surpluses from area C and E are removed, which in this inverse model is a good thing. Hence, the crime prevention intervention shown in Figure 2 produces a net social benefit.

The simple model presented here shows effective crime prevention behavior where only positive behaviors are produced. The price of crime (risk) increases, and the quantity of crime decreases (from q_1 to $q2$). It would be similarly simple to show the converse and manipulate these models to show costs to society. In the case where both supply and demand shift, and the elasticities of one or the other also change, it is theoretically possible to conceptualize a net increase in overall surplus, leading to a net loss in social welfare.[8] The challenge to researchers is to model the various components of these changes, and it is proposed that the crime and prevention model has the potential to be adapted to a range of such purposes.

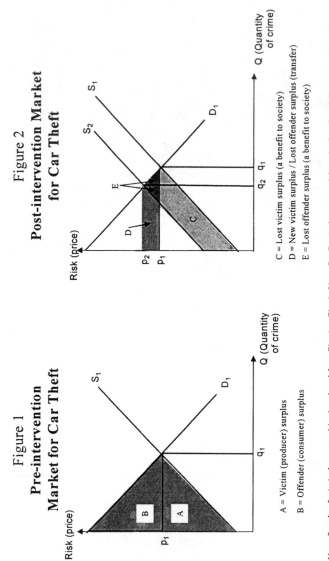

Figure 1
Pre-intervention
Market for Car Theft

A = Victim (producer) surplus

B = Offender (consumer) surplus

Figure 2
Post-intervention Market
for Car Theft

C = Lost victim surplus (a benefit to society)

D = New victim surplus / Lost offender surplus (transfer)

E = Lost offender surplus (a benefit to society)

Note: Supply of criminal opportunities is reduced from Fig. 1 to Fig. 2. Since C + E > 0 then net social surplus is reduced (i.e. net social gain).

Elsewhere, the mechanisms by which crime prevention produces shifts in the supply of criminal opportunities and demand for offending have been described in more detail (Farrell et al., 2000). Increasing the time and effort required to commit an offence, and reducing the supply of criminal opportunities, increases the market risk-price. Reductions in the rewards derived from an offence however, produce a decrease in demand for offences at a given level of risk (since it is less profitable while equally risky). In contrast, an increase in crime is likely to result from an increase in the volume of consumer goods that are suitable for theft. This tracks the mechanism described by routine activity theory, producing an outward shift in the supply curve, and an increase in the supply of criminal opportunities. From a crime prevention perspective, therefore, since more consumer goods typically produce more suitable targets, society might aim to produce goods that are less vulnerable to theft or other crime, and that therefore do not produce the same increase in available criminal opportunities. This is an issue returned to later.

From the basic crime market model that portrays victim and offender surpluses, a range of avenues for exploration can be derived. The elasticity of supply and demand are clearly important. For many types of crime, particularly those committed by opportunistic, unskilled, inexperienced and uncommitted offenders, the demand for crime will be quite elastic (a shallow demand curve). Here, an investment in crime prevention producing even a small reduction in the number of criminal opportunities on the market, or a slight increase in risk, would produce a disproportionately large net social gain. Professional, organized or highly motivated criminals might be expected to have a demand for crime that, while still fairly elastic for the most part, would be less elastic than that of opportunistic offenders. The crime market model would show how the offences they commit would require a more substantial crime prevention effort to produce increases in risk sufficient to prevent or deter these offenders. The simplified supply and demand curves shown as straight lines in Figures 1 and 2 would more realistically be expected to be complex functions. The related issues of the influence of crime displacement and the diffusion of benefits, and the net social cost or benefits that result, are areas outside the purview of the present essay, but present potentially rich veins for exploration by further research.

IV. MEASURING NON-MONETARY COSTS

CBA for crime prevention is not without areas of unresolved debate. The issue of the measurement (or not) of non-monetary costs is a key area of concern. Can and should the psychological and other 'emotional' costs including, potentially, various forms of stress disorder, be incorporated into cost-benefit analysis of crime prevention? To date, the default option for CBA of crime prevention has been to exclude the non-monetary costs of crime. The justifications for this approach vary: sometimes no explanation is given, sometimes the justification is that estimates are not available, sometimes non-monetary costs are deemed irrelevant, and sometimes they are deemed impractical to incorporate since the estimates vary widely. Further, the debate is not confined solely to the field of crime prevention. The more popular debate over the 'costing' of a human life also relates to a range of policy areas, particularly that of public health provision and insurance. It remains a contentious issue (see *Economist* [2001] for a short summary relating to the health debate).

The debate over non-monetary costs is reflected in the terminology. Terminology varies from the optimistic term 'non-monetary costs' (which implies they can still be estimated and compared to monetary costs via a common metric), through 'intangible costs' (which recognizes their existence but seems skeptical of measurement), to the more pessimistic term 'unquantifiable costs' (which, as the name implies, suggests they cannot be quantified and therefore, for policy purposes, effectively do not exist).

Whether to include, and if so, how to measure non-monetary costs, are important issues for the study of crime prevention and for crime policy in general. Two key and related questions seem to underpin the debate The first is: 'Are non-monetary costs important enough to warrant inclusion in cost-benefit analysis?' The second is: 'Can non-monetary costs be estimated?' These questions are tackled after a brief look at the methodologies associated with estimating costs.

Estimation Methods

In general, the economic literature suggests the use of a "shadow market" to evaluate the costs associated with a transaction for which no market exists. A shadow market is typically some existing market that is analogous to the market to be evaluated. In general, there are two methods for evaluating the cost associated with crime (see Gramlich, 1981; Rajkumar and French, 1997; Cohen et al., 1994; Miller et al., 1996; Roman and Harrell, 2001). Each of these models attempts to use different shadow markets to measure a price associated with criminal incidents. The two methods are:

(1) *willingness-to-pay* estimates, which are based on the price one would be willing to pay to avoid damages, such as death or

disability, that result from crime. Methods of estimating will-ingness to pay include: *required compensation*, which esti-mates the price that an individual would have to receive in or-der to risk exposure to a dangerous event; *property-value*, where differences in crime rates and property values are com-pared to estimate the amount individuals will pay to avoid crime and its costs; and, *quality-of-life*, which estimates costs according to degrees of disability;

(2) *victim-compensation* or willingness to accept, the converse of willingness to pay. This is the aggregated amount that would have to be paid to a victim to compensate for his or her tangi-ble and intangible costs. Methods of estimating willingness to accept include: *jury compensation*, which values victim costs at the rate juries compensate victims of crime, including health care, lost productivity and intangible costs such as pain and suffering; *discounted future earnings* estimates, which are based solely on the costs (or averted costs) of lost productivity due to an incident; and *cost of illness*, which uses survey data to aggregate the tangible cost of crime, including health and productivity [Roman et al., 1998].

To date, there is no best practice in benefits estimation, but the most common method of estimation has been victim compensation as estimated by cost of illness As Rajkumar and French (1996) note, this method tends to underestimate true costs because no intangible costs (pain and suffering, fear) are included in the estimate. However, given the high degree of uncertainty in measuring intangible costs, it is often thought to be prudent to exclude them. When it comes to crime, however, the substantial extent of intangibles means that their exclusion in some instances produces potentially misleading findings. The next sections tackle the two questions raised above re-garding the issue:

(1) Are non-monetary costs important?

The answer to this question is an unequivocal 'yes.' For crimes such as rape and domestic violence, the non-monetary costs of the trauma can be far more significant than any actual financial costs in many instances. To exclude non-monetary costs would reduce the apparent impact of these crimes many times over. In practical terms this will make these crimes less likely to be addressed by prevention initiatives, and, when the results come in, it will severely understate the gain derived from any crimes being prevented.

(2) Can non-monetary costs be estimated?

The answer to this question is a definite 'yes,' with the rider that the methods and techniques need to be replicated, revised, and improved upon. The pioneering Miller et al. (1996) work warrants further description in the context of suggestions as to how crime prevention evaluation might build upon it. Miller et al. utilized the victim-compensation model to show how the intangible costs of crime are, as might be expected, far more significant in relation to crimes such as rape than they are for crimes such as burglary. Regardless of the disputed merits of the victim-compensation approach, it is clear that rankings of crime according to their overall costs would be significantly influenced by the exclusion of intangible costs.

Table 1: Tangible and Intangible Costs of Crime

Crime	Tangible Costs	Intangible Costs	Total Costs	Cost Relative to Burglary	Ratio of Intangible to Tangible
Murder	$1,030,000	$1,910,000	$2,940,000	2,100	1.85:1
Rape/sexual assault	$5,100	$81,400	$86,500	62	15.96:1
Robbery/attempt with injury	$5,200	$13,800	$19,000	14	2.65:1
Assault or attempt	$1,500	$7,800	$9,350	7	5.2:1
Burglary or attempt	$1,100	$300	$1,400	1	0.27:1

At least one recent textbook on victims now routinely incorporates such measures in teaching the estimation of the costs of crime (Wallace, 2000:85, Table 5.3). Table 1 shows an adaptation of that presentation, itself an adaptation of the Miller et al. work. The table shows the tangible and intangible costs for five crime types. Tangible costs include medical costs, lost earnings, and public programs relating to victim assistance, which in the U.S. in 1993 were estimated at $150 billion. The intangible costs include pain, suffering and quality of life, which were estimated at $450 billion in 1993 (Miller et al., 1996). When intangible costs of crime are included, crimes come closer to what might be expected in terms of severity. The importance of the intangible costs are clear upon an examination of Table 1. As one example, relative to the tangible costs, the intangible cost of rape is far greater than that for any other type of crime. The cost of rape would be significantly underestimated were intangible costs excluded. It should also be noted here, however, that these estimates are not necessarily definitive. In stark contrast to the value of life placed on murder victims shown in Table 1, one study of a drug dealing gang suggests that the value of the life of a low-level foot soldier may range from $7,500 to $110,000 (Levitt and Venkatesh, (1998:26). Even the higher of these values is far lower than the estimate of the total cost of murder shown in Table 1. While it may reflect differences in components that are costed, as well as methodology, the estimates may also reflect possible variation in the range of values that a life may take depending upon context and circumstances. While it is possible that average low-level drug dealers might value their lives at a far lower level than the average person, it is clearly there is a need for further work to reconcile these figures.

However, it is apparent that it remains standard practice to exclude non-monetary costs from crime prevention evaluations. This practice should change. The pace of change should be accelerated by further studies in this area. Work is needed to refine, improve upon and develop the methodology, and to use alternate methodologies to produce validating or improved estimates. This is required for different times, countries and contexts. Such research seems a necessary step if cost-benefit analysis of crime prevention is to become truly credible.

Nevertheless, the question of whether or not non-monetary costs should be routinely incorporated into CBA of crime prevention remains a tricky one. Ideally, if perfect estimates of those costs existed, they would be incorporated. At present, estimates can vary widely. Estimates can also be subjective: some people would argue that the life of a persistent violent criminal is not worth the same as that of a responsible hardworking taxpayer — the argument can be made that the net loss to society of the former is less than that of the latter. Many non-criminological debates exist, such as: is the life of an elderly person worth the same as that of a young person? Other issues arise in relation to such notions as 'the deserving victim,' such as the person who started the fight but lost. Such measurement issues should not be insurmountable however. This is evidenced by the fact that, at present, crimes of the same type are all implicitly valued equally when crimes are counted. Cases of multiple estimates would simply result in multiple cost-benefit outcomes, bounded by a confidence interval.

Discounting

Crime prevention was once brilliantly defined as the securing of a future non-event (Forrester et al., 1990). From one angle, the phrase also captures the need for 'discounting,' that is, converting past, present and future costs into comparable estimates. There is a time value associated with money: a dollar received today is worth more than that same dollar a year from now. Therefore, it is necessary to value benefits received in the future at something less than their current value. The degree to which future benefits are deflated is the discount rate.

The selection of an appropriate discount rate can be contentious (see Cohen [2000] for an extended discussion). Dhiri and Brand (1999) present a clear and practical statement of its derivation. Three main factors contribute to the formulation of a discount rate: the social rate of time preference; interest rates; and savings rates. The social rate of time preference is simply the rate at which consumers are willing to trade future for current consumption — it is a measure of the preference for deferred gratification. Interest rates and savings rates are linked, and together predict the rate of return to capital had it been invested rather than spent.[9] One factor that does not contribute to the discount rate is inflation, although inflation is often mistakenly used as the rationale for discounting.[10] Clearly, all three of these variables change over time, but a vast literature on discounting helps inform the setting of an appropriate rate.

The applicable discount rate varies over time and space. In the U.K., Dhiri and Brand note that "[t]he standard real discount rate currently used in central government is 6 per cent" (1999:43). In the U.S., it is generally accepted that any discount rate between 3 and 4% can be assumed to be unbiased.[11] The definitive U.S. text on cost-benefit analysis proposes applying various discount rates to a problem in order to generate the equivalent of confidence intervals (Gramlich, 1988). Assuming for present purposes a social rate of time preference of 2%, and a current interest rate of 5%, this discount rate of four percent should offer an appropriately conservative estimate of future benefits. Future benefits are therefore calculated according to Equation 1, where (X_T) is the benefit (cost) occurring in year T and the discount rate is .04:

$$\text{Discounted Future Benefits (DFB)} = \sum_{0}^{T} (X_T / ((1 + D)^T))$$ (1)

Using this equation, each averted crime is discounted for each year during which a benefit is expected to accrue, as determined by the average duration of the intervention (in years) for each type of crime. In Painter and Farrington's (1999) impressive study of the impact of street lighting on crime, for example, street lights had a life expectancy of 15 years, which was therefore the time over which benefits were expected to accrue. A textbook illustration demonstrates the power of discounting. Suppose one were offered the choice between receiving one dollar a year forever at a discount rate of 5%, or $20 at present. It turns out that taking the money up front is a better deal. In fact, in the distant future, after 20 years, the payoff is vanishingly small.

Putting it All Together — And Looking Beyond

When all of these factors are put together, a rather complete picture of a cost-benefit model of crime prevention emerges. It may well be that supply and demand for some criminogenic goods can be readily generated: the number of cars stolen annually can be used to estimate a demand for stolen cars. Police records on prices received for stolen goods might be used to calculate prices. On the supply side, survey data might be used in combination with consumer purchase data to model the 'supply' of anti-theft devices for cars. Multivariate analysis can be used to control for outside factors, such as changes in policing and changes in standard prevention equipment. It is possible that sophisticated models could be developed. Such models might predict how changes in consumer behavior produce changes in the volume of crime.

Another approach may be to apply these same tools at a more micro level, by examining changes in behavior, say, before and after a crime prevention program is implemented. This approach would use the same methods described above, but would use multivariate techniques to isolate the effects of the program. Here, key variables are developed from knowledge of how a program would operate. Costs can be readily tabulated, using market costs for labor, facilities and other costs. An outcome evaluation could be conducted in the usual way, isolating program effects using (quasi) experimental techniques. The 'cost of illness' method (mentioned earlier in relation to victim-compensation method of estimating costs), could then be combined with the outcomes from the evaluation to put dollar values on changes in behavior, by, for instance, creating estimates for the benefits received by society from a car not being stolen. More specific recommendations for conducting these evaluations are beyond the scope of this paper. (See Roman et al., 1998 for further details of such a program as they relate to court-based interventions.)

V. ROUTINE SAVINGS

This section notes some obvious crime prevention efforts that are clearly beneficial but which have not been subjected to cost-benefit analysis. They are often revealed as beneficial by the preferences of those who choose to adopt them.

Case Study of the Car Door

Upon leaving their motor vehicle, most informed people will lock the door. This is because the benefit of locking the door outweighs the cost of the resources expended. The cost (effort) of locking the door is small compared to the potential cost of car crime, even if the risk of car crime is small. In time, locking the door becomes routine, the effort-cost appears miniscule and is outweighed by the psychological benefit of knowing the door is locked, as well as by the actual benefit of reduced crime risk. Locking the door becomes a sensible routine precaution (Felson and Clarke, 1996), so much so that it is often not noticed as an explicitly proactive crime prevention activity.

A car door is more likely to be locked if the car owner has a remote locking device.[12] Just as with doors that swing closed and lock behind you, such facilitators of crime prevention increase the implementation of routine crime prevention. The equivalent in the field of health and safety is the fire door that automatically closes after entry. In both instances, the effort-cost of closing/locking the door is reduced. If costs decrease, net benefit increases. In the model described earlier, this would be shown as a shift inward of the supply curve, reducing quantities of crime and increasing the risk-price.

The car door is one simple example of a routine saving — in terms of costs and benefits — from precautionary crime prevention measures. There are many more, from locking the front door to carrying keys in hand while approaching the car. Taking a cab can often be an implicit crime prevention measure, as can an unwillingness to walk through certain areas at certain times.

So What?

The observation that routine precautions have not been the focus of CBA is significant. It shows that a range of simple and obvious cost-benefit analyses can be undertaken that will empirically demonstrate where benefits outweigh costs. This may allow the study of CBA to progress to a more fruitful stage of focusing upon where and when crime prevention is most beneficial, rather than focusing upon whether or not it is beneficial.

VI. EXTERNALITIES: COST-BENEFIT ANALYSIS AND CRIME POLLUTION

Manufacturers of mobile telephones have a range of possibilities open to them to discourage theft of their devices (Clarke et al., 2001). Car manufacturers have, for many years, had huge variation in their propensity to install anti-theft devices on vehicles. Some manufacturers choose not to implement crime prevention measures in their products because they would incur a small increase in manufacturing costs. It should not, but seemingly still does come as a surprise, that knowingly selling large volumes of criminogenic products results in huge amounts of crime. Arguably this also produces further negative knock-on effects: the expansion of criminal opportunities increases the pool of offenders who pass the tipping point where their perceived utility for crime is greater than the perceived risks —because the 'good' experience shifts those perceptions towards a preference for crime.

As a result, crime research might consider examining the costs and benefits of the absence of crime prevention, rather than solely the costs and benefits of its presence. Doing so may prove that the analysis of the costs and benefits of the absence of crime prevention holds the potential to be a powerful and influential tool by which the baseline of crime prevention standards can be moved upwards.

Focusing upon the well-known example of car manufacturers, the range of crime prevention options available to reduce car theft is fairly large, including: steering-wheel locks, entry codes, alarms, immobilizers (e.g., "the Club"), and tracking devices. Theft of cars for their parts can be made less rewarding by the indelible stamping of identity codes on the most valuable body and engine parts. Admittedly, recent technological advances have made many of these available only in recent years. It is also evident that some measures — a good example is steering-wheel locks — have been introduced as mandatory in some countries. It was clear to all concerned, including policy makers, that the aggregate social benefit of mandatory crime prevention standards was greater than the aggregate social cost of their absence. Hence steering wheel locks became widespread. Barry Webb (1997) briefly describes the fascinating history of car crime and efforts to overcome it — the earliest of which were registration numbers. What is not mentioned is that cost-benefit analysis was implicit to these legislative moves. To policy makers it was clear that the net social benefit of the legislation would far outweigh the crime cost of inaction and the absence of the crime prevention measure. It was also clear that by forcing manufacturers to internalize the crime prevention cost was the means by which to produce the largest net social gain. It appears that there may be a need to develop and apply a methodology that identifies areas where the absence of crime prevention leads to a net social welfare loss.

Externalities

The discussion of market failures that follows needs a brief introduction to the concept of externalities. In general, externalities can be positive or negative, and they arise in situations where a consumer not involved in a transaction is affected by that transaction. Two types of externalities occur. Pecuniary externalities occur where the actions of an actor in the market affect others in the market, and these effects are transmitted in the market, for example by a change in price. This would occur, for instance, where a polluter (probably a regulated monopolist) charges below-market prices to compensate consumers for the deleterious effects of the pollution. Using the automotive examples, this would occur where a manufacturer of a criminogenic good, such as cars, charges a price slightly below the market price to compensate consumers for the costs they face because the manufacturer does not include anti-theft protection.

The other type of externality, the far more common example, occurs where the externalities are orthogonal to the market, and therefore the actions of one actor affect the welfare of others, but there is no market price for that effect. Following the two examples above, this would occur where a polluter does not account for negative pollution externalities in setting a price, or where a car manufacturer excludes prevention technology, but does not compensate consumers for their net loss in social welfare due to increased theft by selling below the market price. If producers simply charge a lower price for a car without anti-theft technology (i.e., with a pecuniary externality), then we have a 'so what' or trivial situation. While this is a empirical question that can, and should, be tested, we suspect that few manufacturers do so.

One other construct deserves explanation. Should the latter situation occur, we are still left with something of a quandary about the appropriateness of third-party (e.g., governmental) intervention. Conservative scholars would likely argue that the market provides solutions to these problems over time, and that most interventions lead to some loss in net social welfare through less efficient markets, and through administrative costs. Without debating these points — and they are eminently debatable — few argue that intervention is inappropriate in the case of public goods. While this discussion is not central to the issues addressed here, crime prevention is, at least in part, a public good. Public goods have two general qualities: they are non-rival (the use of a good by one does not affect the use by others), and are non-exclusive, i.e., everyone is affected. In the case of crime prevention, it is clear that at the macro-level, a program that reduces some crime reduces some crime for all (i.e., it is non-exclusive). It is also clear that crime prevention is, in many instances, non-rival: my use of crime prevention has no effect on your use of it as well. The exceptions might be free-riders and followers. Free-riders seek to benefit from the crime prevention behaviors of others, and underinvest in crime prevention. What we term 'followers' would be people who adopt extra crime prevention measures either to "keep up with the Joneses" or in case they feel that the prevention behavior of others may leave them as the only vulnerable target. The question to answer is whether there are market failures in the provision of crime prevention, and whether crime prevention is a public good. Leaving the latter question aside, in the remainder of the paper we argue that such market failures do exist.

Market Failure

Another of Webb's (1997) examples relating to car crime is the eventual widespread incorporation of locks within car doors, to reduce the ease of theft. This measure was introduced by manufacturers without legislation. It was clear to manufacturers that the extra production costs would be outweighed by the benefit from sales. Thus, it was not due to the benevolence of the car manufacturer that locks were introduced. It was from the pursuit of their self-interest, a response by the market to the fact that consumers prefer a less crime-prone vehicle. In this example, the invisible hand of the market locked the door. However, this example is illustrative more of the exception than the rule: it is more typical that the pursuit of economic self-interest does not lead to crime prevention. It may be more typical that the market fails due to a lack of recognition of the negative externalities associated with the absence of crime prevention. Consumers are typically not well informed either about risks or crime prevention measures. The market equilibrium for in-built crime prevention may be different from that which would maximize overall social welfare. That is why vehicle registration and steering-wheel locks were introduced via legislation rather than via the market.

A Pigouvian Tax for Crime

Alfred Pigou (1877-1959) is credited with being the first to advocate a tax upon industry that produces negative externalities. Hence, manufacturing industry incurs a Pigouvian tax for illegal pollution.

Such a tax forces manufacturers to pay the cost that they are imposing on society. Since it is cheaper to lower the level of pollutants rather than continue to pay the tax, manufacturers quickly internalize the cost by shifting to a less-polluting production process. A Pigouvian crime tax might encourage manufacturers to reduce the level of the viability of products. It could also be used to encourage crime prevention through environmental design (CPTED: see Jeffrey, 1977) and the more routine avoidance of crime facilitators.

Many adaptations to manufacturing processes that might reduce crime would do so at relatively low cost. The cost to the manufacturer of a few pennies would, in many instances, have been largely absorbed during the mark-up process between production and distribution. Yet clearly, such an approach should not be so interventionist so as to interfere with the market, its incentives and its profits. Reducing market efficiency is, firmly, not the aim of these proposals. The avoidance of a specific instance of market failure as it relates to crime — where manufacturers impose large external costs on society in order to reap small rewards for themselves — is a more desirable objective. There should be scope for policy that can meet a Kaldor-Hicks standard whereby manufacturers could be reimbursed from gains by consumers.[13] Victims will be the principal beneficiaries, but society as a whole will benefit, particularly if there is a diffusion of the crime prevention benefits across society. It is not unlikely that, in the long run, manufacturers would also benefit as overall market sizes increased due to consumers moving into markets where crime had previously deterred them from spending.

It is perhaps not over-optimistic to envisage a future in which manufacturers and designers routinely incorporate crime prevention know-how during the development stage. In the near future, white and other electrical goods may have wireless (bluetooth) technologies installed. Such technologies may allow goods to be located to a particular venue, and either traced via a centralized registry or perhaps disabled if reported stolen. One means of encouraging manufacturers to routinely incorporate such wireless anti-crime devices would be through the use of government purchasing power (GPP). If suppliers to government were obliged to incorporate such measures routinely, then it is likely that their transition to the remainder of the market would be speedy.[14]

Developing Pigouvian taxes would require much thought and consideration. Their specifics are outside the scope of this essay. It is not acceptable to impose unreasonable costs upon manufacturers unless the gains are certain. Moreover, such legislation could present difficulties in the context of international markets: higher crime prevention standards in one country could appear as a barrier to entry to products from elsewhere. As with any innovative and potentially beneficial policy, it would not be without critics, and would require great skill in development as well as implementations. Cost-benefit analysis could inform its development as well as evaluation.

A tax to reduce crime externalities would need to be policed. This could take different forms. It could be incorporated into the activities of the police, within existing resources. Perhaps it might be appropriate to develop it within an existing agency undertaking similar activities, such as the Environmental Protection Agency or the Consumer Product Safety Commission. A third alternative might be the development of an independent crime by-product monitoring agency. In the U.K., the strategic development of such a tax and its monitoring (policing) might properly be considered within the domain of the Foresight crime prevention initiative of the Department of Trade and Industry.

What would a broader recognition of the implicit costs of the absence of crime prevention suggest for cost-benefit methodology as applied to crime prevention? First, it would mean a shift in emphasis. CBA relating to add-on crime prevention efforts and projects would continue. In addition there would be CBA to identify products and environments that encourage potentially available crime; and where the costs of avoidance are trivial in comparison to the costs of the crime, a solution would be mandated. This would require an assessment of the current benefits (to manufacturers who save on production costs) in relation to the external costs that the manufacturers impose upon society in the form of crime relating to those goods. Such analyses could provide powerful information that could be directly used to try to implement and encourage built-in crime prevention.

In developing policy responses to reduce the criminogenic qualities of consumer goods, and hence to reduce the supply of criminal opportunities, there may be much to be learned from the progress and pitfalls encountered in relation to environmental protection. In recent years, command and control interventions seem to be beginning to give way to market-based instruments and incentives that encourage reductions in various types of pollution. The market-based instruments seem to come in four basic forms (see, e.g., *Economist* [2001] for a brief overview, or the edited volume of studies edited by Portney and Stavins, 2000). The first is 'tradable permits' whereby companies that produce less pollution than they are permitted to by the government might sell their credit to other companies. It could be fruitful to think through the permutations of 'allowing' car or mobile phone manufacturers, or credit card issuing companies, only a certain number of thefts of each model. Tradable permits, such as acid rain allowance trading programs under the Clean Air Act amendments of 1990 and those included in the Kyoto protocol, are designed to spur innovation and are commonly believed to have led to significant reductions in environmental pollution levels in some spheres (Stavins, 1998). The second market-based instrument for change is 'taxes and charges'. In relation to crime, taxes and charges would alter the prices of good to reflect their crime risks. One possibility might be that the government reduces taxes on goods that have low crime rates and leaves taxes on criminogenic product lines that produce a social cost — along the lines of the Pigouvian tax discussed above. In environmental economics, the third type of market-based scheme is 'the reduction of environmentally-harmful subsidies,' and the fourth is 'the reduction of barriers to the creation of new markets.' While we do not suggest crime-control related policies or examples modeled upon these environmental protection policies, this does not mean that they do not or cannot exist. A significant area of future research may lie in exploring the possibility of applying environmental protection-type policies to the spheres of crime control and prevention. A first step might be for the appropriate government agencies to convene a meeting of environmental protection and crime prevention experts, to encourage cross-fertilization in this arena, and to develop a policy-informing research agenda.

VII. OPPORTUNITY COSTS OF THE FAILURE TO INTRODUCE CRIME PREVENTION — A BRIEF CASE STUDY OF CCTV

This section discusses an issue that is different from externalities, and relates to the fact that the absence of crime prevention in a given situation incurs opportunity costs that are often overlooked. This key issue is demonstrated through the following brief case study relating to CCTV, although the concept applies more generally.

There is now a body of accumulated knowledge demonstrating that closed-circuit television (CCTV) can, when properly implemented and monitored, be effective at reducing crime (see the edited volume by Painter and Tilley [1999], for example). There is also evidence that CCTV can be introduced without infringing upon people's freedoms — providing necessary control mechanisms are put in place to ensure that those monitoring the screens are trained and follow protocols that mean they cannot abuse their position.

CCTV has been shown to reduce crimes of different types under a range of different circumstances. The benefit to victims and to people in general is clear, since crime is reduced and fear of crime is reduced in high-crime areas that are now at least partially protected by CCTV. The freedom of people to move around — particularly since women and the elderly are often likely to modify their behavior to avoid potentially risky areas — is arguably increased. At the same time however, some commentators, particularly in the U.S., still object to CCTV on the grounds of civil liberties. The argument that CCTV infringes upon a person's right to anonymity is that this loss of freedom is a social cost. Opponents answer that this is essentially an argument for a right to anonymously commit crime. However, a more compelling argument may be that policy makers should not ignore the opportunity costs (crime saved, fear reduced) incurred by deliberately failing to introduce a proven crime prevention measure. The role of cost-benefit analysis in this area would be to more formally explore, delineate and quantify the opportunity costs, and to compare them to the 'benefits' of failing to introduce CCTV. Such an analysis may prove that the identification of the opportunity costs of the absence of crime prevention is a general tool that can be utilized to encourage the implementation of crime prevention efforts.

VIII. CONCLUSIONS

The time is ripe for significant progress to be made in the field of cost-benefit analysis as it relates to crime prevention. Things are already beginning to move: the standard for practitioners conducting cost-benefit analysis of crime prevention has clearly been set by the clear and concise monographs of Dhiri and Brand (1999) and the follow-up by Legg and Powell (2000). Welsh and Farrington (1999) have reviewed 13 published cost-benefit analyses with a timely thoroughness. Although it may take some time to become widespread practice, Miller et al. (1996) have paved the way for non-monetary costs to be routinely incorporated into CBA of crime prevention, and, although much further work is clearly required, Farrington and Painter (1999) have initiated moves in this direction.

It is also apparent that cost-benefit analysis has applications for crime prevention that move beyond the existing focus of project and program evaluation. There may be a range of existing crime prevention evaluations that can be retrospectively assessed in terms of costs and benefits. To do so would be, relatively speaking, a cost-efficient exercise in terms of the knowledge derived. We suspect that, should the successful cost-benefit analysis that is implicit to many studies prove founded, it would provide evidence to add to the accumulating body of knowledge that situational crime prevention 'works.' It would also be a quick and easy means of accelerating the study of crime prevention to a level that is credible and comprehensible to those who are influential in public policy decision making. A small demonstration project could assess whether such studies exist, prior to launching into a full-scale assessment of their costs and benefits. An on-site set of research information such as that which must exist within the Research and Statistics Directorate of the U.K.'s Home Office, would seem an appropriate location for such a project.

Cost-benefit analysis of routine activities needs greater delineation. How does an activity or a measure become 'routine' rather than special or unusual? In some cases it must be related to costs of products that facilitate crime prevention (such as 'smart' library and supermarket checkouts that reduce theft at the same time as accelerating processing speed). Efforts at crime prevention education campaigns ('lock it or lose it') imply that routine crime prevention practice can be encouraged.

There is a potentially rich vein of research to be undertaken in relation to crime externalities. Noise is a form of social pollution, and some forms of crime might be viewed through a similar lens. Where manufacturers produce criminogenic products, there is scope for the argument that, by failing to incorporate crime prevention measures, they make minor cost savings at the expense of a larger cost to society. Many precedents exist where such an analysis has been implicit to legislation even if not explicit. Somewhere down the line a form of Pigouvian tax on crime might be considered to encourage the internalization of crime costs, and the relevant monitoring agency identified or developed. Cost-benefit analysis is the appropriate research vehicle for developing such an approach. The related aspects of the field of environmental protection holds the potential to significantly inform these areas of crime control policy.

Counting crimes will never go out of fashion. It is easy, and everyone can understand how many crimes have occurred. However, research on crime requires a common metric via which crimes can be compared. It is likely that the overall social cost of crime is the best common metric. The net social cost approach allows crimes to be compared directly. Miller et. al.'s (1996) work would suggest that, ceteris paribus, preventing one rape is preferable (in cost-benefit terms) to preventing 62 burglaries. A common metric that incorporates non-monetary costs allows the impact of crime prevention measures for crimes of different types to be discussed and evaluated on the same terms. This should allow crime policy to move towards an overall harm reduction approach (where harm is defined as lost social welfare due to crime), rather than the current haphazard approach.

Address correspondence to: John Roman, Justice Policy Center, The Urban Institute, 2100 M Street NW, Washington DC 20037, U.S.A. E-mail: <jroman@ui.urban.org>.

REFERENCES

Austen, J. (1871; reprinted 1997). *Pride and Prejudice.* New York, NY: Penguin Books.

Barr, R. and K. Pease (1990). "Crime Placement, Displacement and Deflection." In: M. Tonry and N. Morris (eds.), *Crime and Justice,* vol. 12. Chicago, IL: University of Chicago Press.

Becker, G.S. (1968). "Crime and Punishment: An Economic Approach." *Journal of Political Economy* 76:169 217.

Clarke, R.V.G. (1998). *Situational Crime Prevention: Successful Case Studies* (2nd ed.). New York: Harrow and Heston.

—— (1995). "Situational Crime Prevention: Achievements and Challenges." In: M. Tonry and D. Farrington (eds.), *Building a Safer Society: Strategic Approaches to Crime Prevention, Crime and Justice: A Review of Research,* vol. 19. Chicago, IL: University of Chicago Press.

—— (1980). "Situational Crime Prevention: Theory and Practice." *British Journal of Criminology* 20:136-147.

—— R. Kemper and L. Wyckoff (2001). "Controlling Cell Phone Fraud in the US — Lessons for the U.K. 'Foresight' Prevention Initiative." *Security Journal* 14:7-22.

—— and D. Cornish (2000). "Rational Choice." In: R. Paternoster and R. Bachman *Explaining Crime and Criminals: Essays in Contemporary Criminological Theory.* Los Angeles, CA: Roxbury.

—— and D. Weisburd (1994). "Diffusion of Crime Control Benefits: Observations on the Reverse of Displacement." In: R.V. Clarke (ed.), *Crime Prevention Studies* (vol. 2). Monsey, NY: Criminal Justice Press.

Cohen, M.A. (2000). "Measuring the Costs and Benefits of Crime and Justice." In: *Measurement and Analysis of Crime and Justice.* (*Criminal Justice 2000,* vol. 4.) Washington, DC: National Institute of Justice. Available at http://www/ncjrs.org/criminal_justice2000/vol4/04f.pdf.

—— T.R. Miller and S.B. Rossman (1994). "The Costs and Consequences of Violent Behavior in the United States." In: A.J. Reiss, Jr. and J. A. Roth (eds.), *Understanding and Preventing Violence: Consequences and Control of Violence*, vol. 4. Washington, DC: National Academy Press.

Dhiri, S. and S. Brand (1999). *Analysis of Costs and Benefits: Guidance for Evaluators.* (Crime Reduction Programme Guidance Note 1.) London, UK: Research and Statistics Directorate, Home Office.

Eck, J. (1993). "The Threat of Crime Displacement." *Criminal Justice Abstracts* 25:527-546.

Economist (The) (2001). "Economic Man, Cleaner Planet." *The Economist* 360(8241):73-75.

Ekblom, P. (1998). "Situational Crime Prevention: Effectiveness of Local Initiatives." In: P. Goldblatt and C. Lewis (eds.), *Reducing Offending: An Assessment of Research Evidence on Ways of Dealing with Offending Behaviour.* (A Research and Statistics Directorate Report.) London, UK: Home Office.

—— H. Law and M. Sutton (1996). *Safer Cities and Domestic Burglary.* (Home Office Research Study No. 164.) London, UK: Home Office.

—— and K. Pease (1995). "Evaluating Crime Prevention." In: M. Tonry and D.P. Farrington (eds.), *Building a Safer Society: Strategic Approaches to Crime Prevention.* (Crime and Justice, vol. 19.) Chicago, IL: University of Chicago Press.

Farrell, G. (2000). "Crime Prevention." In: C. Bryant (ed.), *The Encyclopedia of Criminology and Deviant Behavior.* London, UK: Taylor and Francis Publishers.

—— S. Chamard, K. Clark and K. Pease (2000). "Towards an Economic Approach to Crime and Prevention." In: N.G. Fielding, A.H. Clarke and R. Witt (eds.), *The Economic Dimensions of Crime.* New York, NY: St. Martin's Press.

Felson, M. and R.V. Clarke (1996). "Routine Precautions, Criminology, and Crime Prevention." In: H.D. Barlow (ed.), *Crime and Public Policy: Putting Theory to Work.* Boulder, CO: Westview Press.

Field, S. (1993). "Crime Prevention and the Cost of Auto Theft: An Economic Analysis." *Crime Prevention Studies*, vol. 1. Monsey, NY: Criminal Justice Press.

Forrester, D., S. Frenz, M. O'Connor and K. Pease (1990). *The Kirkholt Burglary Prevention Project: Phase II.* (Crime Prevention Unit Paper No. 23.) London, UK: Home Office.

Gramlich, E.M. (1988). *A Guide to Benefit-Cost Analysis of Government Programs* (2nd ed.). Prospect Heights, IL: Waveland Press.

—— (1981). *Benefit-Cost Analysis of Government Programs.* Englewood Cliffs, NJ: Prentice Hall.

Greenwood, P.W., C.P, Rydell, A.F. Abrahamse, J.P. Caulkins, J. Chiesa, K.E. Model and S.P. Klein (1996). "Implementing the Law: Estimated Benefits and Costs of California's New Mandatory-Sentencing Law." In: D. Shichor and K. Sechrest (eds.), *Three Strikes and You're Out.* Thousand Oaks, CA: Sage Publications.

Hakim, S. and Y. Shachmurove (1996). "Social Cost Benefit Analysis of Commercial and Residential Burglar and Fire Alarms." *Journal of Policy Modeling* 18(1):49-67.

Hesseling, R. (1994). "Displacement: An Empirical Review of the Literature." In: R.V. Clarke (ed.), *Crime Prevention Studies*, vol. 3. Monsey, NY: Criminal Justice Press.

Hooke, A., J. Know and D. Portas (1996). *Cost Benefit Analysis of Traffic Light and Speed Cameras.* (Police Research Series paper no. 20.) London, UK: Home Office.

Hope, T. and S. Field (1988). *Economics and the Market in Crime Prevention.* (Home Office Research and Planning Unit, Research Bulletin 26.) London, UK: Her Majesty's Stationery Office.

Hough, M. and N. Tilley (1998). *Auditing Crime and Disorder: Guidance for Local Partnerships.* (Police Research Group Crime Detection and Prevention Series, paper no. 91.) London, UK: Home Office.

Jeffrey, C.R. (1977). *Crime Prevention Through Environmental Design.* Beverly Hills, CA: Sage Publications.

Kolb, J.A. and J.D. Scherga (1990). "Discounting the Benefits and Costs of Environmental Regulations." *Journal of Policy Analysis* 9(3):381-390.

Legg, D. and J. Powell (2000). *Measuring Inputs: Guidance for Evaluators.* (Crime Reduction Programme Guidance Note 3.) London, UK: Research and Statistics Directorate, Economics and Resource Analysis Unit, Home Office.

Levitt, S. and S.A. Venkatesh (1998). "Drug-Selling Gang's Finances." Working Paper 6592, National Bureau of Economic Research: (June).

Mendelsohn, R. (1981). "The Choice of the Discount Rate for Public Projects." *American Economic Review* 71(March):381-390.

Miller, T., M. Cohen and B. Weirsema (1996). *Victim Costs and Consequences: A New Look.* (National Institute of Justice Research Report Series.) Washington, DC: NIJ.

—— M.S. Galbraith and B.A. Lawrence (1998). "Costs and Benefits of a Community Sobriety Checkpoint Program." *Journal of Studies on Alcohol* 59:462-468.

Painter, K. and D.P. Farrington (1999). "Improved Street Lighting: Crime Reducing Effects and Cost-Benefit Analyses." *Security Journal* 12(4):17-32.

—— and N. Tilley (eds.), (1999). *Surveillance of Public Space: CCTV, Street Lighting and Crime Prevention.* (*Crime Prevention Studies*, vol. 10.) Monsey, NY: Criminal Justice Press.

Pawson, R. and N. Tilley (1998). *Realistic Evaluation.* Thousand Oaks, CA: Sage Publications, Inc..

Portney, P.R. and R.N. Stavins (eds.), (2000). *Public Policies for Environmental Protection* (2nd ed.). Washington, DC: Resources for the Future.

Rajkumar, A. and M. French (1997). "Drug Abuse, Crime Costs and Economic Benefits of Treatment." *Journal of Quantitative Criminology* 13(3):291-323.

Roman, J. and A. Harrell (2001). "Assessing the Costs and Benefits Accruing to the Public From a Graduated Sanctions Program for Drug-Using Defendants." *Law and Policy* 23:237-268.

—— J. Woodard, A. Harrell and S. Riggs (1998). *A Methodology for Estimating Costs and Benefits of Court-Based Drug Intervention Programs Using Findings from Experimental and Quasi-Experimental Evaluations.* Washington, DC: Urban Institute.

Rydell, P.C. and S.S. Everingham (1994). *Controlling Cocaine: Supply Versus Demand Programs.* (RAND Drug Policy Research Center.) Santa Monica, CA: RAND.

Stavins, R.N. (1998). "What Can We Learn from the Grand Policy Experiment? Lessons from SO2 Allowance Trading." *Journal of Economic Perspectives* 12(3):69-88.

Stockdale, J.E., C.M.E. Whitehead and P.J. Gresham (1999). *Applying Economic Evaluation to Policing Activity.* (Police Research Series Paper No. 103.) London, UK: Home Office.

Sutton, M., K. Johnston and H. Lockwood (1998). *Handling Stolen Goods: A Market Reduction Approach.* (Home Office Research Study No. 178.) London, UK: Home Office.

Tilley, N. (1993). *Understanding Car Parks, Crime and CCTV: Evaluation Lessons form Safer Cities.* (Police Research Group Crime Prevention Unit Series Paper No. 42.) London, UK: Home Office.

U.K. Department of Trade and Industry (2000). "Excellence and Opportunity a Science and Innovation Policy for the 21st Century." Cm 4814, (http://www.dti.gov.uk/ost/aboutost/diwhite/).

Van Dijk, J. (1992). "Understanding Crime Rates: On the Interactions between Rational Choices of Victims and Offenders." *British Journal of Criminology* 34:105-121.

Varian, H.R. (1987). *Intermediate Microeconomics: A Modern Approach.* New York, NY: Norton.

Wallace, H. (2000). *Victimology: Legal, Psychological and Social Perspectives.* Needham Heights, MA: Allyn and Bacon.

Waller, I. and B. Walsh (1999). "International Trends in Crime Prevention: Cost-Effective Ways to Reduce Victimization." In: G. Newman (ed.), *Global Report on Crime and Justice.* (United Nations Office for Drug Control and Crime Prevention.) Oxford, UK: Oxford University Press.

Welsh, B. and D. Farrington (1999). "Value for Money?: A Review of the Costs and Benefits of Situational Crime Prevention." *British Journal of Criminology* 39(3):345-368.

—— and D.P. Farrington (2000). "Correctional Intervention Programs and Cost-Benefit Analysis." *Criminal Justice and Behavior* 27(1)115-133.

Webb, B. (1998). "Steering Column Locks and Motor Vehicle Theft: Evaluations from Three Countries." In: R.V. Clarke (ed.), *Situational Crime Prevention: Successful Case Studies* (2nd ed.). New York: Harrow and Heston.

—— (1993). "Steering Column Locks and Motor Vehicle Theft: Evaluations from Three Counties." In: R.V. Clarke (ed.), *Crime Prevention Studies*, vol. 2. Monsey, NY: Criminal Justice Press.

APPENDIX A:
KEY DEFINITIONS

(Reproduced from Dhiri and Brand, 1999)

Inputs are defined as any additional human, physical and financial resources that are used to undertake a project. For example, in an intervention that installs fences across paths at the backs of houses as a target hardening measure to prevent domestic burglary, inputs would include the materials and labor used to install the fences.

Outputs are defined narrowly as the direct products of the process of implementation. They can arise only during the implementation period. Following the above example, the fences installed are outputs and the number of fences installed is an output measure.

Impacts on risk factors are defined as the effects of outputs that *disrupt the causes of criminal events*. Measuring such impacts is therefore a way of monitoring the process through which the intervention is expected to reduce crime. In our fence example, this could be a reduction in non-residents entering the path, thereby reducing the opportunity for burglary.

Outcomes are defined as the consequences of the intervention. These can arise both during and after the implementation period. Key outcomes will relate to the stated objectives of the intervention. In our example, the reduction in burglaries attributable to the installation of fences is the primary outcome. But there are likely to be wider outcomes such as a change in the fear of crime or the reduction in other types of crime. These wider outcomes may or may not be measurable and can be negative as well as positive.

Costs are defined as the monetary value of inputs. Outcomes resulting in negative costs attributed to a program are considered to be benefits.

Benefits are defined as the value of outcomes to society that are attributed to the intervention, expressed in monetary terms. Negative outcomes attributed to an intervention will be referred to as costs.

APPENDIX B:
UNIT OF ANALYSIS

The two key constructs in choosing a unit of analysis are the concept of transfers and opportunity costs and benefits to participants. The idea that costs can be shifted across agencies is not a particularly important insight. However, in practical application, this can create a great deal of difficulty in formulating a cost-outcome analysis. A 'transfer' is simply the shifting of resources from one entity to another. Determining how to account for these transfers can be difficult.

An example will help clarify this issue. If a crime prevention project team assume a part of a facility that was already being used and paid for, (for example, in a police station) but the project does not pay for the facility, then the facility has been transferred to the crime prevention project. If it is assumed that all benefits of the crime prevention project accrue to its public funders, and implicitly the tax-paying public, then it is not necessarily clear how to account for the transfer described above. While the use of the facility clearly is a new cost to the crime prevention project, regardless of whether there is an actual cash outlay, it is not a new cost to the system. If, for example, a crime prevention initiative is funded by the federal or national government, and local government funders (and tax payers) are selected as the unit of analysis, it appears that no cost is incurred by the program. On a larger scale, it is not clear how to attribute the costs of any publicly-funded social program. If no new taxes are required to fund a crime prevention project, than it is not clear that any cost can be attributed to the program, as all funds are simply shifted from an existing public agency.

While the notion that no new costs have been incurred in most public enterprises is technically correct, it is practically specious. Returning to the initial example, there clearly was a cost to the transfer of facilities to the crime prevention project, in that space could have been used for some other activity that would have likely derived some benefit. As such, it is appropriate to consider such transfers as costs to the crime prevention project. In general, it is appropriate to use the analogy of new versus old costs when considering how to apply costs. If a cost occurs as a function of the crime prevention project operations that would not have occurred in the same way had the project not been operating, then it is generally necessary to count that cost.

Next, costs and benefits that accrue solely to program participants must be considered. Consider the instance of a market reduction approach (see, e.g., Sutton et al., 1998) in which there is a crackdown on second-hand sales of stolen goods in a community. Sellers of second hand goods may be foregoing substantial illicit income, as are local consumers who do not benefit from the cheaper-than-legal purchases that were previously available. On the other hand, it may be the case that as a result of the program, a secondhand store gains credibility with the public and increases its legal business as a result. While many analysts may be loathe to include the former as a cost of the program, there may be a preference for including the latter as a beneficial knock-on effect of the intervention. Many analysts recommend excluding both from the analysis.

The final concept in considering a unit of analysis is that of maintaining consistency across both costs and benefits. If, for example, if the unit of analysis selected is the city, then benefits accruing as a result of program operations must be carefully scrutinized. If benefits accruing as a result of program operations include more legal sales from stores, then increases in national or federal sales taxes cannot be considered a benefit. Since it is sometimes extremely difficult to make these judgments, it is generally recommended that the broadest unit of analysis be selected.

NOTES

1. For comments on earlier versions of this paper we are grateful to Nick Tilley, Ken Pease, Paul Ekblom and Peter Reuter.

2. This opening paragraph is really an homage to Jane Austen's satire of 19th century marriage (Austen, 1813 (1997):1).

3. Some commentators aim to define aspects of corrections and probation efforts, youth education programs, court programs and other things as 'crime prevention'. We prefer to call them corrections and probation efforts, youth education programs, courts programs, or other things as appropriate. Just as health and education policy, public holidays and pink ribbons may indirectly influence the crime rate, their main aim is generally not crime prevention, and we do not label them as such. We acknowledge that some offender-based measures and policies may have an implicit or explicit component of criminality prevention, which may (or may not) indirectly influence the crime rate. However, we also acknowledge that criminality prevention is not the same as crime prevention, not

least since other likely offenders may be tempted to take up existing criminal opportunities. Further, 'situational' crime prevention is, in truth, probably the main form of criminality prevention that exists in society, but most criminologists quietly overlook this basic fact.

4. Car manufacturers are certainly making anti-theft devices more standard on cars. Intervention to speed the process several years ago would arguably have avoided millions of car crimes.

5. In the figures, the supply and demand 'curves' are linear for simplicity.

6. This example highlights the issue that there may be a strong case for developing retrospective cost-benefit analyses of crime prevention interventions, such as the introduction of steering wheel locks.

7. This case is actually rather more complicated than presented here, as there is likely a cost to society for this program in multiple ways. For example, consumers likely bear some of the direct cost of the program in the form of increased taxes or fees. Second, this program likely makes the market somewhat less efficient, to the extent that both consumers and producers share the cost of the program, leading to higher prices for cars obtained *legally*, leading to a net loss of social welfare. However, a full treatment of these phenomena is beyond the scope of this discussion.

8. For example, suppose the change from S_1 to S_2 included both a shift as noted in Figure 2, and a change in the elasticity of supply (where the supply of crime prevention became relatively more elastic, i.e., where a small change in price yielded a relatively large change in quantity). In this new model then, the price change might remain the same (i.e., decrease from p_1 to p_2 as shown) but the quantity of crime would likely decrease more than is shown in Figure 1 (i.e., q_2 would move closer to the origin). In this new model then, suppose that the supply curve now goes through the origin. This would split C into an area of lost surplus, and an area of gained surplus. If the area of gained surplus were greater than the area lost by both producers and consumers, than the net cost to society would be negative.

9. For more discussion about discount rates, see Gramlich (1981):88-115; Mendelsohn (1981):239-241; Kolb and Scherga (1990):381-390.

10. While any future benefits will be worth less in today's dollars as a function of inflation rates, inflation is not included as part of the discounting process. If a weight is attached to future benefits to account for inflation (numerator), this weight must be attached as well to the dis-

count rate (denominator), which will also be effected by inflation. The net result is that inflation adjustments cancel out. For more discussion, see Gramlich (1981):94-95.

11. As Gramlich (1981:108) notes, "Given the uncertainties in estimating either one of these rates, use of a real discount rate in the 3 to 4 percent range will probably yield present value solutions that come as close to being correct, or at least unbiased, as is possible in this messy area."

12. For present purposes it is assumed that remote locking devices increase door locking.

13. A Pareto optimal move is where nobody is made worse off but some people are made better off. It might be more realistic in this instance to produce a Kaldor-Hicks standard, where many people are made far better off for only a small internalized cost on the part of manufacturers and designers.

14. The discussion of both bluetooth technologies and the potential to use government purchasing power owe a large debt to discussions with Ken Pease.

LEARNING FROM EXPERIENCE IN PROBLEM-ORIENTED POLICING AND SITUATIONAL PREVENTION:
The Positive Functions of Weak Evaluations and the Negative Functions of Strong Ones

by

John E. Eck
University of Cincinnati

"Science is built up with facts, as a house is with stones. But a collection of facts is no more a science than a heap of stones is a house."

Jules Henri Poincaré

Abstract: *Increasing attention is being paid to the systematic review and synthesis of evaluations of large-scale, generic, crime prevention programs. The utility of these syntheses rests on the assumption that the programs are designed to work across a wide variety of contexts. But many police problem-solving efforts and situational prevention interventions are small-scale efforts specifically tailored to individual contexts. Do evaluation designs and methods applicable to generic programs apply to problem specific programs? Answering this questions requires examining the differences between propensity-based and opportunity-blocking interventions; between internal and external validity; and between the needs of practitioner evaluators and academic researchers. This paper demonstrates that in some common circumstances, weak evaluation designs may have greater utility and produce more generalizable results than very strong evaluation designs. This conclusion has important implications for evaluations of*

Crime Prevention Studies, volume 14, pp 93-117.

place-based opportunity blocking, and for how we draw general conclusions about what works when, and what seldom ever works.

1. CAN WE LEARN FROM EVALUATIONS?

Problem-oriented policing puts great emphasis on the evaluation of responses to problems (Eck and Spelman, 1987; Goldstein, 1990) though some have suggested that evaluations are not sufficiently emphasized (Sherman, 1992). Similarly, evaluations have been used extensively to develop the theory and practice of situational crime prevention (Clarke, 1997). Many of the documented evaluations of these efforts focus on places where crimes occur, and these have been criticized for being methodologically weak (Eck, 1997). Despite the attempts to use evaluations to build knowledge of "what works and what doesn't" at crime places, there are major questions that have not been adequately addressed.

Will collections of findings from evaluations help practitioners learn from their experiences? What can practitioners learn from evaluations of crime prevention at places? How rigorous do evaluations by police and other crime prevention practitioners need to be? In short, do rigorous evaluations of interventions at places help or hinder practitioner learning? Answering these questions is necessary to develop a useful evaluation strategy to guide place-focused crime prevention by police and others.

To anticipate one of the conclusions of this paper, the answer seems to be that rigorous evaluations can hinder learning, but even if they do not hinder learning, they probably do not help. To show why this surprising conclusion is well founded, this paper makes a series of contrasts: between the positive and negative functions of evaluations; between small-scale and large-scale interventions; between small-claim and large-claim interventions; between context-sensitive and context-insensitive intervention; between propensity-based and opportunity-blocking interventions; and between internal and external validity.

Collecting evaluation findings is common when examining large-scale, large-claim interventions. Large-scale interventions are applied uniformly to many people or across large geographic areas. The Drug Abuse Resistance Education (DARE) program, Neighborhood Watch, the use of misdemeanor arrests in domestic violence, and nuisance abatement to curb retail drug markets are examples of large-scale interventions. Additionally, these are examples of large-claim interventions because supporters assert that these programs will be effective if widely adopted. Making a large claim assumes context-insensitivity: i.e., that the program will work in almost any setting. The validity of such claims is always often questionable, which is one reason we conduct evaluations. Scientific evaluations are part of the remedy for exaggeration and overgeneralization of program efficacy. This "debunking" is the *negative function of evaluations.* Assessing the validity of these claims requires not only an understanding of evaluation design, but a clear conception of what we mean by "context" and "context sensitivity."

The context is the social, temporal, physical and legal setting into which an intervention is imposed (Brantingham and Brantingham, 1993). But it is much more than the background. As described by Pawson and Tilley (1997), the intervention interacts with the context to produce the results. The greater the interaction needed to yield a given level of crime or disorder reduction, the greater the context sensitivity of the intervention. If the intervention has no interaction with the context, then the intervention will be context insensitive.

Context sensitivity is the variation in effectiveness caused by implementing the same intervention in different social, temporal and physical settings. The greater the variation, the greater is the context sensitivity. Zero context sensitivity is achieved by universally effective programs and by programs that are ineffective everywhere. Similarly, an intervention that is effective in a few places and ineffective everywhere else may have as much context sensitivity as an intervention that is effective in many places but ineffective in a few places. Effectiveness comes in degrees, of course, so variation in effectiveness across contexts also contributes to context sensitivity.

Researchers also assert that there is a *positive function of evaluations*; that collecting supportive findings builds knowledge of what works. This paper challenges the preceding assertion. The positive function of evaluations rests on shaky epistemological and practical grounds, particularly in the case of small-scale, small-claim interventions. As we will see, the positive function can exist only if evaluations have high internal and external validity. In common circumstances, there is a trade-off between these forms of validity. Additionally, many programs are crafted for very specific circumstances. They may be effective in the context for which they were created, but cannot be expected to be effective elsewhere without substantial tailoring to the new conditions. For the many small-scale, small-claim crime prevention interventions, internal validity is of limited importance and external validity is unimportant. In the world of small-scale, small-claim prevention there are alternative scientific approaches that have greater epistemological validity and are of greater practical utility.

These are the issues examined in this paper. In the next section, I describe how place-focused and situational crime prevention interventions differ from large-scale crime prevention, and why accumulating evaluation findings is inappropriate for these interventions. In the third section, I describe standard approaches to the accumulation of evaluation knowledge, and show why they may be deficient, particularly when applied to small-scale, small-claim interventions.

Another approach to the accumulation of knowledge, one that is on firmer epistemological grounds, is described in the fourth section. The fifth section describes how the negative function of evaluation can be put to use. In the final section, I describe an approach to using weak internal validity designs to guide practitioner learning about effective crime prevention interventions. Over all, this paper argues for a "small science" approach to developing positive knowledge about what works in crime preventions at places. It argues that any scientific approach to building upon evaluation findings must be grounded in sound theory. And it argues that such an approach is more defensible and practical than the approaches currently advocated by most social scientists studying ways to prevent crime.

2. PLACE, SCALE AND CLAIM

Most crime prevention focuses on how to reduce the propensity of offenders to commit crimes. From early childhood interventions (Greenwood et al., 2001), to DARE anti-drug education (Rosenbaum et al., 1994) to prison-based rehabilitation (Cullen and Gilbert, 1982), to drug treatment (Taxman and Yates, 2001), the *modus operandi* of these efforts is to change (potential) offenders' minds so that they will resist taking advantage of tempting crime opportunities when such opportunities arise. Such "propensity-based" interventions are distal to the events they seek to prevent.

An increasingly important alternative approach to crime prevention seeks to block these crime opportunities so that "easily tempted" people will not commit crimes. Opportunity blocking is usually implemented by the application of situational crime prevention (Clarke, 1983). Situational crime prevention, unlike prevention directed at criminal propensities, begins with an assumption that offenders are rational, or at least rational enough (Cornish and Clarke, 1987). It operates by manipulating the proximate risk of being caught, the effort required to successfully complete the crime, the reward from the crime, and the ability to excuse the offence. Situational crime prevention is closely linked to routine activity theory (Clarke and Felson,

1993), which describes the pattern of crime targets and victimization, and to theories of offender movement patterns (Brantingham and Brantingham, 1981), which describe how offenders come to these targets.

Opportunity blocking is particularly adaptable to problem-oriented policing (Clarke, 1997), so it is not surprising that many problem-solving efforts result in the implementation of some form of opportunity blocking. And because many of the police problems are concentrated on short street segments and addresses (Eck, 2000a), much of the effort of blocking opportunities occurs at places.

Places of crime have become increasingly important in criminology. Routine activity points to their importance and this theoretical understanding is supported by empirical descriptions of crime (Eck and Weisburd, 1995). This recognition led to a chapter reviewing place-focused prevention (Eck, 1997) in the congressionally mandated report summarizing evaluation research in communities, schools, labor markets, corrections, families, and policing (Sherman et al., 1997).

In that review of published articles and reports of propensity- and opportunity-blocking interventions, evaluations were assigned an ordinal numerical score that corresponded to Campbell's and Utanloy's (1966) research designs. At the low end were evaluations using cross-sectional non-experimental designs. These received a score of 1. At the other extreme were randomized experiments with close adherence to experimental conditions. These received a score of 5. Evaluations using pre-post designs (without control groups), non-equivalent control group and time-series designs, or multi-site quasi-experiments, received scores of 2, 3, and 4, respectively. Process evaluations were not examined, effectively giving them scores of 0. Depending on the number of evaluations at each score, crime prevention interventions were designated as "works," "promising," "unknown" and "does not work" (Sherman et al., 1997). The purpose of this was to go beyond merely summarizing the evaluation and to weight evaluations by the confidence one has that threats to internal validity had been ruled out.

The chapter on place-focused prevention examined almost 100 separate intervention evaluations. These were divided among types of places where they were applied. Then each form of intervention at a type of place was evaluated. This meant that some interventions were used in more than one type of place: closed-circuit television (CCTV), for example, was examined in retail establishments and when used for controlling outside street crime. No intervention was found that always failed to work. Virtually all interventions identified worked somewhere, if not everywhere. Nevertheless, most evaluations had weak internal validity. That is, the evaluation designs did not eliminate many important potential causes of crime drops, so there was much uncertainty as to what actually caused crime to go down — the evaluated intervention or some other factor? Consequently, few interventions were assigned to either the "promising" or "does work" categories.

In the process of carrying out the (Sherman et al., 1997) review, it became apparent that there were three important differences between place-focused interventions and the interventions being examined in other domains. First, many, if not most[1] of the place-focused interventions were an outgrowth of an earlier analysis of a very specific crime problem. Thus, the interventions being evaluated were tailored to specific contexts. An evaluation of the use of CCTV on school buses, for example, originated as a local concern about vandalism to the buses. Analysts made a careful examination of the location and timing of the vandalism and interviewed students who used the buses (Poyner, 1988). The use of CCTV in this instance was not a part of a large-scale program to install CCTV in all buses in many fleets of buses in many jurisdictions. Nor was it part of a demonstration project to show the effectiveness of CCTV on buses in general. It was an effort to address a very specific problem, and CCTV was the approach selected once the details of the problem had been explored. Though this evaluation helped demonstrate important principles of situational crime prevention, the specific intervention was designed to address a very specific problem. In short, it was a small-claim intervention.

Place-focused situational intervention effectiveness is likely to be highly context sensitive. That is, the measures implemented may be highly effective for the problem they were designed to address and in the local context they were developed, but less effective elsewhere.[2] This stands in stark contrast to evaluations of most propensity-based prevention schemes. Proponents of these interventions often assert that they address some universal, or near universal, problem. Therefore, it is claimed, their intervention is applicable almost anywhere, with limited need for adaptation to local contexts. It is this claim to universal application that makes them particularly vulnerable to the negative function of evaluations.

A second and related issue is that virtually all of the place-focused interventions are small-scale, almost by definition. They were implemented to reduce crime in specific stores, within specific apartment complexes, at specific parking lots, and within specific transport systems. Again, this contrasts with interventions in other domains that were directed at diverse groups of people with varying backgrounds and encountering a variety of life experiences. Small-scale interventions can capitalize on very specific details about a crime problem. Since these specific details vary, even for the same type of crime problem, small-scale interventions also tend to be highly context sensitive.

A third difference is that many place-based interventions are discrete rather than continuous. That is, the problem being addressed is a singular manifestation rather than an ongoing process. Addressing a street corner with drug sales is an example of a discrete intervention. If the intervention is successful, that is the end of the intervention. Providing drug treatment to arrestees is a continuous intervention. As arrestees leave the program, new ones come in. Continuous interventions are built on the assumption that all "clients" share important characteristics that make the program suitable to them. Discrete interventions do not make that assumption. Each intervention is tailored to the client.

These differences between place-focused situational interventions and propensity-based interventions suggest a need to rethink how we build knowledge from evaluations. Can we learn what works to prevent crime at places by collecting evaluations of place interventions? Such an approach is used widely in propensity-based intervention research. Still, it is not evident that the same approach we use to synthesize evaluations of rehabilitation programs, drug treatment regimes, or human capital enhancement programs applies to evaluations of place-focused situational interventions.

3. INTERNAL OR EXTERNAL VALIDITY?

The standard approach to accumulating evidence begins with Campbell's and Stanley's (1966) concepts of internal and external validity. Internal validity is the degree of confidence one has that the intervention caused the reduction in crime, rather than some other factor. This is a subjective assessment based on one's knowledge of the research design used and the likelihood that some other factor caused the change in crime, rather than the intervention. Internal validity is based squarely on the concept of falsification (Cook and Campbell, 1979:25; Popper, 1992). The evaluator has a main hypothesis: that the intervention causes the observed change in the outcome. The evaluator also has a set of rival explanations for what caused the change. Some of these rivals are known and obvious, others are hidden but nevertheless distinct possibilities. If all of these rivals are falsified by the evaluation design, then the only possible cause of the change in the outcome is the intervention. If some rivals cannot be falsified, there is doubt as to whether the change in the outcome was caused by the intervention or the unfalsified rivals. This is like tournaments where contestants are eliminated until only one remains.[3] A great tournament eliminates all but one player, weaker tournaments end before all but the last player have been eliminated.

Internal validity is not an objective description of the state of knowledge. It is a subjective assessment based on what could be. Consider a simple thought experiment. There is an intervention, X, that has been hypothesized to reduce crime, Y. The intervention is field-tested using a quasi-experiment. It is established that Y declined, and this is associated with the implementation of X. Assume, in this case, that the experiment succeeds in demonstrating that X caused the reduction in Y, with the exception that it fails to address a single potential threat to internal validity, T. The failure to rule out T as a possible cause of changes in Y leaves some uncertainty as to whether X or T caused the changes.

Now imagine that unbeknownst to the evaluator a demonic crime analyst has collected data, now secretly stored in a computer file that either falsifies T or to falsifies X. If the crime analyst comes forward, then we know either that T is no longer a rival or that X is not the explanation for the changes in Y. In either case, there is no longer a question of internal validity. We would know with certainty that X is the cause of the reduction in Y, or we would know with certainty that T is the cause of the changes in Y. If the crime analyst does not come forward, then we do not know with certainty whether X or T caused the change in Y. Of course, the demon crime analyst knows the answer, with certainty. For her, internal validity is not an issue. Thus, internal validity serves as a measure of our uncertainty as to what actually caused the observed outcome. When internal validity is very high, confidence in the statement that X caused the change in Y is very high.

External validity is the degree of confidence that we have that if the same intervention were applied again (elsewhere or at a different time), the same results would be forthcoming, holding the evaluation methods constant. This too is a subjective assessment based on one's knowledge of the context sensitivity of the intervention and the distribution of contexts to which the intervention is likely to be applied. The subjectivity of external validity is more obvious since one is making a prediction about hypothetical outcomes in unknown settings some time in the future.

External validity rests on different epistemological foundations from internal validity. There are no rival explanations that can be eliminated since we have not tested X in these other settings. Rather, we have a counterfactual hypothetical: i.e., if X were to be applied in settings S_2, S_3...Sn, then Y will go down in these settings too. There are differences between the context of the original evaluation and the potential contexts where the intervention might be applied. We know little about these potential contexts, and we seldom know much about the relationship between the context of an intervention and the effectiveness of an intervention. This is a serious problem (Pawson and Tilley, 1997).

It is often unclear what might cause the intervention to work differently in different contexts. The evaluation itself could be one factor. So could the population being treated. But there are many other possibilities. In fact, it is impossible to account for all potential contextual factors that might have substantial influences on the effectiveness of an intervention. Further, unlike rival hypotheses, contextual factors must interact with the intervention to produce the outcome (Pawson and Tilley, 1997); they co-produce the outcome. Finally, external validity refers not simply to other contemporaneous settings, but to future settings. Thus, adaptation to the intervention could change the context, making a formerly effective intervention ineffective (Ekblom and Tilley, 2000).

Some researchers ignore external validity altogether. They focus exclusively on internal validity. A recent example of this approach is the congressionally mandated assessment of what programs prevent crime — the Maryland Report (Sherman et al., 1997). Rather than simply summing the outcomes, the evaluation outcomes were weighted by the internal validity of the study to arrive at a conclusion about "what works," "what doesn't," and "what's promising" (Sherman et al., 1997).

Under some conditions, meta-analysis can be used for the same purposes. The advantage of meta-analysis is that one can calculate the overall impact of an intervention, controlling for other factors. Meta-analysis is like a survey of evaluation reports. For each report the researcher codes the effect size — a common metric for outcomes that allows comparison across studies — and the characteristics of the intervention, methods used in the evaluation, and other non-intervention factors that could influence outcomes. The researcher can then examine the impact of the intervention on effect size, controlling for these other factors (Durlak, 1995).

If internal validity is like a spelling bee, various approaches to reviewing the evaluation literature are like establishing the best team by comparing their win-loss records, and then using this information to predict the winner of the next game, or the next set of games. This approach can be made more sophisticated by taking into account "contextual" and "methodological factors" like home field advantage, injuries, and other conditions. At the end of a tournament we know who was eliminated and who was left. After a series of games, we still have a great deal of uncertainty as to who will lose the next game.

The sports betting industry is based on this uncertainty. As in sports betting, betting on an intervention in a new setting, based on past performance, is filled with uncertainty.

The conceptual difference between internal and external validity can be illustrated with Russian roulette. To make the analogy more fitting, we will look at a modified version of Russian roulette. First, at the beginning of the "game" we do not know how many chambers have bullets in them; they could all be empty, all filled, or any number in between. Second, our version will be played with a gun with a very large number of chambers. We play this game until the gun fires. Each firing represents a test of a rival hypothesis. A click represents a rejection of a rival hypothesis. A bang represents the discovery that a rival could be the actual cause of the crime reduction. After several firings we know that the chambers tested are empty. That is, these rivals have been eliminated. That is internal validity.

We can examine external validity by changing our interpretation of each firing. Now a firing represents an evaluation, a click is finding that the intervention worked, and a bang is finding that the intervention did not work. External validity is a forecast based on the premise that because the tested chambers are like the untested chambers future tests will also produce clicks. Such a prediction is dangerous, unless one knows a great deal about the gun loader's procedures and the number of bullets he had available. Such knowledge represents theory.

Generalizing from specific instances rests on principles of induction; repeated discovery of a relationship gives increasing confidence that the relationship will be observed in the future and in other settings. If we can control for contextual differences, our predictions about the future will be more accurate. So if we have multiple evaluations of the same interventions, and they point in the same direction, then we can tell practitioners that if they apply this intervention they will get similar results.

Unfortunately, there is no logical reason to believe in induction (Hume, 1992 [1777].)[4] Further, falsification was developed because induction is an unsound basis for building scientific knowledge (Popper, 1992). Campbell and Stanley (1966:17) recognized this difficulty,

> ...a caveat is in order. This caveat introduces some painful problems in the science of induction. The problems are painful because of a recurrent reluctance to accept Hume's truism that *induction or generalization is never fully justified logically*. Whereas the problems of *internal* validity are solvable with the limits of the logic of probability statistics, the problems of external validity are not logically solvable in any neat, conclusive way. Generalization always turns out to involve extrapolation into a realm not represented in

one's sample. Such extrapolation is made by *assuming* one knows the relevant laws. (Emphasis in original.)

In crime prevention this assumption is seldom valid, and it is most likely to be invalid when we are dealing with context-sensitive interventions.

The conflict between internal validity and external validity gives us another reason to be concerned with the soundness of generalization from evaluations. Consider a randomized trial in which the evaluation team, working with managers in a criminal justice agency, imposes a set of temporary work rules designed to assure the integrity of the experiment. Additionally, the evaluation team monitors adherence to the experimental protocol and the prescribed level of intervention, giving feedback to managers if deviations are detected. Finally, to assure that sufficient cases are accepted into the experiment and to meet project deadlines, the evaluation team interferes with the daily work routines of agency officials and adjusts their workloads.

Now compare this to an evaluation of the same intervention in which the evaluator collects data before the agency begins the intervention and collects the same type of data a few months after the intervention began. The evaluator also examines agency management records to document the intervention. Agency personnel, for the most part, are unaware of the evaluator and the evaluation.

In the first instance, we have an example of an evaluation that probably has high internal validity, but has low external validity because of the experimental management controls. Could we realistically expect other agencies to implement the intervention with the same level of diligence as the evaluated agency? In the second instance, we have an evaluation with a lower level of internal validity, but the delivery of the intervention may be much closer to what can be expected in common circumstances. In other words, the second evaluation has greater external validity than the first. Campbell and Stanley (1966:20) refer to this as the problem of "reactive arrangements."

This concern is not hypothetical. Lipsey (1999) distinguishes between evaluations of demonstrations designed to test efficacy, and those designed to test effectiveness in everyday practical settings. The former includes projects run by researchers that test whether the intervention works under nearly ideal circumstances. The latter include evaluations of agency-implemented programs under close to normal circumstances. In his meta-analysis of juvenile rehabilitation experiments and quasi-experiments, Lipsey found that the evaluations of demonstration efficacy had double the effect sizes of evaluations of practical effectiveness, on average.

This trade-off becomes greater when we consider the impact of special data-gathering efforts used to assess impact. Routinely interviewing experimental subjects has little effect on internal validity, if subjects in the control and treatment groups are handled in the same way, even if the subjects believe the interviews are part of the intervention. But when the intervention is used elsewhere these interviews are not conducted, so the intervention tested is not the same as the intervention exported. Under these conditions, we would expect the outcomes in daily practice to be different from the outcomes measured in the evaluation. This is the external validity problem of the "interaction of testing and treatment" (Campbell and Stanley, 1966:18).

Finally, we have to recall that in crime prevention, the more rigorous the intervention (resulting in higher internal validity), the fewer the number of agencies willing to play host. There are many reasons agencies that deliver crime prevention services may not become a host to an experiment: the evaluator may not ask; the agency may have other pressing business; the agency's leadership may not be sympathetic to evaluations or to the program being tested; or there may be other reasons. Regardless of the reasons, we can be certain that neither the evaluation host agencies nor their contexts are representative of all agencies or contexts that could use the intervention. This is the problem of the "interaction of selection and treatment" (Campbell and Stanley, 1966:19).

Consequently, for reasons that make perfect sense for maximizing internal validity, evaluators sacrifice external validity. There may be ways to ameliorate these problems — avoiding obtrusive measures (Webb et al., 1966), for example can limit the impact of "interaction of testing and treatment" — but field settings make it impossible to eliminate these threats entirely. This raises a diabolical dilemma. We can be confident of the findings and lack confidence that the findings are useful. Or we can generalize to many settings, but lack confidence in the findings we want to apply. This trade-off occurs only when we are interested in the positive function of evaluation.

4. ACCUMULATION OF KNOWLEDGE

These difficulties with generalization suggest that we need to rethink how we assemble knowledge about preventing crime, particularly when we are dealing with small-scale, small-claim interventions. We cannot logically prove an intervention works, though we can demonstrate that an intervention is not universally effective. Evaluations with strong internal validity are probably bad benchmarks for how the intervention will work in everyday practice. Perhaps rigorous evaluations are not suited to this task. If evaluations are inadequate, is there a better alternative?

We must recognize that this problem cannot be solved completely. We can make improvements. The greatest improvement is to pay much closer attention to the theoretical roots of interventions rather than their leafy outcomes. Theories are general propositions about how phenomena interact to cause other phenomena. By their nature theories confer generalizability, at least within the bounds of their scope conditions. An explicit theory describes when and where it is applicable. If an intervention is deducible from this theory, then it should be applicable in the same contexts. The question is whether the theory is correct. Though we cannot be certain if it is correct, we can subject it to hard tests that attempt to demonstrate that it is not. If a theory survives repeated hard tests this is our best explanation, and therefore is our best foundation for developing interventions, given our current state of knowledge.

Is there a better foundation for the formulation of crime prevention interventions other than a theory of criminal activity that has been well tested and has yet to be falsified? No. Even if we expect that some time in the future a theory will be shown to be inadequate, it is currently our best explanation. Since we cannot wait for a better theory before implementing crime prevention interventions, our best current theory should be the basis of such action.

Routine activity theory, situational crime prevention, and related theories of crime events, for example, are our best current theories of why crime concentrates at some places and how these concentrations can be reduced and prevented. Therefore, place-focused programs should be based on this set of theories. The theories do not dictate specific actions, but provide a framework for the creation of context relevant interventions. In this example, the answer to the question, "what works?" to prevent crime at places is "routine activity theory and situational crime prevention." The answer is not, CCTV, lighting, locks, management screening of prospective tenants, nuisance abatement, street redesign or any other particular measure. These are tools that might work in some circumstances but probably do not work in every circumstance (Clarke, 1997).

This raises two questions. First, how does one move from the general best current theory to a specific intervention? Second, what is the role of evaluation in this context? We will address the first question now and reserve the second question to the next section.

Crime prevention programs have to be developed in ways that combine the best relevant current theories with a deep understanding of local contexts. The sources of the theory are obvious. Contextual understanding must be based on thorough analysis of the local problem.

We already have frameworks for such a method. Problem-oriented policing is one such framework, though it makes no specific reference to a theory. Situational crime prevention is another. It provides a coherent theory, and advocates analysis of local context prior to formulation of interventions, but does not advocate a particular delivery mechanism (such as the police). These approaches are very similar to that advocated by Pawson and Tilley (1997), except that Pawson and Tilley appear to emphasize the evaluator's role and I am emphasizing the practitioner's role. As we will see below, evaluations are not well suited for program advocacy or program autopsies, though evaluations can provide valuable information.

We should be mindful that program implementers would prefer not to have to conduct their own analysis of their problem. Or if they are willing, they are likely to do a superficial job. The examples from problem-oriented policing are testament to this position (Scott and Clarke, 2000). Some of this is due to inadequate training and bureaucratic support. Some of this is due to the press of business. And some of this is due to inadequate theoretical and empirical research into problems (Eck, 2000b). Further, the police may be typical of most organizations in this regard. Regardless of the cause, implementers are ill served by evaluators who claim to have positive answers about what works in their circumstances but who have not examined the problem being addressed. Taking practitioners off the hook does no one any good.

5. ROLE OF EVALUATION

Weeding out programs with excessive claims is the main role of strong evaluations. The greater the scale and claim of an intervention, the more important is this negative function. The larger the program, and the more public resources it commands, the greater the need to be sure we are not funding an intervention with little or no return on this investment. So the larger the scale of a program, the higher the level of internal validity required.[5]

Interpretations of negative findings are not straightforward. One interpretation is that the intervention does not work anywhere. However, for the same reasons multiple positive findings do not logically lead to a conclusion of universal generalizability, multiple negative evaluations, from different populations, cannot by themselves demonstrate a program is ineffective. If there exists a sound theory that describes why the intervention should not work, then a rigorous evaluation is a test of this theory. If the theory supporting the intervention is falsified (and the theory antagonistic to the intervention is not), then the best evidence is that the intervention is probably misguided. By a sound general theory antagonistic to the intervention I do not mean the null hypothesis. Rather, we should have a detailed explanation of the crime problem that shows why the intervention is irrelevant or how it makes the problem worse.

The trade-off between internal and external validity is far less of a concern when we focus on negative findings. In essence, we are saying, "If you cannot demonstrate success when extreme measures are being used to assure that the program is working correctly, then it is unlikely that the intervention will work effectively in everyday practice."

Not all evaluations will have negative findings. How do we interpret positive findings? Interventions that survive rigorous evaluations do not have strong claims for generalizability unless they rest on the foundation of a well-tested theory that explains why the intervention is effective. In the absence of such a foundation, we only know that the intervention survived a strong test in a particular context. Without a theory, we have no way of accurately predicting what contexts, in the present or foreseeable future, are suitable for such an intervention. Evaluations with positive findings, but without theoretical support, have very limited utility for policy. They do, however, raise an interesting question: "What explanation of crime is needed to explain the evaluation outcome?" So positive evaluations can stimulate the development of theory, even if they cannot provide strong evidence for what works outside of the contexts within which they were conducted.

6. WEAK EVALUATIONS AND IMPROVEMENT IN PRACTICE

Evaluations have an important negative role for the assessment of large-scale, large-claim crime prevention interventions. In these circumstances, strong evaluations (with high levels of internal validity) are critical. What is the role of evaluation when we are dealing with small-scale, small-claim crime prevention interventions? The answer is that evaluations have an important, but limited negative role.

Before we examine the role of evaluations it is important to recall the setting of many small-scale, small-claim interventions. This can be seen readily in problem-oriented policing projects. These start with the identification of a serious crime or disorder problem.[6] The objective of practitioners is to substantially reduce the problem, if not eliminate it. To determine how the problem can be reduced, problem-solvers engage in a detailed analysis of the problem, sometimes guided by routine activity theory or situational crime prevention. This analysis should reveal ways that the context of the problem can be altered so that the context becomes less suitable for the problem. Drawing from their findings, problem-solvers implement some intervention. They seldom assert that this intervention will work in any other setting. Consequently, problem-solvers do not need to address external validity.

What about internal validity? The evaluation's most important task is to show whether or not the problem has gone down. If it has not been reduced, then the problem-solvers need to re-examine the problem and see if there are other approaches that could be more effective. If the problem has been significantly reduced or eliminated, do practitioners care about rival explanations? To a limited extent, "Yes." It is important to recognize when fortuitous circumstances lead to the demise of the problem, rather than the intervention. But this interest is a distant second to the most important piece of information: that the problem declined.

Knowing the precise unambiguous cause of the decline matters most if one plans to repeat the intervention without a thorough pre-intervention analysis.[7] This is because one would not want to recommend the future use of an intervention when it was not the cause of the decline in the problem. Again, internal validity acts as a check on false claims. Internal validity matters in proportion to one's interest in using the intervention again, in another context, and inversely to the quality of the pre-intervention analysis one used to determine how to intervene. One should not be deceived, however. An intervention can be established, with an internally valid evaluation, to be the cause of a problem's decline, but that does not guarantee that this very same intervention will have the same results if applied again. For purposes of generalization, internal validity is at best a necessary condition, but it is far from sufficient.

But internal validity may not even be a necessary condition. If the next attempt to address a similar problem is also preceded by a detailed analysis, and this analysis points to the use of the very same intervention as before, then the rigor of the evaluation of the earlier intervention is of limited importance.

When dealing with small-scale, small-claim crime prevention interventions, evaluation designs with relatively weak internal validity work well enough. They need to be sufficiently rigorous to show that the problem declined following the intervention, but they need not eliminate all rival hypotheses. Indeed, there can be a great deal of doubt as to what exactly caused the decline in the crime. Simple, pre-post and short time-series evaluations that take into account the most likely rival hypotheses — short-term trends and seasonality, for example — provide sufficient evidence to make decisions about the program. These simple evaluations can be implemented and easily interpreted by practitioners. And they do not create artificial conditions that distort actual practice. Further, unlike textbook rigorous evaluations, they can be accommodated within the way practitioners normally learn from experience.

How good is good enough? Evaluations should help decision makers. So the answer depends on how much certainty decision makers need. Or to put it another way, how much uncertainty they can tolerate. With small-scale, small-claim interventions the principle decision is whether to continue an intervention, whether it should be modified, or whether something else should be done. Not intervening may be more costly than intervening.

Rigorous evaluations are an awkward, inefficient, and unnatural way to learn about what works when we are interested in small-scale, small-claim, discrete interventions.[8] At this scale, learning involves using theory to set the boundaries on how to proceed, and then the use of imitation and trial and error to work out the details. Some hints as to how we can proceed come from civil engineering and the construction of one-of-a-kind structures. Counting the number of bridges standing and comparing this number to the number that collapsed, for example, does not make for success in bridge construction. All we know for certain about standing bridges is that they have not fallen, yet. Rather there is a heavy reliance on theories of physics and materials, plus pre-implementation analysis and planning, coupled with evaluations of catastrophic failures (Dörner, 1997; Petroski, 1992).

Let's see how this might work in crime prevention. A practitioner is faced with a problem that has, so far, been immune to standard operating procedures used by the practitioner's agency. Drawing on a conceptual framework for the problem and likely interventions, the practitioner develops a crime prevention intervention (X_1), tries it on a crime problem (P_1), and looks to see if the problem declined. Though such a framework may be a well-described theory, it is often a general set of shared operating assumptions. If the problem did not change substantially, X_1 will be discontinued and a search for a new intervention will commence.[9] If the problem declined, then the next time some similar problem (P_2) arises, X_1 will be a serious contender for a solution. If there are no other contenders, and no one bothers to closely examine the problem, then X_1 will probably be applied to P_2. If X_1 is context sensitive, then when it is applied to P_2 it will not work as well as it did when first applied to P_1. Practitioners will then adjust their *a priori* expectations for the effectiveness of X_1 when applied to

P_3, P_4, ...P_n. Continued poor experience in the application of X_1 will lead to adjustments (X_2, ...X_m) or the development of a different approach (Z_1).

Theories become involved in this process in two ways. First, they highlight questions that need to be answered during the analysis. Second, they suggest categories of interventions. In the absence of theories, the questions problem-solvers ask will depend on who is conducting the analysis. Some problem-solvers will demonstrate great insight, go beyond the shared assumptions about the problem, and ask questions that are critical to getting to the roots of the problem. Many other problem-solvers will not. In the absence of theory, many problem-solvers will either have difficulty interpreting their analysis in a way that leads them to an effective solution, or they will interpret the results in accordance with the shared assumptions about the problem. To the extent that the standard operating procedures and the proposed intervention are based on the same operating assumptions, X_1 will have limited effectiveness.

The long-term effectiveness of a crime prevention agency depends on how well the agency analyzes the applicability of competing interventions to the crime problems it faces. There are three possible impediments.

First, agency personnel may be unaware of relevant theories. This will slow progress considerably. One can predict that crime prevention agencies that routinely examine new theoretical developments will be more effective in the long run than those that do not.

Second, agency personnel may consistently conduct low quality analyses. In this case, the selection of interventions is likely to be haphazard or rely on a limited range of prevention options. One can predict that crime prevention agencies that conduct high quality empirical examinations of crime problems will have greater long run effectiveness than those that do not.

Third, agency personnel may not be exposed to new ideas from the outside. Paying attention to what has been done elsewhere in vaguely similar circumstances is critical. This directly and indirectly introduces competing intervention options. Direct competitors are almost exact replicas of interventions tried elsewhere. Indirect competitors will be ideas stimulated by the interaction of the new information, experiences with earlier interventions, and analysis of the problem at hand. Indirect competitors may be more valuable than direct competitors. The more possible interventions competing to address a problem, the greater the chances practitioners will find one that fits their problem. So one can predict that the crime prevention agencies that have the greatest exposure to ideas from the outside will be more effective in the long run than those that have the least exposure to outside ideas.

In summary, crime prevention agencies that excel at consistently implementing highly effective programs will have personnel who are well versed in problem theories. They will conduct thorough analyses of their crime problems and will search outside their agency for ideas. They will use information about interventions that have been certified as "works" successfully, but they will not give such interventions priority before undertaking their own careful problem analysis. On the other hand, interventions that have been labelled "does not work" after repeated strong evaluations will be severely discounted.[10]

There are six advantages to this approach:

(1) It does not require evaluations or evaluators to do more than they can. They are better at debunking than building.

(2) It integrates criminological theory with crime prevention practice.

(3) It puts the burden of coming up with effective interventions on the practitioners, and requires them to fit the intervention to the problem rather than to look for "off-the-shelf" solutions This enhances the chances that the intervention will be effective.

(4) Evaluations become a practical tool that can be used by crime prevention program implementers. They do not have to conduct academic-quality evaluations, but can use relatively simple and easily understood procedures to answer a very specific question, "Did the problem decline?"

(5) The use of simple weak designs means that accountability can be increased. It becomes possible for agency personnel to determine, on a routine basis, whether the problem declined.

(6) This approach is better suited to circumstances that change over time, in part because of the intervention. Offenders, victims, and others adapt to crime prevention interventions (Ekblom, 1997). This can strengthen or weaken the effectiveness of interventions. In such circumstances, evaluations need to be easy to use, inexpensive, reasonably quick, and flexible.

In this paper, I have argued that when dealing with small-scale, small-claim crime prevention interventions, adherence to rigorous evaluation criteria is misguided. Standard evaluation practices cannot provide sufficient assurances that a tested intervention will continue to be useful outside the contexts within which it was examined. Standard evaluation practices assume that one is interested in replicating the intervention in other contexts, so it is important to be certain that the intervention, and not something else, caused the drop in crime. Further, standard evaluation practices place too much emphasis on after-the-fact results rather than pre-implementation analysis.

Rather than relying on rigorous evaluations of small-scale, small-claim interventions, practitioners and researchers are better served by applying well-tested theories and conducting thorough analyses of problems before designing an intervention. Simple evaluations can then provide the feedback necessary to make adjustments in the intervention. By sharing information, practitioners can learn what works *to design* effective programs. All of this is likely to lead to faster learning about effective crime prevention and faster adaptation to changing circumstances.

Acknowledgements: I am in debt to Nick Tilley, Ronald V. Clarke, and Francis Cullen for the use of their valuable insights. The fact that I was not able to use them all is my fault, and I take full responsibility for the limitations in this paper.

Address correspondence to: Prof. John E. Eck, University of Cincinnati, Division of Criminal Justice, P.O. Box 210389, Cincinnati, OH 45221. E-mail: <john.eck@uc.edu>.

REFERENCES

Brantingham, P.L. and P.J. Brantingham (1993). "Environment, Routine, and Situation: Toward a Pattern Theory of Crime." In: R.V. Clarke and M. Felson (eds.), *Routine Activity and Rational Choice.* (*Advances in Criminological Theory*, vol. 5). New Brunswick, NJ: Transaction Publishers.

—— and P.J. Brantingham (1981). "Notes on the Geometry of Crime." In: P.J. Brantingham and P.L. Brantingham (eds.), *Environmental Criminology*. Beverly Hills, CA: Sage.

Campbell, D.T. and J.C. Stanley (1966). *Experimental and Quasi-Experimental Designs for Research.* Chicago, IL: Rand McNally.

Clarke, R.V. (1997). *Situational Crime Prevention: Successful Case Studies* (2nd ed.). Albany, NY: Harrow and Heston.

—— (1983). "Situational Crime Prevention: Its Theoretical Basis and Practical Scope." In: M. Tonry and N. Morris (eds.), *Crime and Justice: An Annual Review of Research,* vol. 4. Chicago, IL: University of Chicago Press.

—— and M. Felson (1993). "Introduction: Criminology, Routine Activity and Rational Choice." In: R.V. Clarke and M. Felson (eds.), *Routine Activity and Rational Choice. (Advances in Criminological Theory,* vol. 5.) New Brunswick, NJ: Transaction Publishers.

Cook, T.D. and D.T. Campbell (1979). *Quasi-Experimentation: Design and Analysis Issues for Field Settings.* Chicago, IL: Rand McNally.

Cornish, D. and R.V. Clarke (1987). "Understanding Crime Displacement: An Application of Rational Choice Theory." *Criminology* 25(4):933-947.

Cullen, F.T. and K.E. Gilbert (1982). *Reaffirming Rehabilitation.* Cincinnati, OH: Anderson Publishing.

Dörner, D. (1997). *The Logic of Failure: Recognizing and Avoiding Error in Complex Situations.* Reading, MA: Addison-Wesley.

Durlak, J. (1995). "Understanding Meta-Analysis." In: L.G. Grimm and P.R. Yarnold (eds.), *Reading and Understanding Multivariate Statistics.* Washington, DC: American Psychological Association.

Eck, J.E. (2000a). "Policing and Crime Event Concentration." In: L.W. Kennedy, R.F. Meier and V.F. Sacco (eds.), *The Process and Structure of Crime: Criminal Events and Crime Analysis.* New Brunswick, NJ: Transaction Publishers.

—— (2000b). "Problem-Oriented Policing and its Problems." Unpublished paper.

—— (1997). "Preventing Crime at Places." In: L.W. Sherman, D. Gottfredson, D. MacKenzie, J. Eck, P. Reuter and S. Bushway (eds.), *Preventing Crime: What Works, What Doesn't, What's Promising — A Report to the Attorney General of the United States.* Washington, DC: Office of Justice Programs, United States Department of Justice.

—— and D. Weisburd (1995). "Crime Places in Crime Theory." In: J.E. Eck and D. Weisburd (eds.), *Crime and Place. (Crime Prevention Studies,* vol. 4.) Monsey, NY: Criminal Justice Press.

—— and W. Spelman (1987). *Problem Solving: Problem Oriented Policing in Newport News.* Washington, DC: Police Executive Research Forum.

Ekblom, P. (1997). "Gearing Up Against Crime: A Dynamic Framework to Helping Designers Keep up with the Adaptive Criminal in a Changing World." *International Journal of Risk, Security and Crime Prevention* 2(4):249-265.

—— and N. Tilley (2000). "Going Equipped: Criminology, Situational Crime Prevention and the Resourceful Offender." *British Journal of Criminology* 40(3):376-398.

Goldstein, H. (1990). *Problem-Oriented Policing.* New York, NY: McGraw-Hill.

Greenwood, P.W., L.A. Karoly, S.S. Everingham, J. Hoube', M.R. Kilburn, C.P. Rydell, M. Sanders and J. Chiesa (2001). "Estimating the Costs and Benefits of Early Childhood Interventions: Nurse Home Visits and the Perry Preschool." In: B.C. Welsh, D.P. Farrington and L.W. Sherman (eds.), *Costs and Benefits of Preventing Crime.* Boulder, CO: Westview.

Hume, D. (1992 [1777]). *Enquiries Concerning Human Understanding and Concerning the Principles of Morals* (3rd ed.). Oxford, UK: Oxford University Press.

Lipsey, M.W. (1999). "Can Rehabilitative Programs Reduce the Recidivism of Juvenile Offenders?" *The Virginia Journal of Social Policy and Law* 6(3):611-641.

Pawson, R. and N. Tilley (1997). *Realistic Evaluation.* London, UK: Sage.

Petroski, H. (1992). *To Engineer is Human: The Role of Failure in Successful Design.* New York, NY: Vintage Books.

Popper, K.R. (1992). *The Logic of Scientific Discovery.* London, UK: Routledge.

Poyner, B. (1988). "Video Cameras and Bus Vandalism." *Journal of Security Administration* 11(2):44-51.

Rosenbaum, D.P., R.L. Flewelling, S.L. Baily, C.L. Ringwalt and D.L. Wilkinson (1994). "Cops in the Classroom: A Longitudinal Evaluation of Drug Abuse Resistance Education (DARE)." *Journal of Research in Crime and Delinquency* 31:3-31.

Scott, M. and R.V. Clarke (2000). "A Review of Submissions of the Herman Goldstein Award for Excellence in Problem-Oriented Policing." In: C.S. Brito and E.E. Gratto (eds.), *Problem-Oriented Policing: Crime-Specific Problems, Critical Issues and Making POP Work* (vol. 3). Washington, DC: Police Executive Research Forum.

Sherman, L.W. (1992). "Review of 'Problem-oriented Policing'." by Herman Goldstein. *The Journal of Criminal Law and Criminology* 82:690-707.

—— D. Gottfredson, D. MacKenzie, J. Eck, P. Reuter and S. Bushway (1997). *Preventing Crime: What Works, What Doesn't, What's Promising — A Report to the Attorney General of the United States.* Washington, DC: Office of Justice Programs, United States Department of Justice.

Taxman, F.S. and B.T. Yates (2001). "Quantitative Exploration of the Pandora's Box of Treatment and Supervision: What Goes on Between Costs In and Outcomes Out." In: B.C. Welsh, D.P. Farrington, and L.W. Sherman (eds.), *Costs and Benefits of Preventing Crime.* Boulder, CO: Westview.

Webb, E.J., D.T. Campbell, R.D. Schwartz and L. Sechrest (1966). *Unobtrusive Measures: Nonreactive Research in the Social Sciences.* Chicago, IL: Rand McNally.

Weick, K.E. (1984). "Small Wins: Redefining the Scale of Social Problems." *American Psychologist* 39(1), 40-49.

NOTES

1. Published reports are only suggestive of the use of place-specific analysis that guided the development of the interventions, so it is difficult to get an exact measure.

2. While a specific intervention may be context sensitive, the general concept being used may be far less sensitive. A general concept, however, cannot be implemented directly. It has to be adapted to the specific locale. In fact, that a particular intervention, π, in a specific manifestation of a general concept, X, is one of the many auxiliary hypotheses that evaluators and interpreters of evaluations must make. These auxiliary assumptions too, may be invalid. The slippage between a theoretician's ideal intervention and the program's actual implementation may be substantial.

3. A spelling bee analogy is particularly apt. The winner of a tournament, like a spelling bee, is not the contestant who can spell any word. There are words not used in the contest that might stump the winner. Similarly, in most quasi-experiments, we never eliminate all rival hypotheses, just the most plausible. Someone later might come up with a rival explanation that was not examined, just as it is possible to find a word not used in the spelling bee that stumps the champion. Given the imperfections in field experimentation, this probably is the case in randomized experiments, too.

4. "All inferences from experience, therefore, are effects of custom, not of reasoning" (Hume, 1992 [1777]:43)

5. Ronald V. Clarke, in a personal communication, suggests that when the reduction in crime is very large, then the likelihood of some alternative to the intervention causing the reduction diminishes. That is because there are very few factors that could cause such a large drop. However, when the drop in crime following an intervention is relatively

small, there are many plausible alternative explanations, so a rigorous design is required to sort them out. This suggests a two-stage approach to evaluating situational prevention, when one is interested in widerspread adoption. First, conduct a few inexpensive weak evaluations. Then, if the drop in crime is consistently large, one has sufficient confidence to believe that this intervention should be considered in similar circumstances. Alternatively, if the drop in crime is small or inconsistent, but nevertheless important, then a series of rigorous evaluations should be implemented to test the intervention. Finally, if the drop in crime in the weak evaluations is consistently minor and unimportant, then one can put this intervention near the bottom of the list of plausible responses to problems of this kind. The importance of triaging programs for evaluation is that it recognizes that rigorous evaluations are costly and time consuming, so we would want to use them only for interventions where the expected outcome is important but in doubt.

6. In reality, problem-oriented policing projects can encompass a far greater range of problems than simply crime and disorder. Traffic problems, for example, are important for the police to handle. I am restricting my attention to crime and disorder since we are discussing crime prevention evaluations.

7. I am ignoring "bragging rights" and politically motivated claims of success, though these are very important in some contexts. However, in practice such claims seldom rest on the internal validity of an evaluation. Advocacy feeds on the slimmest of evidence.

8. Given the frequent complaints about the failure of decision makers to take into account evaluations of large-scale/large-claim interventions, it is clear that the use of evaluation results does not come naturally to people in these contexts.

9. This, of course, assumes that there are no rigidities that impede adjusting the intervention for reasons other than effectiveness — political support, budgetary requirements, leadership commitment, and so forth. Two factors make such an assumption less problematic than it at first appears. First, small-scale/small-claim/discrete interventions require fewer resources and political support to implement than other types of interventions, so they can be implemented and discontinued with greater ease (see Weick, 1984). Second, these rigidities may slow decision making, but seldom are they permanent obstacles. The most important question is how rapidly the agency can make changes, not whether it can make changes.

10. The asymmetry between "works" and "doesn't work" labels stems in part from the issue of falsification and the fact that rigorous evaluations require higher quality implementation than is likely in practical settings. These have been discussed earlier in this paper.

CHOOSING AN EVALUATION MODEL FOR COMMUNITY CRIME PREVENTION PROGRAMS

by

Brian J. English
Edith Cowan University

Rick Cummings
Murdoch University

and

Ralph G. Straton
Murdoch University

Abstract: *Community crime prevention programs are used to reduce the incidence of crime in communities and encourage community participation in crime prevention. The evaluation of a community crime prevention program can provide valuable information about the program's appropriateness, acceptability to key stakeholders, efficacy and efficiency, thereby enabling managers to plan improvements. In Australia, however, relatively few programs are evaluated. Where evaluation studies have been undertaken, they have used a narrow range of evaluation models, often focusing solely on measuring project outcomes or impact.*

The aim of the present paper is to increase awareness of the models of evaluation that can inform both the practice and strategic direction of crime prevention programs. It emerged from an initiative of the Commonwealth of Australia Attorney-General's Department, through its National Crime Prevention Program, and the Australian and New Zealand Crime Prevention Ministerial Forum.

In the paper, both a conceptual model and a decision-based process are developed linking the characteristics of a community crime prevention program to the various combinations of evaluation type, approach and methods that comprise specific evaluation models. Several recent evaluation studies are presented to illustrate the range of evaluation models used in community crime prevention

In accord with this framework, our recommendation is that the evaluation of community crime prevention programs will be better served if a wider range of evaluation models are employed to meet the information needs of key stakeholders.

BACKGROUND

As the costs of crime for both individuals and the community rise, crime prevention has become a major concern. Substantial resources are spent on measures to apprehend and punish offenders, and to reduce the likelihood that offences will be committed in the future. Despite these efforts, crime prevention poses a formidable challenge for society, in part because of the range and complexity of the reasons for offending. Community crime prevention programs are a widely used means of reducing the incidence of crime in communities and encouraging community participation in crime prevention.

Community crime prevention can be characterised in a number of ways. Ekblom and Pease (1995) distinguish between action *for* the community, action *through* the community, and action *with* the community. Sherman et al. (1997) focus on the various institutional settings of the crime prevention effort, distinguishing between communities, families, schools, labour markets, places, the police, and the criminal justice system. Each of these institutional settings may vary in the extent to which a crime prevention program may be considered to be a community program.

Despite differing opinions about what community crime prevention is, the central role of the community in crime prevention is widely acknowledged. Felson (1994) believes that most crime is 'ordinary', originating in the routine activities of everyday life. He argues that crime prevention should also be built into these routine activities, emphasising informal social control rather than relying on the distant and often expensive criminal justice system. While this view does not deny that complex psychological, social and structural factors influence criminal acts, it does emphasise the centrality of the local community and its institutions — such as the family, schools, neighbourhood organisations and youth work programs — in crime prevention. Bennett (1995) also has argued that community organisations have particular strengths that make them a useful, even necessary, component in a multi-pronged effort to reduce community crime.

The centrality of local communities in crime prevention is supported by recent research showing that informal social control, and social cohesion and trust among neighbours, are related to lower levels of violence (Sampson et al., 1997). It is also supported by the nature of the *Blueprint Programs* — violence prevention programs that have achieved a high level of effectiveness in reducing violence in the United States (Elliott, 1997). *Communities that Care* is another program, widely implemented in the United States and recently introduced into the United Kingdom and Australia, which recognises the pivotal role of communities in crime prevention. This program aims to build community capacity to plan and implement local, community-wide crime prevention strategies, with increasing evidence of success (Toumbourou, 1999).

A variety of community crime prevention programs are in use in Australia. However, as indicated in a recent national compendium on crime prevention programs (Australia National Anti-Crime Strategy, 1995), fewer than 10% of 170 state and territory crime prevention programs and projects identified had been evaluated. An evaluation of a community crime prevention program can provide valuable information enabling managers to plan improvements.

Accordingly, the present paper aims to increase awareness of the models of evaluation that can guide both the practice and strategic direction of crime prevention, particularly among people at the local level with limited training and experience in evaluation. It emerged from a project initiated by the Commonwealth of Australia Attorney-General's Department through its National Crime Prevention (NCP) program and the Australian and New Zealand Crime Prevention Ministerial Forum. The project was carried out through a partnership between Australian commonwealth, state, territory and local governments (English et al., 1998). The key objectives were to identify, try out and appraise a range of evaluation models for community crime prevention programs, and describe the major issues evaluators should consider in choosing suitable models. Achieving these objectives involved identifying relevant literature through a computerised search of databases for the period 1985 to mid-2001. Over 500 papers on crime prevention programs or their evaluation were identified. Wide ranging consultations with experts in crime prevention also were conducted. An Evaluation Planning Kit for practitioners and policy makers has been produced as an outcome of the project (Straton et al., 1999).

The paper commences with an introduction to the concept of evaluation, and outlines the basic considerations in the choice of an evaluation model. This is followed by an examination of the range and type of community crime prevention programs and a classification scheme for characterising community crime prevention programs to determine an appropriate evaluation model. The paper concludes by describing a number of steps for determining the most appropriate evaluation model for a particular community crime prevention approach. A number of evaluation studies of crime prevention programs are presented throughout the paper to illustrate the use of the different evaluation types, approaches and methods that represent alternative evaluation models.

THE NATURE OF PROGRAM EVALUATION

The Purpose and Definition of Program Evaluation

Program evaluation is the process of delineating, obtaining and providing information which is of use in describing and understanding a program, and in making judgments and decisions related to the program (Straton, 1981). In addition to providing information on the function and outcomes of a program, evaluation studies should provide a description of the context in which a program operates as well as the nature of its actual clients, physical and human resource inputs, and the intervention processes used in its implementation. This description documents what the program actually is — the program reality — in contrast to what was intended or may be assumed about it. Evaluation can also identify the underlying mechanism or causal processes by which the outcomes of the program are achieved — that is, contribute to an understanding of the "why" of the outcomes (Pawson and Tilley, 1994). This is important for a full understanding of why the program may need to be changed or in what circumstances it might be expected to work elsewhere.

To ensure that an evaluation will yield useful information, evaluators should determine the nature of the required information in the planning stages. This will depend upon who the audiences for the information are and the purposes for which they need the information. In short, program evaluation is a process involving deciding what information to gather, obtaining that information, providing the information to key audiences, including stakeholders, and facilitating use of the information by those stakeholders.

Determining Audience Needs

To maximise the usefulness of evaluation information, evaluators must recognise the varying roles and responsibilities of the primary audiences of the information. Mayne and Hudson (1992) suggest that differences in these roles and responsibilities will lead to priority being given to information which is primarily useful either for program management within a relatively short time frame (action-oriented evaluation), or for enhancing knowledge about a particular form of intervention in society (research-oriented evaluation).

Action-oriented evaluation addresses the immediate information needs of those implementing, managing and modifying programs. Mayne and Hudson (1992) point out that managers want to know how and why their programs are working or not working, and so adopt an action oriented perspective on evaluation. Improving their understanding of the program puts them in a better position to make informed management decisions about how it can be improved, transferred to other settings and implemented with other target groups.

Research-oriented evaluation, on the other hand, puts a high premium on methodological rigour because it is seen as a form of scientific inquiry. It is intended for longer-term use, rather than being immediately useful for modifying programs. The review by Sherman et al. (1997) of what works and what does not work in crime prevention represents a research-oriented perspective on evaluation.

In considering these different orientations, Mayne and Hudson (1992) point out that each gives priority to different aims, and so should be judged on that basis. Indeed, it is counterproductive to criticise research-oriented evaluation as not being effective in modifying programs or action-oriented evaluation as being weak methodologically and therefore of limited scientific value. Both are important and complementary in most fields, and particularly in the evaluation of community crime prevention programs.

Ensuring the Usefulness of Evaluation Information

It is often assumed that evaluation information has not been used, or is not useful, unless specific overt decisions (and sometimes actions) have clearly been influenced by the information. However, this is a limited view. Frequently, instrumental use of the information is not feasible because of various contextual, political, ethical or financial constraints, yet the information might increase knowledge and understanding of the program (i.e., conceptual use), or contribute to the acceptance of a position already taken in relation to the program (i.e., persuasive use) (Shadish et al., 1991). Evaluation information may also cause stakeholders to change their thinking about the program, and their behaviour in relation to it, as they learn more about the program through the evaluation process (i.e., process use) (Patton, 1997).

Clearly, the resources expended on evaluation must be justified by the value of the information provided. Therefore, evaluation studies must be focused and conducted in ways that will enhance the likelihood that the information will be useful and used by the key audiences and stakeholders.

EVALUATION TYPES, APPROACHES AND METHODS

An important first step in evaluation planning is the need to determine why the evaluation study is to be undertaken and to consider the alternative evaluation approaches and methods that may be useful.

Evaluation Purposes and Types

An evaluation study may be undertaken for a number of reasons. The most common reasons are to:

(1) determine the impact of an existing program;

(2) provide feedback information on a regular basis to facilitate program management;

(3) obtain guidance on the modification of program inputs and processes;

(4) clarify the underlying program logic; and

(5) assist in program development by identifying areas of client need and the resources that may be used in a new program.

These five reasons for undertaking an evaluation study comprise the key dimensions of the five major evaluation types identified by Owen and Rogers (1999):

(1) Impact evaluation.

(2) Monitoring evaluation.

(3) Interactive evaluation.

(4) Clarificative evaluation.

(5) Proactive evaluation.

This classification shows that, in addition to the evaluation of program impacts, program development and implementation are also appropriate subjects for evaluation research. This is consistent with what Visher and Weisburd (1998:230) call 'the new approach' to crime prevention research. Owen and Rogers (1999) also consider the current state of the program (whether it is currently under development or settled), the components of the program likely to be of major interest, and the timing of an evaluation study in suggesting the evaluation approaches likely to be most appropriate.[1]

Impact Evaluation

Impact evaluation establishes the effects of a program once it has been implemented and settled for a period of time. This may involve determining to what degree program objectives have been met or the assessment of intended and unintended outcomes. The main use of this information is to justify whether the program should continue to be implemented or implemented in other settings and, if so, whether any modifications are required. Thus, it has a strong summative evaluation emphasis. Impact evaluation is usually completed after some logical 'end point' in the program has been reached — for example, where a Neighbourhood Watch program has been fully operational for a year.

Monitoring Evaluation

Monitoring evaluation focuses on program outcomes and delivery for management decision making and accountability purposes. These data are used primarily to account for the expenditure of program funds, including the extent to which key accountabilities have been met by program managers. This type of evaluation is appropriate when a program is well established and ongoing (Owen and Rogers, 1999). It frequently involves keeping track of how the program is progressing. Real time feedback to managers is an important feature of this type of evaluation.

Interactive Evaluation

Interactive evaluation examines program implementation including the extent to which a program is being delivered in the way it was intended to be delivered.

Information from this type of evaluation is used to determine how the implementation of the program could be improved, and it therefore has a strong formative evaluation emphasis. Formative evaluation refers to evaluation designed and used to improve a program, especially when it is still being developed (Joint Committee on Standards for Educational Evaluation, 1994). Consequently, this type of evaluation is conducted as the program is being delivered within its various settings. The information is of particular use to those implementing the program.

Clarificative Evaluation

Clarificative evaluation clarifies the underlying rationale of a program. Program developers use this information to think through and make explicit the logic that supports the program, including assumptions about how its components link to produce the desired outcomes. Whereas clarificative evaluation would usually occur before the implementation of a program, it may also be carried out while a program is operating if it is not clear how it was intended that the program was to be delivered. Therefore, it has a formative evaluation orientation.

Proactive Evaluation

Proactive evaluation focuses on the actual need for a program. The main use of this data is to help planners determine what type of program would meet the identified social need or problem. This type of evaluation is carried out before a program is developed.

An Alternative Framework

Ekblom and Pease (1995) have proposed an alternative framework for distinguishing between various evaluation purposes, which addresses some of the issues inherent in determining the evaluation type. In this framework a major distinction is made between evaluations that address implementation issues (e.g., what practical difficulties were encountered in implementing the program) and those that determine program impact (e.g., was there a real change in crime as a result of the implementation of the program?). While a distinction between implementation and impact evaluation captures some of the variation reflected in the five evaluation types suggested by Owen and Rogers (1999), it does not capture it all. For example, evaluation can also be used for clarifying the underlying logic (referred to as clarificative evaluation), as well as to review current unmet needs (proactive evaluation). Here we have adopted Owen and Rogers's approach as it has the potential to more precisely focus evaluation planning on the wide range of possible information needs.

Evaluation Approaches

Numerous suggestions have been made about how evaluation studies might be conducted, and several authors have analysed and classified these into a few distinct broad approaches to evaluation, providing a description of their rationale and main features (House, 1980; Madaus et al., 1983; Straton, 1985; Stufflebeam and Shinkfield, 1985; Taylor, 1976). There are five evaluation approaches that are most likely to be of use in the evaluation of community crime prevention programs:

(1) goal-based;

(2) decision-oriented;

(3) systems analysis;

(4) professional review; and

(5) illuminative/responsive.

Goal-based

Goal-based evaluation focuses on obtaining information on the extent to which the objectives of the program have been attained. It assumes that program goals represent the most important criteria in judging the worth of the program. However, the results of the study may prove to be inadequate or even misleading if the goals are inappropriate or have been superseded. There also is a risk of ignoring significant unintended effects of the program, which may be either positive or negative.

Decision-oriented

Decision-oriented evaluation identifies the key decisions to be made about the future of the program, and seeks to obtain relevant information. Information about the attainment of existing program goals may not be of high priority, particularly where client need or program context will be different in the future. Instead, the major concern is to what extent the program is likely to be successful in the future in the locations and contexts in which it might be implemented, and how it might be adapted to achieve the required degree of success. This approach may, however, yield information too narrow in scope if the decisions to be faced are not well anticipated or the information needs are not appropriately specified.

Systems Analysis

Systems analysis determines program efficiency, providing information on a few key indicators of program effects (including the extent to which goals have been attained), and program costs. The indicators typically provide only highly aggregated information on what the program effects are and little or no information on how the program might be made more effective or efficient. In essence, the information may be useful for broadly based decisions at the highest levels, but of little use to those directly responsible for improving program delivery and management or for adapting it to different circumstances.

Professional Review

Professional review relies on the judgment of experts from outside the program for determining the key information to gather, the suitability of program objectives and processes, the degree to which it is successful and what changes should be made to the program. It assumes that experts in relevant fields are best placed to determine the criteria and the information to be used in the program's evaluation. The usefulness of the information and the recommendations will be determined by the extent to which the judgments of these professional experts are appropriate to local circumstances and needs and reflect the values and priorities of the key stakeholders.

Illuminative/responsive

Illuminative/responsive evaluation provides a fine-grained depiction of the program, focusing on 'thick' description, an understanding of the complexity of the program and a portrayal of the experiences of program participants, including clients, staff and others affected by the program. This approach assumes that a detailed and intimate view of a program is required to understand its operation and accomplishments well enough to provide a sound basis for making appropriate changes to the program or judgments about its success. The danger with this approach is that the potentially high authenticity of these descriptions and their utility for program deliverers on a day-to-day basis might be obtained at a risk of bias and reduced credibility among those further removed from the program.

As can be seen, every approach to evaluation involves trade-offs. In any evaluation study it is likely that evaluators will need to combine the characteristics of more than one approach to achieve the major purposes of the study. Therefore, evaluators may need to develop a specific evaluation approach tailored for a particular study rather than simply selecting one from a list.

Evaluation Methods

The full range of social research methods may be applied in undertaking evaluation studies, including the various alternative research designs and techniques of data collection and analysis. However, there are a number of program-specific considerations which may make some methods inappropriate for a particular evaluation study. For example, in determining program impact on the incidence of particular types of crime, obtaining quantitative data using an experimental or strong quasi-experimental design would seem the most fruitful method to use. However, ethical, access or other constraints may make it impossible or inappropriate to use such methods. Similarly, the use of naturalistic methods to obtain qualitative data may often be useful for interactive evaluation, but resource constraints and the extensive nature of the program may mean that an *ex post facto* design using quantitative data may be the most feasible method to use.

The very broad division of research methodology into qualitative and quantitative is a useful distinction even though it masks the wide array of different types of data that might be collected and ways of doing so. A number of evaluation methods have been distinguished below which reflect three alternative research design frameworks that might be used to conduct an evaluation study, rather than the various data collection techniques. This has been proposed on the grounds that the choice of design is a broader decision, and that either or both qualitative and quantitative data might be obtained within any of the design frameworks in a particular evaluation study. These evaluation methods are:

(1) experimental and quasi-experimental;

(2) survey and naturalistic; and

(3) *ex post facto.*

Experimental and Quasi-experimental

A high degree of control over where, when, how and to whom an intervention is administered is required in a true experiment so that program effects can be determined by comparing initially equivalent treatment and control groups. However, this level of control is difficult or impossible to achieve in most evaluation settings. It is rare to find experimental methods fully and appropriately applied in program evaluation. Quasi-experimental methods, however, can often be appropriately used in evaluation studies. Quasi-experimental methods adjust to the constraints of the program setting in a variety of ways, including the comparison of non-equivalent groups that have been subjected to different interventions and the assessment of program-related changes over time within groups. Despite their appeal, however, the use of quasi-experimental methods does not always furnish a clear explanation for any observed differences (or lack of them). The interpretation of the findings, therefore, usually relies heavily on the soundness of the logic of the evaluative argument and the evidence used to support it.

Survey and Naturalistic Methods

Survey and naturalistic methods tend to be more descriptive, typically relying on the reports of participants and other stakeholders. These methods are particularly appropriate for obtaining information on the perceptions of a program's context, processes and outcomes. Survey research methods are characterised by a strict adherence to formal sampling designs and a commitment to obtaining high response rates to ensure a representative sample of respondents. They can be useful in identifying the various perspectives held on a program and its effects. Surveys may be difficult to implement well, however, due to problems developing an appropriate sampling frame and differential access to sub-groups within the sample, such as current and previous program participants and non-participants. There is also a tendency towards high refusal rates and 'sanitised' responses among those who think that their access to services or their jobs might be adversely affected by providing negative comments on the program.

Naturalistic methods provide useful in-depth information about a program through the use of extended interviews with open-ended questions and participant and non-participant observation, allowing the detailed exploration of significant issues. These methods have similar problems to those encountered in surveys. The use of deliberative rather than formal sampling procedures makes sampling easier, but may raise serious questions about the representativeness of the information, particularly as resource constraints will usually limit the range and number of sources of information that can be used. This can lead to limited credibility of the information obtained, a shortcoming which may be overcome to the extent that the information clearly contributes to and is compatible with a well-argued case about the nature and achievements of the program.

Ex Post Facto

Many evaluation studies focus on a program that has been in operation for some time, and are initiated and conducted over a relatively brief period. These studies are essentially retrospective rather than prospective. The use of *ex post facto* methods may be required — for example, case control studies where those who participated in the program are compared after the fact with those who did not — as it may not be possible to observe all significant program processes and stages or to follow up a representative sample of program clients during and after their participation to determine outcomes. Useful information about a program can be a product of *ex post facto* studies, but the range of possible alternative explanations for the apparent program context, inputs, processes and outcomes means that plausible conclusions about the program will depend on the strength of the evaluative argument based on this information.

Choosing an Evaluation Method

It is our view that no evaluation method is superior to the other methods — the method chosen will be influenced by the context of a particular evaluation study and its specific purposes and constraints. When deciding the evaluation method to use, evaluators should carefully consider the likely threats to internal and external validity and the measurement validity of the data the study will yield. In addition, the costs involved, access to information sources, the sampling designs and procedures, the ability to maintain the integrity of alternative interventions, the availability of required expertise and time constraints are all factors to be considered in examining these trade-offs. A comprehensive evaluation study is likely to require a combination of methods (Australia National Crime Prevention, 1999).

Evaluation Models in Action: An Example

The three main considerations in selecting a model for an evaluation study are summarised in Figure 1. Taken at face value, this figure indicates that an evaluation type needs to be determined first, as this will reflect the main purposes of the study. Next, an appropriate evaluation approach is specified, followed by a decision on the methods to be used. In practice, however, the decisions about the type, approach and methods frequently are made iteratively so that the particular constraints of the study, such as the time and other resources available, can be accommodated in an optimal way.

Figure 1: Considerations in Selecting an Appropriate Evaluation Model

Evaluation Type	Evaluation Approach	Evaluation Methods
Impact	Goal based	Experimental & quasi-experimental
Monitoring	Decision oriented	
Interactive	Systems analysis	Survey & naturalistic
Clarificative	Illuminative/responsive	Ex post facto
Proactive	Professional review	

The evaluation study of the Neighbourhood Watch program implemented in Britain from 1983 and described by Bennett (1989) is an example of the application of an evaluation model frequently used in this field. A major focus of the study was the program outcomes, particularly the extent to which the program had achieved its objective of reducing victimisations one year after its implementation. This is characteristic of impact evaluation using a goal-based approach: a focus on outcomes directly related to program objectives, in a program which essentially is settled, to determine whether its continuation is justified (Owen and Rogers, 1999).

To determine the program's effectiveness, a quasi-experimental design was employed comprising two experimental areas: a control area and a displacement area (Bennett, 1989). The choice of a displacement area was given particular attention by Bennett, who drew upon the theory (mechanism) underlying Neighbourhood Watch in his discussion. Thus, in general terms, the model used in the planning and conduct of the evaluation study was an *impact evaluation* conducted through a *goal-based approach* using *quasi-experimental methods*.

The extent to which the model used in the Neighbourhood Watch evaluation was optimal, given the information needs of the key stakeholder groups and the various constraints within which the study was conducted, cannot be determined from the description provided. Nevertheless, the choice of model for an evaluation study needs to be fully justified in each particular case, taking into account a range of considerations, including the nature of the program and its context, the information needs and priorities of various stakeholders, the resources available for the study and other constraints, and various methodological considerations. A number of trade-offs will often need to be made so that the extent to which a study yields relevant and important information is maximised.

CHARACTERISING CRIME PREVENTION PROGRAMS FOR EVALUATION PURPOSES

Variations in program focus, program rationale, community context, the ways in which a community is involved and other factors create a wide variety of community crime prevention programs. Evaluators therefore need to consider a range of evaluation models to be able to choose an appropriate model to meet stakeholders' needs. Choosing from a few standard evaluation models is unlikely to provide the information required for making sound program judgments and decisions in many evaluation situations.

Below we examine the various types of program approaches (embodying causal mechanisms and program rationale) that have implications for the evaluation of community crime prevention.

A Classification Scheme for Characterising Programs for Evaluation Purposes

Among the most important general considerations in designing and conducting an evaluation study are:

- its purpose, focus and timing, as these relate to the use of the evaluation information for making judgments and decisions;

- the practicalities associated with collecting relevant evaluation data (i.e., its feasibility);

- the technical adequacy of the evaluation data; and

- the nature of the strategies put in place to safeguard the rights of key stakeholders in the evaluation process (i.e., probity).

Program Considerations

In addition to these general considerations, the choice of evaluation model should be determined by an examination of the program's characteristics, namely:

- the prevention approach that provides the rationale for the program;

- the program type;

- the program specifications; and

- the political context surrounding the program.

Community crime prevention efforts are usually classified as either:

- opportunity reduction/situational approaches, or

- social/developmental approaches (Gant and Grabosky, 2000; Indermaur, 1996; O'Malley and Sutton, 1997).[2]

Crime prevention programs, in common with all social programs, also have embedded within them an assumed causal mechanism. This mechanism is often implicit (or at least not fully explicit) and provides the rationale for the program (Tilley, 1996).

Ekblom and Pease (1995), in common with several other authors, distinguish between two broad causal mechanisms for crime prevention:

- situational-oriented, and

- offender-oriented.

Situational-oriented crime prevention mechanisms assume that crime can be reduced by changing the immediate situation in which offences may occur. As such, situational-oriented crime prevention is based on an opportunity-reduction approach, focusing on specific types of crime, with the emphasis on making both the social and the physical environment less conducive to crime, and on reducing the likely rewards and increasing the likely risks of crime (Clarke, 1997).

Offender-oriented mechanisms, on the other hand, assume that crime is reduced by changing potential offenders generally in terms of the dispositions, motives, knowledge, and skills they bring to situations (Ekblom and Pease, 1995: 600). Accordingly, offender-oriented crime prevention emphasises the centrality of the individual and focuses on his or her personal development in ways that will make criminal activity less likely.

An Australian example of an opportunity reduction/situational approach to crime prevention, cited by Gant and Grabosky (2000), is the introduction of measures in Victorian TABs (licensed betting shops) to limit access to cash. This initiative aimed to deter prospective robbers by increasing the effort and reducing the rewards associated with robberies, thereby making the TABs less attractive targets. The TAB in Victoria progressively introduced time-locking cash boxes, and set a cash limit of $500 on each selling drawer in TAB outlets. These target-hardening initiatives achieved a reduction in the incidence of robberies of between 20% and 48%. A further initiative, fitting time locks to the main safes, was also followed by a decrease in robberies. A decline in the average amount of money stolen in TAB robberies was also observed following the introduction of these initiatives.

In contrast, Gant and Grabosky (2000) use the *PeaceBuilders* program to illustrate a social/developmental approach to community crime prevention. The program's goal was to reduce bullying, violence and other anti-social behaviour through a school-based intervention based on increasing children's resilience and positive behaviours. Participants in the program were students at a school in a southeastern Queensland community with high levels of unemployment, family breakdown and inter-cultural tension. The program addressed risk factors associated with anti-social behaviour, and developed protective mechanisms at the level of the individual, the school and the community. Following the introduction of the program, anti-social behaviour fell, student and parent satisfaction with the school rose, parent involvement with the school increased, staff turnover declined and police call-outs to the school fell from 24 before the program to 4 in the second year after its introduction.

More recently, Ekblom and Tilley (2000) have argued that the distinct separation of reduction/situational approach and social/developmental approach as two causal mechanisms has obscured opportunities for developing a more comprehensive model of causation in crime prevention. They propose a framework for linking situational and offender-oriented prevention which incorporates both theories of causation. Grabosky and James (1995) cite an anti-bullying program developed in Norway as an example where opportunity reduction and social/developmental approaches were combined. In this program, changes were made to playground design (opportunity reduction), pro-social classroom interaction was encouraged, and counselling was provided for children at risk of victimisation (social/developmental). Clarifying the implications for evaluation of the causal mechanism presumed to underlie a community crime prevention program is an important step in evaluation planning.

Implications for Evaluation

The underlying rationale of a program is crucial to program evaluation because it is critical to understanding the "why" of the outcomes. However, the program rationale must be examined for each particular program site because the operation of the mechanism through which a program is expected to effect change will be moderated by community contexts (Pawson and Tilley, 1994). Where it is explicit, the rationale should also be critically examined in an evaluation study because this can assist in identifying what may account for any unintended outcomes (Stake, 1967). In a similar vein, Ekblom and Pease (1995) point out that distinct evaluative requirements attach to different types of prevention (1995:585), while Pawson and Tilley (1994) note that evaluations need to take into account the mechanisms through which effects are assumed to be determined. This carries the implication that an evaluator would use a different evaluation strategy for a program based on an opportunity-reduction approach (e.g., "lock it or lose it" campaigns), compared with a program based on offender-oriented crime prevention (e.g., providing youth at risk of offending with employment opportunities).

In a similar vein, Funnell and Lenne (1990) have suggested that different types of programs would normally be attached to different evaluation strategies because of the distinctive outcome hierarchies related to the purpose of a program. Examples noted by Funnell and Lenne include, on the one hand, programs that seek to influence behaviour (e.g., public education programs, regulatory programs, case management programs) and on the other hand, programs that provide products or services (e.g., security services). The development and use of an outcome hierarchy in planning an evaluation study is outlined by Murray et al. (1993), who provide an example relevant to

the evaluation of community based juvenile crime prevention programs.[3]

A program's specifications are also an important consideration in
the design and conduct of evaluation studies. This is usually expressed in terms of:

- the program setting (e.g., rural, urban, CBD);

- the composition of the target group (e.g., families, students,
  people with disabilities); and

- the type of need or problem being addressed (e.g., crime
  against property, crime against persons).

When considering the evaluation of community crime prevention
programs, evaluators also should take into account the nature of the
community settings of a program and whether the program is initiated by and conducted through local grass-roots means or by external means. This will influence decisions by the primary stakeholders
and will influence what information should be given highest priority
in an evaluation study.

Finally, the political context of a program needs to be taken into
account in the evaluation of community crime prevention programs.
Weiss (1993.94) points out that, while evaluation can be thought of
as a rational enterprise, it always takes place in a political context
embodying a number of significant considerations. The evaluator who
fails to recognize their presence is in for a series of shocks and frus-
trations. This is because, among other things, policies and programs
are proposed, defined, debated, enacted, and funded through political
processes, and in implementation they remain subject to pressures,
both supportive and hostile, that arise out of the play of politics.

Figure 2 shows these three aspects of crime prevention programs
which together form the basis of a classification scheme for crime
prevention programs relevant to their evaluation. The political context
of the program influences all aspects of the program.

Figure 2: Considerations in Characterising Community Crime Prevention Programs for Evaluation

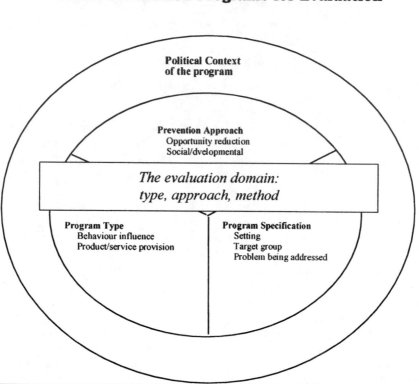

Characterising Programs for Evaluation Purposes: An Example

An analysis of Neighbourhood Watch programs, in a generic form, provides an illustration of the characterisation of a community crime prevention program in preparation for planning an evaluation study.

Based upon the Neighbourhood Watch programs implemented throughout the London Metropolitan Police District in Britain in 1983, Bennett (1989) suggests these programs typically include four main components, or variants of them. These components are:

- a network of community members who watch out for and report suspicious incidents to the police;

- the personalised marking of valuable property;

- home surveys to advise on the minimum level of protection required; and

- a public information campaign to raise awareness of the importance of crime prevention.

To characterise such programs in a way that is useful for evaluation purposes, the underlying *prevention approach* (in terms of the assumed underlying causal mechanisms), *program type* (as reflected in its main purpose and outcome hierarchy), and *program specification* (the particular program setting, target group and problem focus) need to be identified. Once these elements have been identified, the implications of particular constraints surrounding the program (the political context) can be determined. This could include, for example, determining the implications of any disagreements between key stakeholders about how the information related to the evaluation should be disseminated.

Prevention Approach — Opportunity Reduction

Neighbourhood Watch is based on a prevention approach embodying the view that crime can be reduced by changing the situation in which offences might occur, and reflects a focus on the role of modulators of crime, in this case surveillance by community members (Ekblom and Pease, 1995) A Neighbourhood Watch program therefore has an opportunity reduction-approach embodying a situational-oriented causal mechanism.

Ekblom and Pease (1995) point out that there are significant implications for evaluating situational-oriented approaches to crime prevention such as Neighbourhood Watch. These include the possible unintended side effect that reducing the opportunity to offend in one locality may lead to these crimes being displaced to other places, targets or types of crime. This displacement may be into nearby areas used for comparison purposes in the evaluation study, with the result that intervention effects could be overestimated. More generally, Chen (1990) points out that understanding the theory underpinning a particular social intervention is essential for identifying the important program elements that ought to be used in focusing an evaluation study, as well as in articulating the presumed causal mechanisms in order to develop appropriate outcome measurement.

Program Type — Advisory Program

Funnell and Lenne (1990), as noted earlier, suggest that different types of programs attach themselves to different evaluation strategies because of the distinctive patterns of outcomes and outcome hierarchies that each type is expected to achieve. They distinguish between programs that intend to influence behaviour and those that provide a product or service. Programs that seek to influence behaviour are further subdivided into advisory, regulatory or case management programs. Examples of advisory programs, also often referred to as public information programs, include health promotion programs and telephone advice services. Neighbourhood watch may also be thought of as an advisory program: police, insurance companies, local government and security firms give information and advice to Neighbourhood Watch groups in an effort to reduce crime (or the fear of crime).

Advisory programs have a unique outcomes hierarchy that should guide the evaluation process. Evaluation tasks at the lowest level of the outcomes hierarchy for these programs include determining the extent to which the desired number and type of people have been contacted. Evaluation tasks at higher levels in the hierarchy include determining the extent to which the desired number and type of people involved in Neighbourhood Watch exhibit the desired changes in action or behaviour, such as improving the physical security of their homes.

Program Specification – Neighbourhood-based, Problem-specific

The program specification includes the setting in which the program is implemented, the target group, and the need or problem being addressed. In Australia, Neighbourhood Watch has been implemented in an enormously wide range of social and geographical areas. Mukherjee and Wilson (1987) reported that in New South Wales there were over 1,000 Neighbourhood Watch districts covering more than 1 million households. Some of these are in inner-city and outer-suburban areas; others are in regional areas. Each of these settings will present its own unique problems for evaluation, such as the feasibility of collecting certain types of evaluation data.

The target group of a Neighbourhood Watch program is all households in a particular area. An evaluation study may need to identify the range of types of households and how factors such as household resources and other characteristics are related to the extent and degree of program uptake. Furthermore, the specific nature of the problem being addressed, or the relative importance of various aspects of the general overall problem (e.g., car theft, other property theft and property damage), will also have significant implications for evaluation.

SELECTING AN APPROPRIATE EVALUATION MODEL FOR COMMUNITY CRIME PREVENTION PROGRAMS

Evaluation studies have an important role to play in providing information on the nature and performance of community crime prevention programs. The cornerstone of any evaluation study should be the extent to which the information it provides is useful to the program's stakeholders and the other users of the information. This information can be of particular use in improving program effectiveness and efficiency where the information is valid, relevant, broad in scope and important for making significant program judgments and decisions.

Obtaining such information depends on using an appropriate evaluation model to guide the planning and conduct of an evaluation study. The evaluation model chosen and the way it is applied should enhance the information's appropriate, effective and ethical use. The choice of evaluation model should take into account the nature and specific characteristics of the program. However, evaluators also need to consider the extent to which the generally accepted standards for evaluation can be met when choosing a particular evaluation model such as those outlined in the Program Evaluation Standards (Joint Committee on Standards for Educational Evaluation, 1994).

Figure 3 shows a conceptual representation of the various considerations in choosing or constructing a model for an evaluation study of a community crime prevention program. Figure 2 also indicates that these characteristics can only be properly understood by taking account of the political context surrounding the program.

As discussed earlier (see Figure 2), the conceptual framework identifies three characteristics of community crime prevention programs of particular concern for evaluation purposes, namely the prevention approach, program type and program specifications. Recapping, there are two widely recognised broad approaches to prevention: the opportunity-reduction approach and the social/developmental approach (O'Malley and Sutton, 1997). Program types may be classified as those seeking to influence behaviour and those providing a product or service (Funnell and Lenne, 1990). There are three aspects of the program specifications that are important for evaluation — the program setting, the target group and the particular need or problem being addressed. A further important consideration for evaluation is the political context within which a program operates.

Figure 3: Considerations in the Choice of an Evaluation Model

Program considerations		Evaluation considerations		SPECIFIC EVALUATION MODEL
-Prevention approach -Program type -Program specification	→	-Type -Approach -Method	→	

↑	↑	↑
Informed by: *Political interests,* *processes and decisions*	*Informed by:* *Stakeholder/audience's* *forthcoming judgments* *and decisions*	*Informed by:* *Evaluation practice standards* *and criteria*

As also shown, the conceptual framework draws attention to the variations in evaluation type, approach and method that comprise particular evaluation models. In combination, the five evaluation types and five generic evaluation approaches previously referred to (see Figure 1) represent the essence of alternative evaluation models. Again recapping, the different evaluation types reflect the major purposes for which an evaluation study may be undertaken. The evaluation approaches, on the other hand, provide alternative bases for determining the high priority information to be gathered in an evaluation study and in making judgments of worth and merit about the program. However, an evaluation model is only fully specified when linked with particular evaluation methods. The various combinations of these evaluation types and evaluation approaches are illustrated in matrix form in Figure 4. For each cell of the matrix, there are a variety of methods which might be used. While certain methods will tend to be more compatible with particular evaluation types and approaches, there are many alternatives worthy of consideration. A process for determining the most appropriate model(s) is described next.

Figure 4: Matrix of Evaluation Types and Approaches

	Evaluation Type				
Evaluation Approach	Impact Evaluation	Monitoring Evaluation	Interactive Evaluation	Clarificative Evaluation	Proactive Evaluation
Goal based					
Decision oriented					
Systems analysis					
Professional review					
Illumina-tive/re-sponsive					

Process for Selecting an Appropriate Evaluation Model

Figure 5 outlines how each of the elements in the conceptual framework can be brought together to select an appropriate evaluation model (Cummings and English, 1998).

Figure 5: Process for Selecting the Most Appropriate Evaluation Design

Step 1	Identify the program characteristics Prevention approach Program type Program specifications
Step 2	Determine the evaluation study purposes Identify key stakeholders Identify judgments/decisions to be made and associated information needs Develop study purposes
Step 3	Identify appropriate evaluation model Identify appropriate evaluation types Select appropriate evaluation approaches compatible with types Identify most suitable methods for each combination of type and approach, taking into account how relevant evaluation standards and criteria will be met
Step 4	Negotiate the preferred model with key stakeholders

Step 1. Identify Program Characteristics

The first activity is to identify the characteristics of the program that have implications for evaluation. This information is usually available in official program documents such as program planning specifications or funding proposals. If the information is not available from documents, then it needs to be identified through discussions with key stakeholders such as program managers. The program characteristics need to be explicit in order for the evaluation to be clear about the focus and boundaries of the program. Where the program has more than one focus in a particular area of interest, they all should be identified, preferably with a priority assigned to each focus. This priority list of prevention approach, program type and program specifications needs to be described explicitly to stakeholders, who, in turn, should verify its accuracy.

Step 2. Determine Evaluation Study Purposes

The process of identifying the purposes of the evaluation study involves discussion between the evaluation sponsors and the key stakeholders of the program. The identification process usually starts by examining who is responsible for the program, who funds it, who works in it, and who are the clients or participants. Discussion with these stakeholders is likely to identify additional stakeholders. Eventually, those with direct responsibility for the program or who are directly affected by the program or the evaluation need to be singled out as the primary stakeholders. It is generally individuals from this group who are used to represent stakeholder interests.

Once the primary stakeholders are identified, it is necessary to identify the decisions or judgments they intend to make about the program and about which they hope the evaluation study will provide them with information. It is often a difficult task to get a clear picture at this point, given that they often have very different backgrounds, areas of responsibility and particular interests in the program. However, a set of key decisions, judgments or issues needs to be delineated to provide a focus for the evaluation. For example, the purpose of an evaluation in the community crime prevention area may be to describe the goals, operation and outcomes of the program; determine the impact of the program on vandalism and youth in the area; compare the costs and benefits of the program; and, make recommendations about the program's suitability for continuation and/or transfer to another setting.

Step 3. Identify Potential Evaluation Models

Once the stakeholders, their decisions or judgments, and their information needs are identified, the process of identifying the most appropriate evaluation model can commence. First, the evaluation types are examined to determine which ones might be compatible with the purpose of the evaluation. Five types of evaluation were identified earlier. In determining which type may be appropriate, Owen and Rogers (1999) suggest that several dimensions need to be considered, including the main reason for undertaking the evaluation, the degree to which the program has been implemented, the key aspects of the program upon which the evaluation will focus, and the timing of the evaluation in relation to the delivery of the program. The various evaluation approaches are considered next.

In the community crime prevention area, 12 of the possible 20 combinations of type and approach appear to be especially relevant, and these are shown as shaded cells in Figure 6. The remaining eight combinations have a high level of incompatibility between the approach and type. For example, it is unlikely that an evaluation study focussing on collecting information about how a program was designed would be compatible with the goal based approach which focuses on how well the goals of the program have been achieved. From the possible combinations available, a short list can be drawn by looking at how well each combination of type and approach will address relevant evaluation standards. The 'utility' standards ((Joint Committee on Standards for Educational Evaluation, 1994), which are intended to ensure evaluations address the information needs of key stakeholders, including timeliness, are considered particularly important in determining the appropriate combinations of type and approach.

Figure 6: Matrix of Evaluation Types and Approaches Appropriate to Community Crime Prevention Programs

	Evaluation Type				
Evaluation Approach	Impact Evaluation	Monitoring Evaluation	Interactive Evaluation	Clarificative Evaluation	Proactive Evaluation
Goal based					
Decision oriented					
Systems analysis					
Illuminative /responsive					

The next step is to identify the methods which are most suitable for each combination of type and approach. The framework identifies five major evaluation methods; experimental, quasi-experimental, survey, naturalistic and ex post facto. The choice of the most appropriate methods is based on a combination of the types of information required and relevant evaluation standards and criteria (such as feasibility, propriety and accuracy criteria). Some methods will better suit the type of information required, the structure of the program, ethical considerations, and the financial and time constraints on the evaluation study. Nevertheless, in general all methods are potentially useful.

Step 4. Negotiate Final Design with Stakeholders

Once the shortlist of appropriate models is developed and checked against relevant evaluation standards and criteria, the problem of determining the preferred model remains. Here, the process becomes very specific to the individual program under consideration at a particular time. The program type and specifications are critical considerations in determining which model is likely to be most appropriate. In addition, specific issues — such as, the budget, the feasibility of using certain data collection and reporting methods given the structure and operation of the program, the political environment in which the program and the evaluation are operating, and the personal preferences of the individual key stakeholders — need to be considered. Importantly, these matters need to be negotiated with the stakeholders, particularly the client or sponsor of the evaluation. In most instances, there are trade-offs made to arrive at the most acceptable model.

EVALUATION MODELS IN USE IN COMMUNITY CRIME PREVENTION

Below we classify a number of evaluations of community crime prevention programs to illustrate the various combinations of evaluation type, approach and methods that reflect the particular evaluation models currently being used. The examples have been chosen from recently published reports of evaluation studies using the following criteria:

- The crime prevention program is community-based, being a preventive effort either for, with or through the community.

- The study is an example of program evaluation, including either or both research-oriented and action-oriented evaluations.

- The evaluation study was completed within the past 15 years.

- The examples represent a range of programs and evaluation models.

Table 1 presents a summary of the characteristics of the selected evaluation studies. More detailed summaries of the evaluations follow below.

PREVENTING ALCOHOL-RELATED CRIME THROUGH COMMUNITY ACTION

- Impact evaluation
- Goal-based
- Survey and naturalistic methods

This evaluation study, conducted by Homel and associates (Homel et al., 1997), illustrates a goal-based impact evaluation which employed a range of methods to provide evaluation data, in particular survey and naturalistic methods. The purpose of the study was to examine the extent to which key program activities had reduced alcohol-related crime, violence and disorder in and around licensed (liquor selling) premises in a major tourist location in Queensland, Australia. The study also examined the extent to which these effects were maintained over the longer term.

Homel et al. (1997) point out that previous research had revealed that inappropriate drink promotions that encourage mass intoxication are a major risk factor for violence. The clear implication is that if the level of intoxication decreases, then the level of associated violence should also decreases.

Table 1: Classification of Community Crime Prevention Programs for Evaluation Purposes

Study Authors	Program Characterization			Evaluation Type	Evaluation Model	
	Prevention Approach	Program Type	Program Specification		Evaluation Approach	Evaluation Method(s)
Homel et al., (1997)	Opportunity reduction/situational	Behaviour influence	Urban, alcohol-related crime	Impact	Goal-based	Survey & naturalistic
Kessler & Duncan (1996)	Opportunity reduction/situational	Behaviour influence	Urban, narcotics	Impact	Goal-based	Quasi-experimental
Crawford & Jones (1996)	Opportunity reduction/situational	Behaviour influence	Urban, burglary	Interactive	Decision-oriented	Naturalistic
Ekblom (1992)	Opportunity reduction/situational Social/developmental	Behaviour influence	Urban, range of crimes	Impact	Decision-oriented	Quasi-experimental

Study Authors	Program Characterization			Evaluation Model		
	Prevention Approach	Program Type	Program Specification	Evaluation Type	Evaluation Approach	Evaluation Method(s)
Iuliano (1995)	Social/developmental	Behaviour influence	Urban, truancy & offending	Interactive	Illuminative/responsive	Naturalistic
Wundersitz (1994)	Social/developmental	Behaviour influence	Remote, illegal vehicle use	Interactive	Illuminative/responsive	Naturalistic

Several strategies (developed in the light of the association between levels of intoxication and levels of violence) were implemented with the aim of decreasing the level of intoxication of patrons in and around the licensed premises. These included the formation of a community forum and several community-based task groups to oversee and direct the program, and the development of model house policies and associated codes of practice for the responsible serving of alcohol. There were also improvements in the external regulation of licensed premises by the police and licensing inspections.

Study Characteristics

During the evaluation study, data were collected before implementing any changes, as well as throughout and following the implementation period. This enabled changes over time to be monitored and used to assess the impact of the various intervention strategies. A control area was considered but not included because of budget constraints. The information collection procedures included community surveys, interviews with licensees, direct observation of serving practices at licensed premises, and the analysis of incident reports.

Findings

The findings suggest that there had been major changes in the responsible serving of alcohol, including more responsible promotions. The rates of physical violence also dropped by 52%, from 9.8 per 100 hours to 4.7 per 100 hours over the year the program was implemented. Security and police data also revealed evidence of a decline in violence and street offences. However, the study found that, two years after the program had ceased its implementation phase, the rates of physical violence had increased again to 8.3 per 100 hours. This finding was interpreted by the evaluators as indicating the importance of maintaining community monitoring in programs where communities seek change and are empowered to bring about the changes. The evaluation team also underlined the importance of participatory approaches to program design, implementation and evaluation in community crime prevention.

COMMUNITY POLICING OF NEIGHBOURHOODS

- Impact evaluation
- Goal-based

- Quasi-experimental

In evaluating this program, Kessler and Duncan (1996) conducted a goal-based, impact evaluation, which employed a quasi-experimental design. The purpose of the evaluation study was to assess the impact of community policing in reducing crime in four neighbourhoods of Houston, Texas. The programs conducted in two of the neighbourhoods were initiated in response to citizens' complaints about the widespread use and availability of drugs and the associated crime, and were referred to as the *War on Drugs* and the *Link Valley Drug Sweep* campaigns. These programs involved the mobilisation of the community and the police to board up abandoned properties, close 'crack houses' and arrest drug dealers. Volunteer local citizens also cleaned up neighbourhoods by removing trash and hypodermic needles. One of the neighbourhoods was swept clean and access was restricted to residents only.

In contrast, the Blocks Organising Neighbourhood Defence (BOND) programs in the other two neighbourhoods were Neighbourhood Watch programs. These programs focused on creating processes whereby citizens could work continually with police to improve safety and security. This involved:

- identifying residents who were willing to participate in the BOND programs;

- training residents in crime prevention techniques

- teaching residents proper crime and suspicious behaviour reporting techniques;

- establishing an organisation through which to communicate neighbourhood problems to police and residents; and

- identifying support activities.

As crime patterns developed, the use of networks and newsletters allowed residents to make informed decisions about how to deal with problems as they occurred, such as instituting foot patrols during certain hours and in particular areas where burglaries were occurring.

Study Characteristics

The evaluation study used statistical data collected over the course of the implementation of the program to assess its effectiveness. Data such as calls for service (calls made by citizens to police), recorded crime (crime reported by citizens that is recorded) and narcotics crime (arrests by police) were collected for the four neighbour-hoods. Time-series analysis was used to track the changes in these variables over a number of years before the programs were implemented through to approximately 12 months after their commencement to allow lagged effects to be examined.

Findings

The results did not allow any clear generalisations to be made about the effectiveness of the programs. None of the four programs produced results that conformed to the hypothesis that community policing programs would bring about a temporary increase in calls for service and recorded crime, followed by a long-term decrease. For example, the War on Drugs program appears to have been successful in motivating citizen involvement and cooperation with police in that there were increases in calls for service and recorded crime. But the authors found no evidence for an eventual reduction in this neighbourhood's problems.

Similarly, while the citizens of the Link Valley Drug Sweep program were highly motivated and worked closely with the police, there was no evidence of increased reporting to police, or indeed of any significant impact on the measures examined. In one of the Neighbourhood Watch programs, calls for service showed significant change by temporarily decreasing — but this was the opposite of what was hypothesised for this type of community policing program. In the second Neighbourhood Watch program, recorded crime increased gradually. The authors stated that over all the best conclusion may be that the programs had no impact (Kessler and Duncan, 1996:657).

The authors remarked that police departments appear to not yet know the solutions to providing an effective community policing service. They stressed that the search must rely on rigorous evaluations and empirical research findings. The authors noted limitations to the evaluation study, including difficulties associated with the quality of the records and documents about the programs, and concern over the reliability and validity of the measures used. Other considerations could include the use of a wider range of information collection procedures and sources to address a wider range of questions, such as changes in the type of crime, the seriousness of the crimes, who are the perpetrators of crimes and so on, so as to fully appreciate the impact of this type of program.

TRANSFERRING CRIME PREVENTION INITIATIVES

- Interactive evaluation
- Decision-oriented
- Naturalistic

This study illustrates the use of a decision-oriented, interactive evaluation, which employed a naturalistic method (Crawford and Jones, 1996). The purpose of the evaluation study was to provide information that would assist in the successful transfer of the Kirkholt Anti-Burglary Project to Tenmouth, a city in the southeast of England.

The Kirkholt Project had three main aims, which were also adopted in the Tenmouth Project:

- the reduction of burglary in the targeted area;
- the delivery of the crime reduction mechanisms through a multi-agency approach; and
- the eventual local community ownership of the project.

The aims of the project were summed up by the authors as an attempt "to devise a joint plan between the statutory and voluntary agencies, commercial sector and the community towards frustrating the activities of burglars and the fear they provoke and make it work!" (Crawford and Jones, 1996:25).

Study Characteristics

The report on the evaluation study begins with a discussion of the nature of evaluation. It asserts that evaluation in the area of community crime prevention is preoccupied with determining whether the program objectives have been achieved, using before and after surveys. This preoccupation prevails despite wide recognition, in the view of Crawford and Jones (1996), that any outcome in this area will be determined by its policy context and implementation processes. This means accepting that the transference of community crime prevention initiatives (e.g., from one location to another) will need to be informed by a thorough understanding of the mechanisms, contexts and outcomes of these preventive efforts and their interrelationships through process, or interactive, evaluation (cf., Pawson and Tilley, 1994).

The interactive evaluation of the Tenmouth Project included the use of observational methods as well as semi-structured interviews.

This dual data collection strategy enabled the evaluation team to assess the gap between what was said would be done and what was actually done, an important consideration given the purpose of the evaluation study.

The key issues explored in the evaluation study were informed not only by investigating the similarities and differences between Kirkholt and Tenmouth (e.g., in terms of social and demographic factors) and what is meant by success (e.g., is interagency collaboration an end in itself or a means to achieving an end?), but also by the evaluation team's knowledge of the social processes that constitute crime prevention efforts. These key issues included:

- the importance of understanding the structure and decision-making processes of community crime prevention initiatives;

- the nature of community participation;

- the extent of implementation; and

- the nature and extent of interagency involvement.

Findings

A number of findings emerged from the evaluation study which informed the process of transferring the Kirkholt Project to Tenmouth. Of particular importance, according to Crawford and Jones (1996), was an assumption that communities, including the commercial sector, would be intimately involved in the Tenmouth Project. They point out that "there was, however, little community involvement during the life of the project, largely because the technical parameters of the project had already been set by Kirkholt" (Crawford and Jones, 1996:34). Moreover, despite the fact that communities with significant crime problems are typically those which lack the necessary social structures to support community ownership, these same communities are being asked to help themselves in the prevention of crime. In summing up the results of this evaluation study, Crawford and Jones (1996) argue that, in the quest for a quick fix, community crime prevention technologies, including evaluation, have lost sight of the complex social relations in which programs become embedded.

CREATING SAFER CITIES

- Impact evaluation

- Decision-oriented

- Quasi-experimental

This evaluation study (Ekblom, 1992) illustrates the conduct of a decision-oriented, impact evaluation, using a quasi-experimental method. The purpose of the study was to contribute to the development of a wide range of projects established in 20 local areas in England, and funded through the Safer Cities Programme (SCP). Ekblom (1992) states that "the function of the SCP evaluation is to contribute to the development of SCP, in particular through the decision to continue with the programme and the direction of that continuance" (1992:50).

In describing the nature of the SCP, Ekblom (1992) underlines how it drew on existing experience in crime prevention initiatives to identify three main objectives:

- to reduce crime;

- to lessen the fear of crime; and

- to create safer cities within which economic enterprise and community life could flourish.

A wide range of projects had been funded to achieve these objectives, incorporating both situational (e.g., target-hardening) and offender-oriented (e.g., educational initiatives) preventive action.

Study Characteristics

In the evaluation study, two principal types of data were collected, one focusing on the extent to which the SCP projects were implemented according to their blueprint (process evaluation), and the other focusing on the extent to which the three main objectives were being met (impact evaluation). In discussing the issues involved in determining the extent to which the SCP objectives were being achieved, Ekblom (1992:37) suggests that the evaluation study faced:

Extremely difficult conditions which centre on having to detect the effects of a set of preventative schemes which are very diverse in size and nature (some being extremely modest), which may or may not be successfully implemented, which start up at different times, which possibly overlap, and whose locations are not merely scattered but unknown in advance (and) these effects have to be detected against a background of non SCP preventative activity in the SCP areas themselves.

Consequently, two complementary approaches to comparison were adopted, one involving comparisons with a number of areas (cities and boroughs) which were not participating in the SCP, and the other involving comparisons within the SCP project areas. Both types of comparison involved investigating "before and after" changes within the constraints faced by most quasi-experimental methods.

Findings

The findings of the evaluation study were not reported in Ekblom's paper, which is concerned with the rationale for focusing and conducting the SCP evaluation. This includes a detailed explanation of one approach to overcoming some of the difficulties that evaluation consultants face when they are funded to inform real time policy-level decisions about big 'P' programs such as the SCP. In this evaluation study, these difficulties included what counted as SCP action (ranging from mere provision of advice about a project through to core schemes fully funded by the SCP), and how to design out, as far as possible, the influence of other preventive initiatives that were funded to address the same problems. Ekblom (1992:50) concludes by saying:

> We have also attempted to be honest regarding the uncertainty that will inevitably surround the final results, and frank about the risk of measurement failure which we have striven to keep to a minimum within the resources available to us.

REDUCING THE RISK OF LEAVING SCHOOL EARLY AND DEVELOPING OFFENDING BEHAVIOUR

- Interactive evaluation
- Illuminative/responsive
- Naturalistic

This evaluation study (Iuliano, 1995) was selected as an illustration of the use of an illuminative/responsive, interactive evaluation that employed naturalistic methods, embedded within a participatory action research design.[4] The purpose of the evaluation study was to bring to light the experiences of all the participants in the program in order to develop new directions, as well as to provide information to other schools that may be interested in implementing a similar project.

The evaluation report notes that the original project concept of recruiting unemployed young people to act as mediators or supervisors to reduce fighting and bullying in schools was developed in France. This idea was further developed in South Australia, where young unemployed adults were employed to act as mentors to young truants who were at risk of leaving school early and developing offending behaviour. Iuliano (1995:22) states that:

> A mentor's role will be to support school attendance, to coach students to be successful at school (improved learning outcomes), to act as a behaviour coach and a link and advocate between the family and school.

Study Characteristics

The illuminative/responsive approach adopted for this evaluation study started from the position that sustainable change in how programs are designed and implemented emerges from the understanding generated when the experiences of the participants are brought to light and new directions are created from these experiences. Evaluation data were obtained from three primary sources:

- workshops for mentors and other participants in the program (e.g., family members),
- interviews with the young people experiencing difficulty attending school, and
- document and records analysis.

The uniqueness of adopting a participatory-action research design to obtain these data is also reflected in the interview process, in which the interviewee (referred to as a speaker) was invited to reflect about and interpret his or her experiences.

Findings

The findings of the evaluation study brought to light several issues that are not usually addressed by other approaches, particularly those that restrict their focus to the extent to which the goals of the program have been achieved. These included, for example, the findings that:

- some of the mentors had been working with students in schools where the school appeared to have no knowledge of the program or that mentors were working within their school; and

- a second group of mentors recruited into the second round of the program did not experience the more formal processes of selection, induction and training as required in the first round, and this may have explained certain changes in satisfaction with the program.

Examining the extent to which program activities are implemented as intended is particularly important when the effects of programs are being evaluated since the observer needs to be convinced that the observed effects are a result of the program expected to be implemented and not some other version of it.

To sum up, the participatory action research design employed in this evaluation study starts with the assumption that the individuals directly affected by social interventions are in the best position to reflect on their experiences and develop new ways of improving the processes and outcomes of value to them. This involves assisting these key stakeholders to develop the questions of concern in the evaluation study and ending with a process of negotiated change that addresses their interests and expectations.

REDUCING RECIDIVISM FOR ILLEGAL VEHICLE USE

- Interactive evaluation
- Illuminative/responsive
- Naturalistic

This study, conducted by Wundersitz (1994), provides an illustration of an interactive evaluation study using an illuminative/responsive approach and naturalistic methods which, unlike the Iuliano study described earlier, did not employ a participatory action research design. The purpose of the evaluation study was to assess the impact of a series of youth camps held in South Australia, which provided opportunities for young offenders to learn new skills and to increase their self-esteem and self-discipline. This, in turn, was expected to encourage lawful and constructive behaviour.

A recruitment process selected 10 Indigenous youths, of whom seven were serving a custodial order and three were on community-based orders. All 10 youths had a history of illegal vehicle use and had been involved in high-speed car chases. The report notes that from the outset there was general recognition that the goals of the program could not be achieved through a single camp or even a series of camps. The camps were seen to be only one part of a broader strategy aimed at decreasing the likelihood of recidivism for illegal use of motor vehicles and associated offences. The program also had a number of secondary objectives, including establishing closer working relationships between the police and the South Australia Department of Family and Community Services personnel to facilitate improved interagency cooperation and understanding of youth offending.

Study Characteristics

The evaluation study focused on the experiences of the youth, police and various other participants in the camps with the aim of improving how these camps were run in the future as well as obtaining some preliminary data about their perceived impact. The evaluation data were, for the most part, obtained through interviews before and after the camps. The rates of offending before and after the camps were also obtained from records held by Family and Community Services and the police, although it is noted that there were some unexplained discrepancies in this data.

Findings

The interview data suggested that the camps were regarded positively by the youths as well as by the police officers and the staff at the centre where a majority of these youths were serving a custodial order. Indeed, the police were seen as 'good blokes'. Moreover, experiences such as rock climbing in the first camp, having family members to talk to in the second camp, and an opportunity to see how traditional Indigenous people lived in the third camp, were all viewed as positive experiences by the young people. The police officers, on the other hand, underlined the importance of giving each young person an opportunity to accept responsibility for themselves and others. The police also felt that they and the young people had increased their understanding of each other.

One of the strengths of evaluation studies which adopt an illuminative/responsive approach is that suggestions for improvement are closely tied to the perceptions of the people directly affected by the program. In the present case, these suggestions included ensuring that there was continuity of both individual police and youth participation in the three camps, a greater involvement of Indigenous adults who were related to the young people concerned, and the involvement of the young people who participated in the pre-planning stages of the camps. Indeed, in view of the purpose of the evaluation study, namely to improve how future camps would be run, the views of the key stakeholders clearly were an essential component.

REFLECTIONS ON CURRENT PRACTICE

The above-described evaluation studies of community crime prevention programs were selected and categorised in terms of the program characteristics and evaluation models. As shown in Table 1, a range of models have been used. A number of conclusions can be drawn from these particular cases and our wider review.

Evaluation Types

The evaluation studies all involve impact or interactive evaluation. This is not intended to imply that other types (Owen and Rogers, 1999) are not being employed in evaluating community crime prevention programs. There are many examples of what Owen and Rogers refer to as proactive evaluation in the field of community crime prevention (e.g., literature reviews that have been conducted to inform program development in the social/developmental area). Nevertheless, few examples were found of clarificative evaluation and monitoring evaluation.

Evaluation Approaches

Goal-based evaluation approaches were found to dominate the evaluation of community crime prevention initiatives. In the literature search, it was rare to find examples of evaluation studies that are illuminative/responsive, in spite of the contribution such studies can make to how programs actually work in practice and the issues that need to be addressed in steering program delivery as it was intended, or currently is thought to be most productive.

Evaluation Methods

Experimental or quasi-experimental methods are very commonly adopted in evaluation studies of community crime prevention programs. In fact, one commentator has noted that evaluation appears to be 'method driven', i.e., motivated by a desire to implement strong designs. This may be related to what appears to be a research orientation to evaluation in this area, as opposed to an action orientation (Mayne and Hudson, 1992). The latter is usually more responsive to the information needs of a range of program stakeholders and decision makers.

Alternative Models

The choice of an evaluation model in a particular case should, from the point of view of best practice, emerge from the complex interplay of:

- an understanding of the nature of the program;

- the judgments and decisions of importance to key stakeholders;

- the various types, approaches and methods available to conduct an evaluation study; and

- the extent to which commonly accepted standards of practice can be met.

Based on the present analysis, program evaluation in community crime prevention does not appear to be taking full advantage of the wide range of alternative models that can result from this interplay. The likely consequence is that the full benefit of the evaluative efforts, in terms of useful, relevant and important information, is not being realised.

RECOMMENDATIONS FOR EVALUATION PRACTICE IN COMMUNITY CRIME PREVENTION

Program evaluation is concerned with making value judgments about a program (Scriven, 1991). These judgments may take a number of forms, including the determination of the value of the program over all, or of particular aspects of it, with a view to making decisions on program changes, expansion, termination and implementation in other settings. Making soundly based judgments requires information that is relevant and important to the judgments and decisions. This would usually include information on the social and physical context of the program and how it achieves its effects, as well as information on its outcomes (Pawson and Tilley, 1995). When planning and conducting an evaluation study, it is important to consider the likely uses of the information provided by the study. Evaluators should ensure that the scope and quality of the program information are appropriate to the nature and significance of the judgments and decisions to be made.

Merely having information about a community crime prevention program will not help decision makers and other key stakeholders to make the best judgments and decisions about it. The basis for making these judgments should also be included. These can be derived from a variety of sources, including the program objectives, government or agency policy, widely held community values, ethical standards, the performance of other programs with similar objectives, and the current status quo in the local community or in other comparable communities. Their relevance will depend partly on the main purposes of the evaluation study (Owen and Rogers, 1999).

To ensure that the information produced by an evaluation study will be useful to the people making judgments and decisions about the program (usually the major stakeholders), stakeholders' information needs and priorities must be determined and included during the planning, design and conduct of the study. Stakeholders should be consulted about the purposes of the study, the critical variables to be measured and the information to be obtained, as well as the standards important to them.

There are a number of different models that can be used to evaluate community crime prevention programs. These models help evaluators decide the evaluation questions and procedures to be used (Posavac and Carey, 1997). Each model reflects a different combination of evaluation type or purpose (Owen and Rogers, 1999), evaluation approach (e.g., goal-based, decision-oriented) (House, 1980), and evaluation method.

An appropriate evaluation model should reflect these three key aspects and should also incorporate currently accepted standards of evaluation practice, such as those outlined in the Program Evaluation Standards (Joint Committee on Standards for Educational Evaluation, 1994). These standards are concerned with the utility of the information, the feasibility of collecting it, its technical adequacy and ethical practice in the conduct of an evaluation study.

In short, evaluation is essentially about the development of a defensible argument about a program, focusing particularly on what it does and in what context, what its effects are, why the effects eventuate, and to what extent the effects are replicable and generalisable to other settings and populations (Cronbach, 1982; Pawson and Tilley, 1994; Tilley, 1996). Consequently, we believe the evaluation of community crime prevention programs will be better served if a wider range of models are used to meet the information needs of the stakeholders in community crime prevention. It is important that the evaluation model used to guide an evaluation study is 'optimal' given the specific relevant considerations applying in that case. An evaluation model is more likely to be optimal if careful and systematic consideration is given to the full range of available models.

The reasons for the lack of evaluation of community crime prevention programs have not been studied extensively, but political and financial considerations probably have a strong influence. The limited knowledge and experience of many program managers of evaluation theory and practice may also be an important factor. This is not to say, however, that just conducting more evaluations will serve a useful purpose. What is needed are high quality, highly informative evaluations driven by the information needs of primary audiences.

Another influence on the extent of evaluation activity is the fact that the implementation and resourcing of community crime prevention programs and their evaluation are a part of the broad political process within the community, and so must compete for resources with other social programs and initiatives (O'Malley, 1997). In addition, evaluative evidence is often seen as bad news since program objectives are often over-optimistic and are rarely fully met — facts that evaluation might expose. Evaluators must recognise these factors when planning and conducting evaluations if the evaluations are to produce evidence that is not only useful, but is actually used (Weiss, 1993).

Acknowledgments: This project was funded by the National Crime Prevention Program - Towards a Safer Australia, an initiative of the Commonwealth Government. This article has been published with permission from the Australian Government's National Crime Prevention Program, under which the research has been conducted. Correspondence should be directed to Dr. Brian English.

Address correspondence to: Brian J. English, Associate Professor, Institute for the Service Professions, Edith Cowan University, Bradford Street, Mount Lawley, Western Australia 6050. E-mail: <b.english@ ecu.edu.au>.

REFERENCES

Australia National Anti-Crime Strategy, Lead Ministers (1995). "National Anti-Crime Strategy Crime Prevention Compendium for Australian States and Territories." Adelaide, AUS: Crime Prevention Unit, South Australian Attorney-General's Department.

Australia National Campaign Against Violence and Crime (1997). "Evaluation Models for Community Crime Prevention." (Project brief.) Canberra, AUS: National Campaign Against Violence and Crime.

Australia National Crime Prevention (1999). "Pathways to Prevention: Developmental and Early Intervention Approaches to Crime in Australia." Canberra, AUS: National Crime Prevention, Attorney-General's Department.

Bennett, S.F. (1995). "Community Organizations and Crime." *Annals of the American Academy of Political and Social Science* 539:72-84.

Bennett, T.W. (1989). "The Neighbourhood Watch Experiment." In: R. Morgan and D.J. Smith (eds.), *Coming to Terms with Policing: Perspectives on Policy*. London, UK: Routledge.

Chen, H. (1990). *Theory driven Evaluations*. Newbury Park, CA: Sage.

Clarke, R.V. (1997). "Introduction." In: R.V. Clarke (ed.), *Situational Crime Prevention: Successful Case Studies* (2nd ed.). Guilderland, NY: Harrow and Heston.

Crawford, A. and M. Jones (1996). "Kirkholt Revisited: Some Reflections on the Transferability of Crime Prevention Initiatives." *The Howard Journal of Criminal Justice* 35:21-39.

Cronbach, L.J. (1982). *Designing Evaluations of Educational and Social Programs*. San Francisco, CA: Jossey-Bass.

Cummings, R. and B.J. English (1998). "A Framework for Selecting an Appropriate Design for a Programme Evaluation Study." Paper presented at the National Australasian Evaluation Conference, Melbourne, Australia, October.

Davis, R.C. and B.G. Taylor (1997). "A Proactive Response to Family Violence: The Results of a Randomized Experiment." *Criminology* 35:307-333.

Ekblom, P. (1992). "The Safer Cities Programme Impact Evaluation: Problems and Progress." *Studies on Crime and Crime Prevention* 1:35-51.

—— and N. Tilley (2000). "Going Equipped. Criminology, Situational Crime Prevention and the Resourceful Offender." *British Journal of Criminology* 40:376-398.

—— and K. Pease (1995). "Evaluating Crime Prevention." In: M. Tonry and D.P. Farrington (eds.), *Building a Safer Society: Strategic Approaches to Crime and Justice.* (*Crime and Justice: A Review of Research,* vol.19.) Chicago, IL: University of Chicago Press.

Elliott, D. (1997). "Editor's Introduction." In: M.A. Pentz, S.F. Mihalic and J.K. Grotpeter (eds.), *Blueprints for Violence Prevention.* (The Midwestern Prevention Project, book one.) Boulder, CO: Center for the Study and Prevention of Violence, Institute of Behavioral Science, University of Colorado.

English, B.J., R.G. Straton and R. Cummings (1998). *Evaluation Models for Community Crime Prevention: Conceptual Foundations.* Perth, AUS: Institute for Social Programme Evaluation, Murdoch University.

Felson, M. (1994). *Crime and Everyday Life: Insights and Implications for Society.* Thousand Oaks, CA: Pine Forge Press.

Funnell, S. and B. Lenne (1990). "Clarifying Program Objectives for Program Evaluation." *Program Evaluation Bulletin* (New South Wales Office of Public Sector Management) 1:1-13.

Gant, F. and P. Grabosky (2000). *The Promise of Crime Prevention* (2nd ed.). Canberra, AUS: Australian Institute of Criminology.

Grabosky, P. and M. James (1995). *The Promise of Crime Prevention.* Canberra, AUS: Australian Institute of Criminology.

Hagan, F.E. (1997). *Research Methods in Criminal Justice and Criminology* (4th ed.). Boston, MA: Allyn and Bacon.

Homel, R, M. Hauritz, R. Wortley, G. McIlwain and R. Carvolth (1997). "Preventing Alcohol Related Crime through Community Action: The Surfers Paradise Safety Action Project." In: R. Homel (ed.), *Policing for Prevention. (Crime Prevention Studies,* vol. 7). Monsey, NY: Criminal Justice Press.

House, E.R. (1980). *Evaluating with Validity.* Sage, CA: Beverly Hills.

Indermaur, D. (1996). "Towards Effective Crime Prevention in Western Australia." Paper presented at the launch of the State Government Crime Prevention Strategy, Perth, August, 1996.

Iuliano, G. (1995). *How Do We Draw the Lines: The Evaluation of the STOMP Program.* Adelaide, South Australia: Window Media Pty Ltd.

Joint Committee on Standards for Educational Evaluation (1994). *The Program Evaluation Standards* (2nd ed.). Thousand Oaks, CA: Sage.

Kessler, D.A. and S. Duncan (1996). "The Impact of Community Policing in Four Houston Neighborhoods." *Evaluation Review* 20:627-669.

Madaus, G.F., M.S. Scriven and D.L. Stufflebeam (1983). *Evaluation Models: Viewpoints on Educational and Human Services Evaluation.* Boston, MA: Kluwer-Nijhoff.

Marshall, C. (1984). "The Case Study Evaluation: A Means for Managing Organizational and Political Tensions." *Evaluation and Program Planning* 7:253-266.

Mayne, J. and J. Hudson (1992). "Program Evaluation: An Overview." In: J. Hudson, J. Mayne and R. Thomlison (eds.), *Action-oriented Evaluation in Organisations: Canadian Practices.* Toronto, CAN: Wall and Emerson.

Mukherjee, S. and P. Wilson (1987). "Neighbourhood Watch: Issues and Policy Implications." *Trends and Issues in Crime and Criminal Justice,* paper #8.

Murray, G., R. Homel, T. Prenzler, K. Wimhurst and I. O'Connor (1993). "A Framework for Evaluating Community Based Juvenile Crime Prevention Programs." Brisbane, AUS: Centre for Crime Policy and Public Safety, Griffith University.

O'Malley, P. (1997). "The Politics of Crime Prevention." In: P. O'Malley and A. Sutton (eds.), *Crime Prevention in Australia: Issues in Policy and Research.* Sydney, AUS: The Federation Press.

—— and A. Sutton (1997). *Crime Prevention in Australia: Issues in Policy and Research.* Sydney, AUS: The Federation Press.

Owen, J.M. and P.J. Rogers (1999). *Program Evaluation: Forms and Approaches* (2nd ed.). St Leonards, New South Wales, AUS: Allen and Unwin.

Patton, M. (1997). *Utilization-focused Evaluation: The New Century Text* (3rd ed.). Thousand Oaks, CA: Sage.

Pawson, R. and N. Tilley (1995). *Realistic Evaluation.* London, UK: Sage.

—— and N. Tilley (1994). "What Works in Evaluation Research." *British Journal of Criminology* 34:291-306.

Posavac, E.J. and R.G. Carey (1997). *Program Evaluation: Methods and Case Studies* (5th ed.). Englewood Cliffs, NJ: Prentice-Hall.

Sampson, R.J., S.W. Raudenbush and F. Earls (1997). "Neighborhoods and Violent Crime: A Multilevel Study of Collective Efficacy." *Science* 277:918-924.

Scriven, M. (1991). *Evaluation Thesaurus* (4th ed.). Newbury Park, CA: Sage.

Shadish, W.R., T.D. Cook and L.C. Leviton (1991). *Foundations of Program Evaluation: Theories of Practice.* Newbury Park, CA: Sage.

Sherman, L.W. (1997). "Thinking about Crime Prevention." In: L.W. Sherman, D. Gottfredson, D. MacKenzie, J. Eck, P. Reuter and S. Bushway, *Preventing Crime: What Works, What Doesn't, What's Promising.* Washington, DC: Office of Justice Programs, National Institute of Justice, United States Department of Justice.

—— D. Gottfredson, D. MacKenzie, J. Eck, P. Reuter and S. Bushway (1997). *Preventing Crime: What Works, What Doesn't, What's Promising.* Washington, DC: Office of Justice Programs, National Institute of Justice, United States Department of Justice.

Stake, R.E. (1967). "The Countenance of Educational Evaluation." *Teachers College Record* 68:523-540.

Straton, R.G. (1990). "Research of the Evaluation Process in Australia." *Evaluation Journal of Australasia* 2:2-12.

—— (1985). *Curriculum Evaluation: Approaches and Planning* (2nd ed.). Waurn Ponds, Victoria, AUS: Deakin University Press.

—— (1981). "Social Indicators and Programme Evaluation." Response prepared on behalf of Murdoch University to the Australian Bureau of Statistics, "Social Indicators: A Discussion Paper." Perth, AUS: Murdoch University.

—— R. Cummings, B. English, J.M. Owen and H. Peerless (1999). *Evaluation Planning Kit: A Guide for Planning Evaluations of Community Crime Prevention Projects.* Perth, AUS: Institute for Social Programme Evaluation, Murdoch University.

Stufflebeam, D.L. and A.J. Shinkfield (1985). *Systematic Evaluation: A Self-instructional Guide to Theory and Practice.* Boston, MA: Kluwer-Nijhoff.

Taylor, D.B. (1976). "Eeny, Meeny, Miney, Meaux: Alternative Evaluation Models." *North Central Association Quarterly* 50:353-358.

Teeters, N.K. (1995). "Fundamentals of Crime Prevention." *Federal Probation* 59:63-68.

Tilley, N. (1996). "Demonstration, Exemplification, Duplication and Replication in Evaluation Research." *Evaluation* 2:35-50.

Toumbourou, J.W. (1999). *Implementing Communities That Care in Australia: A Community Mobilisation Approach to Crime Prevention.* (Trends and Issues in Crime and Criminal Justice Series, Paper No. 122.) Canberra, AUS: Australian Institute of Criminology.

Visher, C.A. and D. Weisburd (1998). "Identifying What Works: Recent Trends in Crime Prevention Strategies." *Crime, Law and Social Change* 28:223-242.

Weiss, C.H. (1993). "Where Politics and Evaluation Research Meet." *Evaluation Practice* 14:93-106.

Wundersitz, J. (1994). *Evaluation of the Preventative Component of Operation Bother: The Camps*. Adelaide, South Australia: Young Offenders Unit, Family and Community Services.

NOTES

1. While Owen and Rogers (1999) include the evaluation approach as an important characteristic in establishing the type of an evaluation, this aspect has been treated separately in this paper.

2. Gant and Grabosky (2000) extend this classification to distinguish two additional considerations: programs based on the importance of community development, which use social/developmental approaches to integrate individuals more fully into their community; and prevention measures by criminal justice agencies, which use opportunity reduction/situational approaches at whole-of-community level to reduce motivation to offend.

3. Target-hardening strategies, such as improving street lighting and other environmental interventions, suggest that another program type, 'environmental design', may be needed.

4. Participatory action research can be defined as a qualitative method which enables participants to create their own descriptions of their lived experience, attach their own meaning to this experience, and develop their own pathways of change through that meaning.

EVALUATING MULTI-AGENCY ANTI-CRIME PARTNERSHIPS: THEORY, DESIGN, AND MEASUREMENT ISSUES

by

Dennis P. Rosenbaum
University of Illinois at Chicago

Abstract: *Inter-organizational partnerships are widely praised as a vehicle for planning and implementing complex, comprehensive community interventions. This article explores conceptual, design, and measurement issues relevant to the evaluation of coalitions, with particular reference to anti-crime initiatives. A general theory of partnerships is outlined that goes beyond organizational models to focus on the complexity of intervention strategies: domains of influence, causal mechanisms, intervention targets, and partnership services. To fill a large gap in our knowledge of coalition effectiveness, impact evaluations should include a mixture of strong research designs with counterfactuals, a theory (or multiple theories) of change, a blend of quantitative and qualitative methods, measurement and analysis at multiple levels, and multiple case studies for understanding the dynamics and external relationships of each partnership. The primary substantive issue for public safety partnerships is the failure to be inclusive, thus undermining their greatest strength. Finding the proper role for "the community" has been a continuous challenge as law enforcement agencies and strategies tend to be overrepresented.*

THE ORIGIN AND THEORY OF ANTI-CRIME PARTNERSHIPS

In the endless search for more efficient and effective methods of crime prevention, criminal justice scholars in Western Europe, North America, and Australia have noted the tendency for greater government investment in "partnerships" and "coalitions." (e.g., Crawford,

1997; Rosenbaum et al., 1998). There is no single definition of a partnership, but essentially, we are talking about a cooperative relationship between two or more organizations to achieve some common goal. When it involves multiple partners, typically representing diverse interest groups, a partnership can also be referred to as a coalition, which, Butterfoss et al., (1993) describe as "interorganizational, cooperative, and synergistic working alliances."

Recent interest in partnership building has grown worldwide and the forces behind this trend are probably numerous. Researchers have attributed this renewed interest to the elevated importance of "community" in local government processes and a corresponding dissatisfaction with the effectiveness of traditional service bureaucracies (e.g., Crawford, 1997). In the law enforcement field, there is also a desire for change caused by the problems of: (1) perceived racial inequalities and injustices in the delivery of police services, which regularly produces a cry for better police-community partnerships; (2) the judged ineffectiveness of traditional reactive police methods, which opens the door for problem-oriented policing and prevention models; and (3) the absence of a coordinated, "criminal justice system" to handle public safety issues, which has frustrated those seeking effective justice and deterrence.

In essence, the new discourse on public safety among Western nations gives special attention to "prevention," "community," "partnerships," and "problem solving" as the defining features of an idealized local government that is more effective, efficient, and just than traditional response schemes. This discourse has yielded a wide variety of configurations in practice. Urban coalitions or partnerships often have a strong community focus that reaches far beyond the walls of the criminal justice system. Kubisch and her colleagues (1995:1), for example, describe "comprehensive community initiatives" (CCIs) in this manner:

> ...they all have the goal of promoting positive change in individual, family, and community circumstances in disadvantaged neighborhoods by improving the physical, economic, and social conditions. Most CCIs contain several or all of the following elements and aim to achieve synergy among them: expansion and improvement of social services and supports, such as child care, youth development, and family support; health care, including mental health care; economic development; housing rehabilitation and/or construction; community planning and organizing; adult education; job training; school reform; and quality-of-life activities such as neighborhood security and recreation programs.

While many of these interventions are considered outside the purview of law enforcement, they are certainly consistent with the basic principles of social crime prevention and partnership building. Indeed, the international importance of this approach to crime prevention is captured in the unanimously approved resolution of the 1990 United Nations Congress on the Prevention of Crime and Treatment of Offenders, which states that crime prevention must...

> Bring together those with responsibility for planning and development, for family, health, employment and training, housing and social services, leisure activities, schools, the police, and the justice system in order to deal with the conditions that generate crime. [United Nations, 1991, cited in Crawford, 1997:56].

This approach has been adopted more widely in Canada and Western Europe than in the United States, but the latter has been talking about the importance of this approach for many years. Indeed, the President's crime commission report in 1967, which launched the "war on crime" in the United States, reached a conclusion similar to that found in the United Nations resolution, but emphasized the importance of non-government resources in crime prevention:

> While this report has concentrated on the recommendations for action by governments, the Commission is convinced that government actions will not be enough. Crime is a social problem that is interwoven with almost every aspect of American life...Controlling crime is the business of every American institution. Controlling crime is the business of every American [U.S. President's Commission... (1967):xi.]

Scientific Rationale for Partnerships

The absence of research knowledge to defend current crime control practices provides the first justification for exploring new ways of doing business. Our knowledge of the causes and correlates of crime is substantial, but our understanding of crime control and prevention strategies remains rather primitive, as reflected in sustained crime rates and our inability to document, scientifically, the effectiveness of most anti-crime programs (for reviews, see Rosenbaum et al., 1998; Sherman et al., 1997). In the United States and (to a lesser extent) in other countries, the government has responded to crime by dumping large sums of money into the criminal justice system, producing an enormous and costly set of tactics for conducting a protracted "war" against drugs and crime. The underlying theory of action used to justify this approach places a high value on deterring or incapacitating repeat offenders, with law enforcement agencies serving as the primary, and often, only mechanism for change.

Many of us in the crime prevention field have argued, over many years, that the criminal justice system cannot, by itself, solve the complex problems of crime, drugs, and disorder in our society. (In the short run, maybe, but not in the long run.) Resources from outside the system are desperately needed, as well as new ways of thinking about these problems from the inside (Lavrakas, 1985; Rosenbaum, 1986, 1988). In a nutshell, given the multiple and complex causes of crime and drug use, a growing chorus of scholars argue that a new approach in needed, one that tackles these problems from multiple angles, applying a multitude of strategies. This line of reasoning has been used to justify the creation of ant-crime/drug "partnerships" or "coalitions" — a group of organizations that can bring distinctive but complementary skills and resources to the table and can produce coordinated and targeted responses to public safety problems.

In this chapter, I will explore issues in the theory, measurement, and evaluation of partnerships. Because crime prevention coalitions are not well studied, I will draw upon a more extensive body of research literature in the areas of health promotion and drug prevention to inform our thinking about interagency and comprehensive approaches in the public safety domain. The chapter will address the core question of how to conceptualize and evaluate partnerships, highlighting the unprecedented obstacles that evaluators must face and overcome. In the final analysis, policy makers need to know whether the partnership approach to crime prevention is an effective alternative to more conventional single-agency/single program schemes.

Theoretical Justification for Partnerships

The rationale for creating comprehensive anti-crime coalitions is grounded in theory and research on the nature and causes of crime/drug abuse, as well as the practical benefits envisioned by these inter-organizational arrangements.

Etiology

Both theory and research strongly suggest that the target problem (or cluster of problems) is complex and multi-dimensional. To illustrate, in the area of substance abuse, a large body of research has identified a range of specific causes and risk factors for adolescents, including structural and sociological variables, e.g., age, gender, social class, race, community, and region (Radosevich et al., 1980), so-cial interactional variables, e.g., drug use among family and peers, school environment, religiosity (Jessor and Jessor, 1977; Kandel et al., 1978), and individual psychological factors, e.g., personality traits, behavioral patterns, and motivation. (For a review, see Hawkins et al., 1992a.) In essence, a host of risk factors associated with substance use have been identified that cover the gamut of individual, family, peer, and community characteristics. From a prevention and policy standpoint, these risk factors can be addressed individually or collectively. Often, drug prevention programs are focused on one or two causal factors and are managed by a single agency, but given the diversity of known causes, comprehensive programs are easily justified. Indeed, researchers have argued that comprehensive, community-wide strategies are likely to have larger and more sustained effects than single-strategy or single-agency approaches (Benard, 1990; Cook and Roehl, 1993; Hopkins et al., 1988), especially when they target known risk factors.

Consistent with this hypothesis, the evaluation literature provides several examples of positive program results when communities adopt comprehensive approaches to drug and alcohol prevention. The Midwest Prevention Project in Kansas and Missouri has been a big success story (Pentz et al., 1989), utilizing mass media education, school-based education, parent education and organizing, community organizing, and changes in health policy to produce desired reductions in adolescent use of cigarettes, alcohol, and marijuana. The Minnesota Heart and Health Program (MHHP) is another comprehensive initiative that has achieved substantial reductions in cigarette smoking in three communities through school-based education, cardiovascular risk factor screening, health education, community mobilization, continuing education of health professionals, mass media education campaigns, and both adult and youth education (Johnson et al., 1990).

The inherent attractiveness of the community-wide coalition model and these early successes have led to the development of other major initiatives. These include the Communities that Care model (Hawkins et al., 1992b), the Community Partnership Program (Cook and Roehl, 1993), the Fighting Back initiative (Klitzner, 1993), and many others.

The etiology of violence is similarly complex, suggesting the need for complex, multi-level interventions. An extensive body of research indicates that delinquency and youth violence are caused by a wide range of factors, including poor parenting and childhood maltreatment (Hawkins et al., 1998; Loeber and LeBlanc, 1990; Schuck and Widom, in press), personality deficits (Wilson and Herrnstein, 1985), peer group influences (Spergel, 1990; Thornberry et al., 1993), community social disorganization and structural characteristics (Bursik and Grasmick, 1993; Jencks and Mayers, 1990; Leventhal and Brooks-Gunn, 2000; Sampson, 1997), and environmental opportunities (Clarke, 1995; Felson, 1998; Rosenbaum et al., 1998). While much of this research has focused on specific risk factors, again, some authors have called for integrated and ecological perspectives on human development, recognizing that different structures and systems interact and have differential effects on individuals at various stages in the life cycle (e.g., Bronfenbrenner, 1988; Farrington et al., 1993). Thus, for example, the adverse effects of child abuse can be compounded by inferior education, lack of economic opportunities, inadequate health and public services (including police), the absence of positive role models, weak collective efficacy among neighborhood residents, peer pressure to join youth gangs, and easy opportunities for criminality. A compounding of processes and institutions in one's environment can conspire to lower one's probability of living a productive, healthy, and crime-free life (see Schuck, 2001). Recognizing the complexity of this etiology, some researchers and policy analysts have proposed comprehensive, multi-level interventions as a strategic approach to increasing public safety in urban settings.

In addition to providing a general rationale for partnerships, social science research can be used to shape our thinking about the types of interventions (and therefore, types of evaluations) that are needed to address crime and delinquency problems. Connell et al., (1995), for example, illustrate how an extensive body of research findings on urban communities and youth can be used to inform the design and evaluation of comprehensive community initiatives. Community variables can have direct and indirect effects on individual youth. This knowledge can aid partnerships by pointing them in the direction of important causal factors, best practices, and variables needing attention by evaluators.

A THEORY OF PARTNERSHIPS

Partnerships or coalitions represent a unique hybrid organism in the world of social interventions. Beyond the difficulty of defining these entities is the problem of adequately conceptualizing them for the benefit of advancing theory, measurement, evaluation, and knowledge utilization. Before laying out various configurations, I offer a few words about the theoretical basis for hypotheses regarding the effectiveness of partnerships. In other words, why should partnerships work and work better than other approaches? The partnership model is based on several key assumptions and postulates:

(1) Crime and drug problems are complex and deeply rooted, requiring complex, innovative, and comprehensive solutions.

(2) Partnerships are better suited than individual agencies to identify and accurately define the target problems of greatest concern in a given community. They are more likely to include diverse perspectives and theories about crime and drug causation.

(3) Partnerships are better suited to developing creative targeted interventions because they include a diverse group of individuals representing a diverse group of organizations with different philosophies of intervention.

(4) Multiple interventions are more effective than single interventions. Multiple interventions hold the potential of increasing the total quantity (dosage) and/or quality of the "treatment."

(5) Applying similar reasoning, multiple agencies are more effective than single agencies. Representing different organizational cultures and services, partnership members bring more "new" ideas and resources to the problem-solving arena.

(6) As a corollary of 4 and 5 above, interventions that emanate from different domains — individual, family, peer group, neighborhood, community institutions and government — will maximize the total impact on the target audience. Multiple interventions by multiple agencies create the opportunity for the target group to be exposed to more than one intervention and thus experience cumulative effects.

(7) As a corollary of 4 and 5, exposure to different strategic mechanisms at different levels of intervention may yield new synergistic effects. That is, new effects can be created from the combination of two or more interventions — interventions that produced no effects or different effects singularly.

These assumptions and postulates offer some clues about the mechanisms or processes by which change is expected to occur. In sum, several avenues are hypothesized for partnerships to outperform single-agency approaches on crime and drug prevention outcomes: First, by "putting heads together" a partnership may result in new, innovative approaches that would not have been conceived without the "collision" and synthesis of diverse perspectives. Second, the application of resources from multiple agencies may increase the *quantity* or "dosage" of the intervention. Third, partnerships may lead to the coordinated application of resources in a manner that changes the nature or *quality* of the interventions and their effects. The presence of such synergistic effects would serve to demonstrate that "the whole is greater than the sum of the parts."

Of course, the mere presence of a partnership or coalition does not guarantee these effects. Additionally, we must assume that the partnership is functioning like a "well-oiled" machine and that it can guarantee strong implementation. Often these additional assumptions do not hold up against reality. Thus, to further articulate a theory of partnerships, some key factors that facilitate or inhibit the functioning of such groups will be reviewed later.

In the meantime, if the above assumptions are valid, then partnerships can be expected not only to reduce crime and drug abuse, but to serve a number of other functions as well (see Butterfoss et al., 1993; Kubisch et al., 1995). Partnerships, in theory, are expected to:

(1) increase organizational accountability;

(2) reduce fragmentation and duplication of services;

(3) build public-private linkages;

(4) increase public awareness of (and participation in) anti-crime initiatives;

(5) strengthen local community organizations; and

(6) permanently alter the way agencies "do business" by giving more attention to strategic planning, data-driven decision making, prevention, interagency cooperation, and community participation in local governance.

A theory of partnerships should go beyond group dynamics and group processes to delineate the various strategic intervention approaches employed by the group. My colleague and I have emphasized that partnerships may pursue multiple theories of change based on multiple theories of causality (Schuck and Rosenbaum, in press). Building on this framework, I am proposing that partnerships can be conceptualized in terms of several key dimensions:

- *Domains of Influence*: Does the partnership seek change through a single domain or through multiple domains of influence in the target's environment? These domains include individuals, families, small groups, peer groups, schools, churches, neighborhood organizations, social service agencies, and larger social, political, or economic entities.

- *Causal Mechanisms*: Does the partnership seek change through a single causal mechanism or through multiple processes? In the case of crime prevention, these mechanisms are diverse, including increased social control, increased support and modeling, reduced environmental opportunities for criminal behavior, increased threat of punishment, increased economic opportunities, improved parenting, increased educational opportunities, increased public awareness and knowledge of crime prevention and legal sanctions, etc.

- *Intervention Targets*: Does the partnership seek to change the behavior of one segment of the community or multiple groups within society? Crime prevention interventions can focus on high-risk youth (e.g., gang members) or all school-aged youth; one "hot spot" or multiple neighborhoods; young offenders or older victims; These choices are often confounded with race, class, and gender distinctions.

- *Partnership Services*: Does the partnership employ the services of a single agency or multiple agencies to implement the program? In theory, a partnership can use multiple agencies for planning, but a single agency for implementation of services. This partnership services dimension is likely to be related to "domains of influence" (above), but they are separate. (e.g., multiple agencies could focus their services on strengthening the role of families in crime prevention).

This theoretical framework suggests that partnerships can result in many different intervention strategies and multiple definitions of "comprehensive." Furthermore, this framework suggests that partnership effectiveness will be determined by the interaction effects generated from various combinations of domains, causal mechanism, targets, and partnership services. Our knowledge in this arena is extremely limited. Will a partnership be more effective, for example, if it pursues a single causal mechanism (e.g., increased youth supervision) across multiple domains (e.g., family, school, church, police) or if it pursues multiple causal mechanisms (e.g., supervision, parenting, job opportunities) through a single domain of influence (e.g., the family)? The answer will depend on the amount of variance in crime-related outcome measures that can be explained by various domains, processes, target groups, partnership services, both individually and in combination. Basic research is suggestive, but evaluation research across multiple sites with multiple controls is the best way to test various components of this model.

A theory of partnerships must pay special attention to the inter-organizational capacity to respond to problems with creativity, intensity, and/or coordination of interventions. The proposed model of partnerships suggests that interventions have many important characteristics that predict success — *Who* will be doing *what* to *whom* with the support of what *service agencies*? Coalitions have the ability, in theory, to move horizontally and vertically, that is, to reach across organizational boundaries and to reach outside the local community to leverage relevant resources. Coalitions are also hypothesized to have greater flexibility and more options for responding to local problems, including the capacity to employ more sophisticated data-driven approaches to planning and decision making. Coalitions also imply a sharing of power and decision making among participants, and oftentimes, encourage the devolution of authority from central government to local communities, under the assumption that achieving a high degree of community self-regulation is a desirable goal.

In sum, the value of partnerships, in theory, lies in their responsiveness to the etiology of complex problems, their ability to encourage interagency cooperation both inside and outside the criminal justice system, their ability to attack problems from multiple sources of influence and to target multiple causal mechanisms, and their potential for satisfying the public's growing desire for input, information sharing, and connectedness with local government. In theory, partnerships represent the capacity to achieve new, intensive, and more comprehensive interventions by "putting heads together" to generate new ideas and by leveraging and coordinating resources from multiple sources. Within this partnership framework, each agency brings a unique set of skills, experiences, resources, and intervention strategies to the table. The partnership provides a mechanism to exploit this capital by developing and implementing comprehensive and coordinated community-wide strategies at different levels (see Cook and Roehl, 1993; Florin et al., 1992; Chavis et al., 1993; Klitzner, 1993; Prestby and Wandersman, 1985).

Contribution of Organizational Theory

Drawing on the organizational literature and the work of Katz and Kahn (1978), several authors have sought to conceptualize partnerships as "open systems" (Florin et al., 1985; ISA Associates, 1993). An open system is characterized by a dynamic, continuously changing relationship with its external environment. An open organization or partnership needs to import and transform resources to produce products, such as action plans and activities. Open systems survive and thrive by continually gathering resources, creating information feedback loops for self-regulation, and restoring a steady state or equilibrium after any disruption to the system by its environment. Open organizations can reach a particular goal through many different paths, depending on the circumstances present in the environment. Thus, there is no single "right way" to achieve a stated goal or objective.

Applying an open-systems approach to voluntary community organizations, Prestby and Wandersman (1985) hypothesize that coalitions are likely to remain viable if they: (1) acquire the necessary resources (e.g., skills, experiences, technology, funding from member organizations); (2) create an organization; (3) create a structure (e.g., leadership, prescribed roles, formal rules and procedures) that allows the group to set goals and meet both individual and organizational needs; (4) engage in activities, including both strategy-related actions and activities that serve to maintain the organization; and (5) achieve short-term and long-term outcomes relevant to the coalition's goals. In essence, a partnership must have more than resources — participants must figure out how to utilize these resources in an organizational context so as to maintain social cohesion among members and achieve the goals of the group.

This model complements the strategic intervention-focused elements of partnership theory I have outlined. In essence, group resources, structure, dynamics, and strategic functions are all important for achieving the desired impact on the target audience. The relative importance of various factors for predicting success in the real world is an empirical question. Now that a series of demonstrations and occasional evaluations have been completed, we can begin to test these models.

PARTNERSHIPS IN PUBLIC SAFETY

Coalitions are not new to urban problem solving. Comprehensive community initiatives in the United States stretch from the settlement houses of the 19th century to the War on Poverty in the 1960s to the community development projects that have continued to date (see Halpern, 1994; Hope, 1995; Kubisch et al., 1995; O'Connor, 1995). Public safety was not excluded from the comprehensive model, as demonstrated by the classic Chicago Area Project, started in 1931 to encourage community self-help and prevent juvenile delinquency (Shaw and McKay, 1942). The Boston Mid-City project in the 1950s and the Mobilization for Youth program in Manhattan in the 1960s attempted to replicate the basic idea behind the Chicago Area Project (see Marris and Rein, 1967; Miller, 1962), as they sought to mobilize community involvement across grass roots, social service, faith-based, and government organizations. Aside from these innovative projects, efforts to prevent crime and delinquency through comprehensive coalitions or partnerships have been rare in the United States, primarily because of the lack of political will to support preventative action at this level. In other countries, partnerships are valued so highly that they are legally required. In Britain, for example, the Crime and Disorder Act of 1998 mandates that local partnerships be formed among the police, local authorities and other agencies for the purpose of preventing crime and disorder (Hough and Tilley, 1998). In recent years, the law enforcement community in the United States, through community policing initiatives, has developed a range of new partnerships. The breath and depth of those partnerships varies dramatically. In this article, I will give special attention to the role of law enforcement in public safety partnerships because they are typically the recipients of government funding for such initiatives and have positioned themselves, historically, as the central actor in the public safety arena.

Involvement in partnerships by law enforcement agencies appears to be on the rise. National survey data (Roth et al., 2000) indicate that the number of U.S. law enforcement agencies who report participating in "partnership-building activities" has grown from 58% in 1995 to 80% in 1998.[1] At both points, the five most common partnership activities were: joint crime prevention programs (e.g., Neighborhood Watch), regular community meetings, joint projects with businesses, projects with residents to reduce disorder, and citizen surveys.

In the U.S. most police-driven partnerships are dyadic in nature, whereby the police maintain separate two-party relationships with citizen groups, businesses, schools, other city agencies, universities, and other entities. The two most popular law enforcement partnerships, by far, have been with citizen groups to establish Neighborhood Watch programs and with schools to deliver the Drug Abuse Resistance Education Program (D.A.R.E.). Despite their widespread use and popularity in the Western world, neither program has been able to produce consistent crime and drug prevention effects under controlled conditions (see Rosenbaum, 1987; Rosenbaum and Hanson, 1998). Despite their poor track record on hard outcome measures, both initiatives have adjusted their approach to new urban environments and promise better results in the future (Rosenbaum, 2002, and forthcoming).

The movement toward community and problem-oriented policing has encouraged law enforcement agencies to reach beyond dyadic relationships to establish more expansive and formal inter-agency partnerships (For evaluations, see Rosenbaum, 1994.) In some cities, the emphasis on "problem oriented" policing (Eck and Spelman, 1987; Goldstein, 1990) has resulted in formal partnerships with other city agencies to deliver street-level services as a team. Some of these teams have citywide jurisdiction to address specific problems, such as abandoned and deteriorating housing (e.g., Oakland's Beat Health Unit, see Mazerolle et al., 1998; Rosenbaum et al., 1994), while others are neighborhood-based and address all safety-related neighborhood problems within that geographic area (e.g., Salt Lake City, see Rosenbaum and Kaminska-Costello, 1997). A related pattern is the growth of neighborhood-based "mini city halls" or "one-stop shopping centers," where community policing officers share an office with employees of social service agencies (e.g., Nashville, see Roth et al., 2000). But often, the work arrangement at these one-stop centers is best described as parallel work rather than coordinated work between agencies. Finally, problem solving can be centrally coordinated through the mayor's office, where city agencies are directly accountable to citizens who request city services in writing (e.g., Chicago, see Skogan and Hartnett, 1997). In Chicago, a more efficient and equitable delivery of services may have played a big role in the well-documented reductions in crime and disorder.

The promise of partnerships has led to a number of government-sponsored national demonstration programs. The U.S. Department of Justice has funded several key initiatives to demonstrate the value of collaboration for addressing public safety issues. The Community Responses to Drug Abuse Program (CRDA) in nine cities encouraged police departments and community organizations to join forces, along with other social service agencies, to combat local drug markets and to provide services to high-risk youth. A national evaluation of CRDA found that partnerships were productive and educational to all parties. Some conflict between group members did arise because of the mixture of professional and community representatives who generally advocated divergent approaches to program planning and implementation (Rosenbaum et al., 1994). Community groups wanted to implement program activities quickly to achieve early success, while agency employees favored a more strategic, and protracted planning process.

The partnership concept was expanded further in the 1990s, when the Department of Justice funded initiatives than were more comprehensive in nature, while retaining law enforcement in a central role. Two projects are highlighted here because of the lessons learned for research and practice.

Comprehensive Communities Program

The 16-site Comprehensive Communities Program (CCP) was initiated in 1994 "to demonstrate an innovative, comprehensive and integrated multi-agency approach to a comprehensive violent crime/community mobilization program " (U.S. Bureau of Justice

Assistance, 1996:1). With funding of roughly $2 million each, cities were encouraged to engage in strategic planning that involved partnership building, data-driven problem identification and problem solving, and documentation of results. The government established two defining principles for CCP: (1) Communities must take a leadership role in developing partnerships to combat crime and violence; and (2) State and local jurisdictions must establish truly coordinated and multi-disciplinary approaches to address crime and violence-related problems, as well as conditions that foster them.

The national process evaluation found that most CCP sites were able to create new partnerships or broaden existing partnerships to include representation from the community, private sector, and many levels of government (Kelling et al., 1997, 1998). The partnerships almost always led to the implementation of diverse programs, but were especially important for strengthening community policing and community mobilization strategies. CCP was credited with improving police accountability systems in some cities (e.g., Boston) and changing neighborhood service delivery systems in others (e.g., Baltimore, Salt Lake City, and Columbia, SC). CCP sites with a history of partnership building and federal grant writing experienced more success with implementation than sites where CCP represented an entirely new way of doing government business. In terms of crime outcomes, many of the sites reported substantial reductions in target neighborhoods during the two-year demonstration period (U.S. Bureau of Justice Assistance, 2001), but a rigorous impact evaluation was not conducted, and crime rates were on the decline nationally during this period.

The CCP evaluation uncovered some of the problems that can emerge with multi-agency partnerships. Although most participants expressed strong satisfaction with their coalition, some complained of limited involvement in the planning and implementation process, and hence, expressed more negative views. Also, coordination of services was not always achieved or even considered desirable. That is, some sites were able to function effectively without regular meetings of all members because a central administrator (typically in the police department) served as a grant manager and broker of independent services. Across all the sites, when meetings and street-level interactions did occur between partnership agency representatives, they were not always conflict-free. For example, the relationship between law enforcement and social service representatives was occasionally strained because they held divergent views of how best to respond to delinquent youth. Generally, police personnel expressed a preference for punitive strategies (i.e., arrest and prosecution), while social service personnel were inclined to recommend prevention and rehabilitation services. In addition, social service agencies sometimes questioned why the bulk of the federal funding was retained for law enforcement purposes when youth prevention and intervention services are so poorly funded in general.

The CCP evaluation is also noteworthy because it provided an inside look at the communication patterns between partnership members. Through survey-based network analysis, we were able to shed light on the social structure of the CCP partnerships and better understand the role of particular individuals within the network (Rosenbaum, 1998a). Across eight cities, the overall pattern of contacts between partnership members confirmed what Heinz and Manikas (1992) call the "hollow core": i.e., a doughnut-shaped cluster with no one individual or group at the center of the communication network. This pattern of results supports the notion that partnerships, while needing leadership, are not necessarily dominated or controlled by representatives from a single agency.

CCP also taught us about the challenges that organizations face when they take seriously the idea of creating a full-blown partnership with new structures, policies, and practices. Salt Lake City, for example, created a highly innovative organizational entity called, Community Action Teams (CATs). These neighborhood-based teams, which met weekly to engage in local problem solving, were initially composed of a police officer, probation officer, city prosecutor, community mobilization specialist, youth/family specialist, and community relations coordinator. After working together closely, the members of each CAT team became highly cohesive, bonding with each other and the local community. As a functioning entity, however, the CATs encountered serious bureaucratic obstacles due to their formal linkages to traditional government agencies. Leveraging and selectively applying the resources of their parent organizations (the original concept) was not possible in the early stages because of rigid hierarchies of communication and authority, political turf and distrust among parent agencies, weak accountability and supervision, and variable levels of commitment from the top administrators. Thus, to make it work, Salt Lake City realized that it needed coordination, cooperation, and commitment from all the parent organizations. This implies the need for a new management structure that supercedes the parent organizations on selected operations, but finding the right configuration has been difficult.

Weed and Seed

The most visible Department of Justice partnership initiative involving law enforcement has been the Weed and Seed program, with more than 200 communities involved today. Weed and Seed is a comprehensive, multifaceted anti-crime program started in 1991. During the initial 18-month demonstration period, 19 programs were given approximately $1 million each to a achieve the following objectives (Roehl et al., 1996): (1) to develop a comprehensive, multi-agency strategy to control and prevent violent crime, drug trafficking, and drug-related crime in targeted high-crime neighborhoods; (2) to coordinate and integrate existing as well as new federal, state, local, and private-sector initiatives, criminal justice efforts, and human services and to concentrate those resources in the project sites to maximize their impact; and (3) to mobilize residents in the targeted sites to assist law enforcement in identifying and removing violent offenders and drug traffickers from their neighborhoods, and to assist other human service agencies in identifying and responding to service needs in the target area. The agriculturally-derived program title suggests a two-prong strategy of "weeding" out violent criminals in the target neighborhood through law enforcement and prosecution efforts and "seeding" the area with prevention, intervention, treatment, and revitalization services.

Both process and impact evaluations of Weed and Seed were conducted, yielding numerous insights. In terms of the partnership structure and management, the U.S. Attorneys Office (federal prosecutor) was the lead agency and thus, the U.S. attorney often chaired the steering committee. Law enforcement agencies were heavily represented on the steering committee, which typically included the local chief of police, local district attorney, Federal Bureau of Investigation, Drug Enforcement Agency, Bureau of Alcohol, Tobacco and Firearms, and law enforcement coordinators from the U.S. Attorney's Office. Interagency cooperation among federal, state, and local law enforcement agencies, for the purposing of developing and implementing weeding strategies, was relatively successful across the sites. In contrast, interagency cooperation among federal, state, and local prosecutors was not as successful. Too often the local district attorney's office, which handled 92% of all Weed and Seed cases, felt excluded by the "feds" from the planning and decision-making process, and received no federal grant funds for their efforts.

The most innovative component of Weed and Seed — the seeding of preventative social services — was also the biggest disappointment during the initial demonstration period. As the evaluators note, "Many seed committees were unable to function effectively" (Roehl et al., 1966). The reasons for this limited success were numerous, ranging from insufficient funds for seeding activities (less than one-fourth of the total funds on average) to inadequate attention from program leaders. From a multi-agency partnership perspective, the composition of the seeding committees was also a critical oversight. Local agencies — including police, mayor's office, city services, and large nonprofit organizations — were overrepresented on many seeding committees. The federal lead agency was active in only 2 of the 19 sites, and too often, community leaders and citizens were underrepresented and without a voice. The evaluators summarized the problem on a positive note: "the stronger, more active seed committees began with or evolved into a membership comprising substantial numbers of community representatives with decision-making authority over seeding funds." (Roehl et al., 1996:9). In sum, for future programs the evaluation findings underscore the importance of bringing the right people "to the table" from the beginning, including representatives from the district attorney's office and from the target neighborhoods. As it turns out, community representation is also critical to prevent neighborhood residents from becoming angry and resentful of "weeding" activities, which happened in several locations. Community policing officers and strong partnership leaders played critical roles in bridging the gap between conflicting interests.

A subsequent cross-site analysis, using data from eight of the original 19 sites, identified a range of factors that seemed to contribute to successful implementation and impact of the Weed and Seed initiative (Dunworth et al., 1999).[2] In terms of community setting variables, successful sites were those with (1) a pre-existing network of community organizations and community leaders, (2) a limited presence of deep-seated, intractable crime problems, such as gangs, (3) proximity to commercial areas with potential for economic development, and (4) more stable, less transient neighborhood populations.

In terms of program design, the evaluation concluded that the proper mix and sequencing of "weeding" and "seeding" activities are important predictors of success. Specifically, successful sites were more likely than their counterparts to: (1) build community trust by implementing seeding activities at the same time as weeding; (2) sustain weeding activities to prevent the resumption of criminal activity; (3) combine high-level interagency task forces with street-level police presence as an anti-drug trafficking strategy; and (4) maintain an active prosecutorial role at both the local and federal levels. One important lesson here is that, contrary to the widespread belief that weeding activity is a one-shot event that must precede seeding activity, successful sites appreciate the need for simultaneous and sustained activity on both fronts.

The efficient use of limited resources to produce maximum impact is another important design consideration. The Weed and Seed findings suggest that greater success is achieved when the funds are concentrated on a narrowly defined (smaller) target population, and when administrators are able to channel and leverage other funds for the initiative. Thus, programs that are able to increase the dosage or intensity of the intervention are likely to have greater success than programs that focus on large target areas with no supplemental funds or resources applied to the initiative.

Finally, the Weed and Seed evaluation suggests that leadership styles and partnership dynamics are important for success. Weed and Seed is, indeed, a coalition of separate organizations with different objectives and constituents, and therefore, being able to work together smoothly toward a common goal is essential. The results suggest that successful sites were characterized by: (1) leadership that encouraged cooperation rather than confrontation; (2) a "bottom-up" approach to identifying problems and solutions; and (3) extra efforts to build capacity among local organizations. Giving community organizations and leaders an equal role in developing and implementing the Weed and Seed initiative can be very difficult for law enforcement agencies, but appears to be a sound long-term strategy for building healthy partnerships and creating self-regulating communities.

These findings tend to replicate those generated from the national evaluations of CRDA and CCP, and thus contribute to a growing literature of the factors needed to create a fully functioning, cohesive partnership involving law enforcement. Collectively, these studies suggest that public safety partnerships can be dissected and effects can be estimated with multi-site comparisons, although caution is warranted because of design limitations. They also stimulate important questions about the generalizability of partnerships and about "community involvement" in these coalitions, as discussed below.

PARTNERSHIP LIMITATIONS AND THE ISSUE OF "COMMUNITY"

Anti-crime partnerships, notwithstanding their many theoretical strengths, face numerous and sometimes serious obstacles to implementation. Findings from many national and local evaluations imply that organizational reform is needed *inside* the participating agencies to prepare them for a true partnership with each other. In policing, for example, rigid hierarchical bureaucracies, alienated police cultures, and political agendas limit the organization's ability to interact with other organizations and the community with openness, equality, and responsiveness (see Greene, 2000; Rosenbaum et al., 1998). According to the partnership literature, however, the most pervasive obstacle to a fully-functioning partnership is *external* to any given agency and involves the question, "Who should be 'at the table' and what challenges does this membership roster present?" Partnership composition and the role of "community" are forever troubling.

A partnership's greatest strength is also its greatest weakness, namely, the diversity of agencies and constituencies represented, and therefore, the diversity of views and orientations to social problems that must be negotiated to reach decisions. A common theme among evaluation reports is the limited participation and role prescribed for "the community" and those most affected by the partnership's interventions. There is little question that government bureaucracies and even professional social service agencies have not done enough to reach out to grass roots organizations and community leaders in low-income, high-crime neighborhoods. Community involvement is usually desirable at all points in the process, from strategic planning to program implement to evaluation and feedback. I should note, however, that achieving this goal is a multi-faceted challenge to government agencies, and many of these officials would like to see "the another side of the story" told.

So here's the other side. I have distilled the lists of criticisms of greater community involvement to arguments that have some basis in social science research (for a review of relevant research, see Rosenbaum et al., 1998). Here are some key points they are making:

- Getting community members to participate in anti-crime programs, especially in low-income, high-crime neighborhoods, is extremely difficult due to feelings of hopelessness and despair, fear of retaliation, deep-seated distrust of government agencies and the police in particular, and the widespread effects of poverty on human functioning.

- Those who do participate do not necessarily represent "the community." They are more likely to be civic-minded "do-gooders." Communities are not homogeneous, and the leaders of various factions will compete for legitimacy and power, making it difficult to determine who should be invited to the partnership.

- Having professionals and grass roots representatives at the same table is problematical because of their incompatible styles of work and philosophies of intervention. Professionals, who attend meetings daily, tend to dominate the discussion. Nonprofessionals want immediate action without much research or planning.

- Agency representatives tend to complain that having the community involved requires a large partnership, which is inherently dysfunctional and very slow to act. Partnership efficiency requires that the group be "lean and mean" rather than democratic.

- Partnership members need to discuss confidential information about neighborhood problems, troubled families, and troubled individuals. Community members cannot have access to this type of information without violating individual privacy.

- Many problems can be solved without the involvement of citizens. Police departments, relying on police records, have engaged in extensive problem-solving activities.

Of course, many of these arguments have forced academics and policy makers to rethink whether partnerships are appropriate for all crime-related problems and all circumstances. For example, the demand for community participation stems, in part, from the fact that partnerships typically focus on geographically defined neighborhoods. Tilley (2000) has argued, however, that a strategic emphasis on "neighborhood" and "community" in crime prevention is overrated because not all crime-related problems are neighborhood-based. Some patterns of crime extend beyond neighborhood boundaries.

Partnerships with broad representation also assume that a rational planning process will result from collective input and discussion. Yet experience indicates that having diverse input is no guarantee that the emergent plan of action will be based on the best available scientific information regarding the problem, best practices for intervention, or the democratic "will of the people." We should not assume that the average person on the street is thinking about causation and social policy in a rational way. For example, survey data from the Fighting Back partnerships indicate that most citizens view drug abuse as a disease, but feel that it is caused by social ills (e.g., poverty, disenfranchisement, broken homes), and believe that the best solutions are education, community awareness, and law enforcement (Klitzner, 1992). These contradictory beliefs highlight the need for researchers and policy experts to be involved in the planning process and hopefully increase the probability that rational thinking will prevail in group decision making.

While we must acknowledge the limits of citizen participation in partnerships, we must also be suspicious of efforts to maintain the status quo when the call for neighborhood-based governance is so strong and the complaints about municipal police agencies are so widespread. One of the big lessons from anti-crime partnership evaluations is that a room full of law enforcement officials will inevitably result in a law enforcement solution to the problem. Police organizations have a tendency to prescribe the same set of solutions (e.g., crackdowns, saturated patrols, stakeouts, targeted enforcement) regardless of the nature of the problem. Unless the "toolbox" of ideas at the partnership table includes alternative perspectives and approaches, problem solving will continue to be "business as usual" in the public safety realm. In recent years, law enforcement has reached out to other city agencies for problem solving, but this too has its limits. The solutions tend to be enforcement-oriented. Furthermore, research suggests that when interagency partnerships are strengthened, such coordination runs the risk of driving out citizen involvement (Duffee et al., 2001; Warren et al., 1974).

As a further complication, professionals who complain about community involvement quickly forget that the presence of aggressive "zero-tolerance" policing in urban neighborhoods requires the "consent of the governed." Enforcement strategies require careful planning, including community input and endorsement. To achieve this, the police and the community must have a solid working relationship built on mutual respect and trust. This type of partnership simply does not exist in many American neighborhoods, as reflected in public opinion polls, complaints of police misconduct, and numerous Justice Department investigations of local police organizations (see Ramirez et al., 2000).

Finally, law enforcement efforts to encourage citizen participation are typically limited in scope. The police, when they do reach out to the community, would like citizens to serve as their "eyes and ears" but not to become too serious about strategic planning or crime control initiatives (Buerger, 1994; Friedman, 1994; Rosenbaum, 1988, 1998b). Over many decades, the American police have worked hard to maintain sole ownership over the crime issue and convince politicians and citizens that public safety is the exclusive responsibility of professional crime fighters. Budgets are maintained and images polished when public safety is attributed to uniformed officers who work for a professional law enforcement agency (Crank and Langworthy, 1991).

But we should not be too harsh on law enforcement agencies. Apparently, the problem of recognizing and incorporating the role of the community is not unique to law enforcement-led coalitions. Private foundations have funded numerous community-focused coalitions with the hope that local institutions would join forces to empower local citizens and build community capacity. Yet evidence of this phenomenon in partnership composition is hard to find. A national study of 1,650 coalitions by Rosenbloom, Dawkins, and Hingson (cited in Chavis et al., 1993), found that only 35% involved the target populations in the coalition and only 20% included citizen action groups. Nevertheless, as our society continues to increase in diversity, and as law enforcement seeks greater efficiency by targeting high-crime neighborhoods, citizen participation at all stages of the intervention process will be a necessity rather than a nicety.

THE CHALLENGE FOR EVALUATION RESEARCH

We know a fair amount about partnership dynamics and activities, but very little about partnership effects. This knowledge gap exists, in part, because partnerships present enormous challenges for evaluation researchers and other stakeholders. Most evaluations focus on a single intervention designed and implemented by a single agency. As I have suggested here, partnerships, especially non-dyadic partnerships, are much more complex, thus making them more difficult to study (see Connell et al., 1995; Fulbright-Anderson et al., 1998; Klitzner, 1993). The obstacles to evaluation, as noted in the literature, include:

- *the complexity of the interventions.* Comprehensive initiatives are characterized by horizontal complexity (working across different organizations and sectors) and vertical complexity (working at the individual, family, and community levels);

- *the complexity of contextual variables.* Partnerships emerge from, and are influenced by, a specific constellation of political, economic, demographic, and geographic conditions;

- *the dynamic, changing nature of the intervention.* Partnerships and their products are typically dynamic and evolving entities, and making it difficult for evaluators to "hit a moving target" or analyze bi-directional causality.

- *the diversity of intervention processes and outcomes.* Partnerships, by their nature, are unique and complex, which leads them to select diverse inputs, processes, outputs, and outcomes. Often, partnerships attempt to impact several goals simultaneously. Establishing conceptual and operational definitions of these variables is a big challenge for evaluators;

- *the lack of optimal conditions for traditional experimental research.* With community-wide and comprehensive partnerships, the evaluator's ability to use random assignment or find equivalent comparison groups can be restricted.

These obstacles, collectively, suggest that partnerships are quite difficult to study using traditional scientific methods. The complexity of behavior in social organizations, when embedded in the larger community context, poses a serious challenge to causal inference and scientific inquiry of any type. But all is not lost. There are sensible approaches that can be employed to advance our knowledge of partnership processes and effects.

Evaluation Design

Given the complex nature of partnerships and comprehensive interventions, it has become fashionable to discard traditional quantitative methods and assume that "anything goes" in the way of methods for evaluating these initiatives. This would be a serious mistake, for we would be "throwing out the baby with the bath water." The standards of scientific validity needed to answer the question, "Did the intervention make a difference?" have not changed, regardless of our ability to follow them. (For a detailed discussion of validity and major threats to validity in social science research, see Shadish et al, 2002). Along these lines, I agree with Chen (1990) that evaluations should be judged by whether they meet several basic criteria: (1) Are they responsive to the needs of stakeholders? (2) Are they relatively unbiased in terms of producing reliable and valid results? (3) Are they trustworthy in terms of controlling for confounding factors? and (4) Are the findings generalizable to conditions, populations, and problems beyond the immediate setting?

Of course, randomized experimental designs, with units that have an equal probability of being assigned to either the experimental or control groups, are the best for protecting against major threats to evaluation validity (Shadish et al., 2002), and thus represent the "gold standard" in the field. I do not agree with evaluators who claim that such experiments are inappropriate or impossible for the study of comprehensive partnerships. More intelligent lobbying of government officials (on the need for large-scale experiments), and more creative input on the part of evaluators (to capitalize on emergent opportunities) may change the approach to funding and program evaluation. Experiments can inform us about whether the partnership as a whole ("molar" treatment) is producing effects, and if properly utilized, they can inform us about whether specific components of the partnership ("molecular" treatment) are working, although the latter is more difficult.[3] In the meantime, there are several approaches that can lead to credible evaluations and reasonable causal inferences. Good design, theory, and measurement all play critical roles.

Carefully designed quasi-experimental evaluations, involving the use of comparison groups, should be considered whenever possible.

This may require comparisons between a substantial number of communities or cities on particular outcome measures, but this expectation is not unreasonable for national studies. At this point in history, I am saddened to report that the critical importance of a credible "counterfactual" (i.e., data indicating what would have happened in the absence of the intervention) has been lost on many evaluators of partnerships and other complex interventions. The counterfactual model is at the heart of all causal inference. In a quasi-experimental design involving a comparison group, a test of causal hypotheses may be limited to either an assessment of overall partnership impact (versus no partnership) or an analysis of the effectiveness of a specific intervention component. But regardless of the design type, including qualitative case studies, counterfactual information remains essential for making causal statements (see Hollister and Hill, 1995; Granger, 1998).

Determining the appropriate unit of analysis is an important design consideration, especially for evaluations that involve selecting or matching appropriate units. The evaluator must be able to answer the question, "Is the partnership seeking to change the behavior of individuals, families, peer groups, community organizations, neighborhoods, and/or formal organizations?" By developing a theory of intervention, this question can be more easily addressed.

In the absence of an independent comparison or control group, communities or other units of analysis can be used as their own comparison in a simple pre-post treatment design. Multiple measures of the outcome before and after program implementation — referred to as an "interrupted time series design" — is preferred over the simple pre-post design because it allows for more reliable prediction of outcomes than a single pre-test score. Of course, time series analysis can be strengthened if the researcher has a solid theoretical understanding of how the intervention is expected to "behave" over time and what contextual variables may appear as plausible rival hypotheses for the observed change. Statistical modeling can be used in a variety of ways to create counterfactuals and estimate program effects (see Hollister and Hill, 1995).

There are dozens of research designs with various strengths and weaknesses. The evaluator should attempt to "mix and match" design elements (e.g., type of control group, presence of pre-test and/or post-test measures, timing of interventions) to strengthen causal inference and provide opportunities to test different threats to validity (see Shadish et al., 2002).

The Case Study Method

The case study approach is considered a desirable alternative to the experimental framework for evaluating partnerships, although the two are not incompatible and can be used jointly. Case studies are intended to produce rich and detailed information about interventions, from start to finish. They are often associated with naturalistic, qualitative field work (Guba and Lincoln, 1981), but they can also incorporate quantitative data collection (Yin, 1989). Through a variety of methods, the evaluator can construct a complete picture of how the partnership was developed, how it functions, its short-term effects, and the full context in which these processes occur.

The case study method is now a popular approach for studying innovation in criminal justice. Case studies have been especially useful for describing community policing and problem-solving initiatives by law enforcement (e.g., Capowich and Roehl, 1994; Green et al., 1994; Hope, 1994; McElroy et al., 1993; Sadd and Grinc, 1994; Skogan and Hartnett, 1997; Wilkinson and Rosenbaum, 1994). The primary focus of these studies, however, is often internal organizational reform or police driven problem-solving projects. Rarely do they give much attention to the partnership issues that emerge in a neighborhood context between the police and the community (for exceptions, see Lyons, 1995 and Skogan and Hartnett, 1997).

The strength of the case study approach lies in its ability to capture the complexity and fluidity of a comprehensive partnership. This approach is not concerned with isolating one or two causal factors, but rather seeks to measure a host of variables working simultaneously in a particular context. In this regard, the case study approach is similar to the "realistic evaluation" approach advocated by Pawson and Tilley (1997), which assumes that interventions are conditioned by the context in which they occur and that greater attention should be given to the mechanisms of change. To be useful for impact analysis, case studies must go beyond mere description. The value of the case study approach rests heavily on the ability to construct a theory of change or logic model that explains how the partnership functions and why it should be expected to produce certain effects (see Duffee et al., 2000, for a listing of theoretical constructs relevant to community policing partnerships). The case study method can be used as a vehicle for inductive theory construction or deductive theory testing.

Theory-based Evaluation

Adopting a theory-of-change approach to evaluating comprehensive partnerships is very sensible. Such an approach serves to bridge the gap between the seemingly conflicting demands for strong causal statements on the one hand and a fuller understanding of comprehensive, context-driven interventions on the other. Carol Weiss (1972, 1995) has been advocating a theory of change approach to evaluation for many years, and others have promoted this approach for evaluating comprehensive community initiatives (see Fulbright-Anderson et al., 1998) and other social interventions (see Rogers et al., 2000). As Weiss notes (1995:66), theories of change are simply "theories about how and why the program will work." Theory-based evaluation is applauded for its ability to make explicit the theory of intervention by articulating the relationships among inputs, activities, short-term outcomes, and long-term outcomes. This specification of linkages in graphic form, using boxes linked by arrows, is called a "logic model," which illustrates the program's theory of how change is expected to occur (see Coffman, 1999; Connell and Kubisch, 1998). The primary benefit of this approach is that it makes explicit what are often implicit linkages between variables in the model. Connell and Kubisch (1998) offer three reasons for using a theory of change approach when evaluating comprehensive community initiatives:

- the planning and implementation of the initiative will be sharpened. There will be less ambiguity among stakeholders about what outcomes are expected and what activities and processes are needed to achieve them;

- the measurement and data collection processes will be facilitated. The theory of change will suggest how and when to measure various constructs identified in the logic model, from inputs to mediating processes to outcomes.

- the problems associated with causal attribution of impact are reduced. If stakeholders agree, in advance, on the theory of change, then observed changes between relationships can be used to support or question the causal assumptions behind the theory.

Thus, specifying a theory of change can be helpful to both practitioners (who should be thinking seriously about what they are trying to achieve and how) and evaluators (who should be thinking seriously about measuring and testing intervention-related assumptions and sub-assumptions). But the theory of change approach is not a panacea and does not entirely solve our dilemma with respect to partnerships and causal inference. Despite the glowing endorsements for this approach, it is problematic as a stand-alone methodology (see Cook, 2000; Shadish et al., 2002). First, contrary to the impression left by some advocates, there are often multiple theories of change that can be offered for a single program, and the mechanisms of action for each are not always clear. This can be a problem in that stakeholders often hold conflicting, not well articulated theories of intervention. Second, if causal inference is a high priority, the direction of causality and timing of effects (i.e., how long it takes before x will cause y) is assumed without sufficient empirical justification. Third, oftentimes more than one theoretical model can fit a particular data set. Fourth, this approach assumes reliable measurement, especially since the focus is on capturing change in relationships over time.

In sum, an approach that relies exclusively on theory testing, without adequate controls, in a context where dozens of variables are considered important, is likely to encounter serious problems. In essence, theory-based evaluations, like case studies, cannot circumvent the standard threats to validity when generalized causal inference remains a priority of the evaluator. As Granger (1998:222) points out, theory-based evaluations can yield scientifically credible and generalizable results "if evaluators attend to the need for sufficiently credible counterfactuals at all stages of their work." To achieve this, the evaluation must include strong theories, representative samples, multiple methods and designs, serious testing of alternative hypotheses, and plans for replication.

In sum, theory-based evaluation offers a powerful tool for gaining insight into complex interventions, but should be combined, whenever possible with case study methods, experimental methods, and alternative designs to enhance scientific validity. Other single system evaluation designs — such as longitudinal designs, individual growth curve models, within-experimental control designs, and multiple time series control methods — should be considered when traditional control groups are absent (see Kim et al., 1994). Also, high quality measurement and sound reasoning will be extremely important in the final analysis.

CONCEPTUALIZATION AND MEASUREMENT

Careful and detailed measurement is a very important component of a successfully executed partnership evaluation. To a large extent, the theory of change and the research design will dictate the basic measures and measurement points. But substantially more detailed information can be obtained through various field observations and interviews. Because of the evolving nature of partnerships, qualitative field documentation is absolutely critical and should be used to modify and update the original model. Indeed, conducting interviews with participants is essential for formulating various theories of intervention in the early stages of the evaluation.

Typically, evaluators are able to conceptualize interventions (including partnerships) as having several distinct components: program inputs, program activities and processes, short-term outcomes, and long-term outcomes. Measurement in each of these domains is important (see Cook and Roehl, 1993 and Klitzner, 1993 for detailed frameworks).

Measuring Input and Contextual Variables

By measuring input and contextual variables, the evaluator is able to define the elements that comprise the "partnership" and establish baseline data on external conditions. Whether or not one adopts an "open systems" approach to partnerships, there is little question that a host of contextual factors may influence the nature and effectiveness of the partnership. Furthermore, the measurement of contextual factors allows the evaluator to test plausible rival hypotheses for observed outcomes.

To begin with, the demographic context is likely to affect partnership activities and outcomes. The evaluator should measure the size and composition of the target area as well as geographic boundaries. Almost inevitably, the physical definition of the target area will create political and practical problems if it divides natural communities or catchments areas for government services. Also, partnerships appear to be more effective when resources are concentrated in smaller areas (Dunworth et al., 1999).

Measuring the social and community context will aid the evaluation in many ways. The magnitude of social problems within the target and comparison areas will provide essential baseline data for estimating partnership-induced change. Also, given that community crime rates are heavily influenced by structural variables and the degree of community social disorganization (Sampson, 1997), this knowledge will provide a context for judging the likelihood of intervention success and the generalizability of the findings.

The social context of the target community can be important for shaping the definition of the target problem and levels of community support for the partnership. If community definitions of the problem are consistent with those offered by the partnership, then one can predict stronger community support for partnership actions and greater local ownership of the problem. In multi-ethnic and multi-income areas, the success of the partnership can be affected by who is invited to define the problem and set partnership priorities, who takes on leadership roles, and who feels included in the decision-making process (ISA Associates, 1993; Dunworth et al., 1999). The widespread assumption of homogeneity within ethnic communities is virtually always false, and self-appointed community leaders are often challenged by persons representing other interest groups. Also, whether the lead agency in the partnership is viewed as a part of, or apart from, the target community (i.e., having legitimacy and credibility) is hypothesized to affect the level of community cooperation.

Governmental and organizational context are likely to affect the partnership. Communities vary substantially in terms of the quantity of resources available to address social problems, their willingness to work in partnerships, and the stability of local government. Each of these factors can facilitate or inhibit the formation of a solid, working partnership in predictable directions. Recent changes in local government, for example, can disturb the planning of coalition efforts. When officials are voted out of office, the lead agency person or other key members of the partnership can be removed and support for the initiative can quickly dissipate.

Current and previous government responses to the target problem(s) are important for gauging the innovativeness and effectiveness of any partnership actions. National studies show that anti-crime partnerships are more successful when they have a history of positive working agency dyads, and a history of securing external funding for public safety initiatives (Dunworth et al., 1999; Kelling et al., 1997). Past behavior is always a good predictor of future behavior, and, of course, must be taken into account when seeking to estimate the independent effects of creating a formal partnership: i.e., was the observed change due to the new partnership or the city's history of good working relationships between agencies?

When new funding is involved, the evaluators need to ascertain whether the proposed partnership strategies are unique and distinctive from previous programs or are simply being used to justify additional funding for ongoing initiatives. If previous programs are still operational, yet different from the partnership's initiative, then they should be viewed as a threat to the validity of any statements about partnership effectiveness. For example, the Boston Gun Project ("Ceasefire") —the youth anti-violence project widely touted as a success — was introduced in the mid-1990s alongside numerous other anti-crime interventions organized by schools, churches, and community organizations. Yet the evaluators did a nice job of reviewing, and attempting to rule out, these rival explanations for the reduction in youth violence (Braga et al., 1999).

Finally, measuring the level and type of involvement in the partnership by government officials, technical assistant providers, and evaluators is critical for understanding the external validity of the effects. Foundations and government agencies appear to desire a greater role for themselves, researchers, and outside experts in the process, while local participants are naturally skeptical of outside help beyond mere funding. Whether evaluation findings can be replicated in other settings depends on the careful documentation of their respective roles. Regardless of how they view themselves, outsiders become insiders — the greater their involvement in the process, the more they become an integral part of the intervention itself. Consequently, they must become subjects of the evaluation and defined as input resources for any replication attempts.

Formation of Partnerships

Understanding the reasons why partnerships come into being will help to predict their level of success. Partnerships emerge in response to specific incidents or problems, a recognized need for community-wide or regional planning, and/or new funding opportunities (e.g., when the federal government requires the formation of a partnership to receive funds). Whether agencies are participating for the money, to achieve shared goals, or for political gain can make a difference in their willingness to invest time and resources in the partnership. Whether agency representatives are involved because they are the most knowledgeable and most appropriate individuals within their parent organizations or because they were the most expendable says a great deal about the organization's initial commitment to the partnership.

The research literature suggests that agencies are likely to join a partnership and work together successfully when they feel the benefits exceed the costs (Mizrahi and Rosenthal, 1993; Schermerhorn, 1975; Whetten, 1981). The benefits (and predictors) of participation include prior mutual respect, perceived need for collaboration, funding or legislative mandates, a history of working together, and the expectation of payoff from sharing resources. Participation is unlikely when agencies have a history of disrespect and conflict, when turf or jurisdiction is threatened, and when agencies fear they will not get sufficient credit for their contribution. Perhaps the most critical factor in the early stages of partnership formation is agreement on a mission or purpose for the group (Gray, 1985). If the organizations can find a good reason to join forces that does not compromise their individual identities, then cooperation is more likely. Commitment to the collaboration is facilitated by a belief among participants that working together will yield positive results (Schermerhorn, 1975).

Measuring Program Activities and Processes

The evaluation of complex partnerships requires careful attention to the processes associated with program planning, program development, and implementation. During these processes, certain partnership characteristics and dynamics will determine the group's viability and success with implementation.

Planning Process

Planning is arguably the central activity of partnerships. Partnerships hold meetings, conduct needs assessment and other forms of research, and engage in other planning activities. Groups adopt various approaches to planning, but the current trend in law enforcement is to follow a data-driven problem-solving model with local researchers participating in the partnership. This approach is embodied in the Justice Department's Strategic Approaches to Public Safety Initiative, or SACSI (see Coldren et al., 2000). This framework suggests numerous measurement points, from problem identification to evaluation. It suggests that evaluators should be attentive to whether the planning process is strategic and/or data-driven. To what extent does the group rely on research findings and available statistics (as opposed to opinions and political agendas) to prioritize and define problems? To what extent does the group employ a strategic approach that has a long-term perspective? Are the groups engaged in "ready-aim-fire" planning (i.e., moving from establishing a working group to creating an action plan), or do they prefer the "ready-fire-aim" approach (i.e., moving immediately to implementation without any serious planning?) (ISA Associates, 1993). The group's approach to planning will depend on its leadership, composition, and dynamics, as well as contextual factors discussed earlier.

Type of Partnership

Partnerships come in all shapes and sizes. They vary in purpose, objectives, scope of activities, philosophy, history, membership size and composition, organizational structure, degree of formality, budget, number and function of staff, and many other dimensions. Researchers have proposed several classification schemes for categorizing partnership types, some of which have redeeming value for the theory of partnerships outlined here.

First, partnerships can be classified by *membership composition*. Cook and Roehl (1993) found that 250 community partnerships could be characterized as one of three types: (1) *Leadership*: coalitions whose members are primarily political, social, and/or business leaders; (2) *Grass roots*: coalitions whose members are primarily citizens, often from the target community; and (3) *Professionals*: coalitions whose members represent government, for-profit, and non-profit agencies that provide direct services to the community. In practice, partnerships can also include combinations of these groups and exhibit diversity within each. Coalitions often include representatives from various government and social service agencies, as well as elected officials, private businesses, voluntary organizations, community/grass roots organizations, churches, and other groups with a vested interest in the community. Evaluators need to ask whether the "right" people are at the table in the right numbers for the task at hand. Too often evaluators rely on members of the partnership to determine whether the composition of partnership is correct. An effort should be made to collect data from organizations that are *not* involved in the partnership to find out why. The size and composition of partnerships may influence partnership cohesion, creativity, and productivity.

Second, partnerships can be classified by their *strategic action orientation*. For example, community-wide coalitions generally adopt one of two approaches to action — *empowering* the community or *centralized coordination* of services (ISA Associates, 1993). A similar typology, but one defined by both group composition and action orientation, emerged from the national COPS evaluation (Roth et al., 2000). The authors proposed two types of law enforcement partnerships: (1) *Task force partnerships*, composed of law enforcement agencies addressing a particular crime problem such as gang or drug activity, and (2) *Programmatic or tactical partnerships*, composed of police and non-police groups seeking to provide prevention services or programs, such as D.A.R.E., Neighborhood Watch or citizen patrols. The COPS research team went further to describe two types of community policing partnerships which are common today, and these too can be distinguished by membership: (3) *problem-solving partnerships*, where the police typically work with other city departments responsible for code enforcement, housing, social services, zoning, public works, and parks and recreation; and (4) *community partnerships*, where the police meet with citizens and community leaders to address neighborhood safety issues.

Third, partnerships can be classified by the *number of partners*. Does the partnership include only two parties or does it involve multiple organizations? Many law enforcement partnerships are correctly classified as dyads. The police are particularly good at teaming up with citizen block clubs, business groups, schools, and community organizations, but each dyad is a separate, non-overlapping partnership. With a range of partnership sizes, researchers can test hypotheses about the relationship between size and effectiveness in planning and implementation.

Fourth, and perhaps most importantly, partnerships can be conceptualized in terms the *degree of collaboration*. Members' roles and relationships to one another can define the level of collaboration, ranging from superficial to substantial. For example, Crawford (1997) distinguishes between "multi-agency relations," where agencies merely come together to address a given problem, and "inter-agency relations," which "entail some degree of fusion and melding of relations between agencies" (p.119). Multi-agency relations, which are much more common, require no real change to each organization's structure or function, while interagency relations are likely to produce new forms of work and organizational configurations. In a similar vein, the national evaluation of COPS concluded that community policing partnerships in the U.S. can be placed on a continuum ranging from "true collaboration in all phases of work" at one end to "mere involvement" of the parties at the other. Kelling and his colleagues (1997) have gone further to define the points on this continuum as: "collaboration, coordination, cooperation, consent, indifference, objection, passive protest, defiance, and active opposition."

Leadership

Strong leadership is considered the key to successful partnerships. Partnerships engage in a range of activities, including prioritizing and defining problems, analyzing the target problem, reviewing the literature for "best practices," designing new intervention strategies (action plans), coordinating the implementation of these strategies, monitoring partnership effectiveness, and adjusting to feedback received from the environment. Multi-agency partnerships need someone who can get people to the table, help them formulate a collective vision, motivate them to participate fully, and keep them interested in coming back. Leaders are expected to oversee the planning process and build consensus regarding definitions of the problem and coordinate desired strategies of intervention.

Research suggests that success with implementation and group maintenance is associated with good leadership (Bailey, 1986; O'Sullivan, 1977). Thus, evaluators should measure the strength and style of leadership: Is the group leader highly visible or a behind-the-scenes manager? A consensus builder or an autocrat? Seen as highly effective and admired by the group or disrespected? All too often, effective leadership is absent in partnerships. Some of this is intentional, as partnership members seek to avoid a "power grab" out of respect for other members of the group.

Structure

Coalitions, like any organization, need structure to function smoothly. Is there a lead agency that can handle the administrative responsibilities? Is there staff? Is there a core planning group or steering committee? Are there appropriate subcommittees? Are there regular meetings of these groups, and is communication structured and coordinated through a central leadership? Coalitions seem to perform better when these conditions are in place and when expectations are clear (Ellis and Lenczner, 2000).

Decision-making Responsibility

The process by which decisions are make in the partnership should be carefully studied. Decision-making is likely to be linked to the group's structure and style of leadership (e.g., autocratic or laissez-faire, formal or informal). The literature suggests that coalitions have greater success with program implementation and maintenance when they exhibit a higher degree of formalization through rules, roles, and procedures (Schermerhorn, 1981; Chavis et al., 1987). Without decision-making structure, partnerships can disintegrate.

Partnership Dynamics

The health and vitality of the partnership will be reflected in the social dynamics among group members (Cook and Roehl, 1993). A group's ability to reach agreement on target problems and intervention strategies, and its ability to execute a plan of coordinated action, can be affected by whether members of the group get along, respect one another, and work well together. Thus, the social relations and communication patterns among coalition members constitute a topic ripe for evaluation research. Dimensions worthy of attention include:

- *Social Cohesion*: To what extent can the partnership be characterized as a cohesive group, where members feel positively toward one another, enjoy working together, and are committed to make the partnership a success? Research indicates that partnerships are more likely to survive and thrive when members are active, satisfied, and committed to the group (Prestby et al., 1990; Wandersman et al., 1987). Establishing a positive organizational climate is an essential condition for a working partnership, especially the creation of social cohesion among members (Giamartino and Wandersman, 1983) and good internal communication (Hall et al., 1977).

- *Conflict or Cooperation*: Good organizational climate implies limited conflict among members. Yet conflict is unavoidable in interagency partnerships, especially with large and diverse groups. Therefore, evaluators should measure the nature and extent of conflict and the methods used to resolve it.

- *Coordination*: To what extent are agency representatives able to work together effectively to achieve internal goals, such as defining the target problem, developing intervention plans, establishing channels of communication, and adapting to external feedback? Coordination occurs when agencies within the group take into account each other's actions when making decisions.

- *Interaction Patterns*: Communication among a high percentage of the group's members is considered a sign of a healthy "inter-organizational network," where all participants are linked to one another (e.g., Aldrich, 1979). Long-standing coalitions are characterized by frequent meetings with high attendance and good channels of internal communication (Chavis et al., 1987).

  For mapping interaction and communication patterns within anti-crime coalitions, network analysis can be a valuable tool (see Rosenbaum, 1998a). This is a solid analytic strategy for describing and illuminating social relations (see Wasserman and Galaskiewicz, 1993, 1994, for reviews). Network analysis can be used to determine the centrality of individual actors, the total pattern of communication among all actors, and the existence of clusters or subgroups within the network. If attrition problems can be minimized, network analysis can be useful for testing hypotheses about changes in network relationships over time at either the individual or organizational level.

Other Partnership Traits

There are other partnership characteristics that may be important to success but are not covered here for lack of space. In addition to the above, these include the ability to secure diversified funding, attract and retain volunteers, use up-to-date technology, provide professional development opportunities, and engage in regular evaluations (Ellis and Lenczner, 2000). The ability to exploit state-of-the-art information technology should become increasingly important.

Implementation Activities

Creating a partnership that is socially cohesive and well managed is a far cry from implementing activities or programs. Documenting the translation of action plans into action is essential for producing results and making causal inferences about the effectiveness of specific interventions or mediating variables. If the partnership has developed a logic model, which implies the relevant theory (or theories) of change, this scheme should be used as the guiding framework for developing a measurement plan: i.e., what activities should be measured, when and how should they be measured, and how should they be linked to one another and to specific outcomes?

In addition to internal activities (e.g., interagency planning and coordination) and external activities (e.g., direct service delivery), partnerships often interact with non-partnership agencies to leverage resources and broker services. Partnerships do not exist in a vacuum and should be evaluated in terms of their linkages to external entities. The degree of formalization and intensity of these relationships varies, but they are considered important for achieving short-term outcomes. Every member agency has its own network of organizations with which it interacts.

Finally, as any good evaluator knows, the gap between theory and practice can be enormous, and most impact evaluations show "no difference" between the experimental and control groups. When no impact is observed, evaluators can be left scratching their heads unless careful measurement has been taken along the way. There are two general sets of reasons for finding "no difference" or no impact on program outcomes (Weiss, 1972): Either the intervention did not set in motion the causal processes/activities identified as important in the theory or logic model (referred to as "program failure") or the processes/activities were implemented "by the book" but did not cause the expected effects (referred to as "theory failure"). When programs are not implemented according to theory (or the guiding logic model), which commonly occurs, then evaluators are unable to test the validity of the original model. However, if partnership initiatives change and evolve over time, then evaluators must be quick to adjust process measures accordingly. Often, this is not possible with quantitative measures, which guarantee reliability through their inflexibility. Good qualitative work will be needed to capture some of the new activities, although certain impact analyses will be permanently lost.

We cannot condemn partnership members for not conforming religiously to the original plan. Many events can occur in a complex environment that necessitate a change of plans or actions, and, in fact, community-based, comprehensive approaches are frequently modified. For example, in a qualitative study of eight community-wide health prevention coalitions in Canada, Robinson and Elliot (2000) found that the full-scale use of comprehensive approaches was rare, and that agencies preferred to implement elements of the model and adapt them to local conditions. Local context plays a big role in tailoring programs to local needs and resources, as I have learned from conducting several multi-site national studies of partnerships.

Change in activities may reflect a modification of theory or simply a change in implementation. In either case, the evaluator must be extremely vigilant to measure what actually happened in the field. Measuring the type, intensity and duration of any "treatment" is important for establishing the construct validity of the "cause" and "effect" variables. The careful measurement of particular variables is the foundation that allows researchers to: (1) know which concepts are being captured; (2) determine whether co-variation of "cause" and "effect" occurs over time; and (3) rule out other possible causal factors. In addition to adjusting measurement, the evaluator should be quick to revise the theory of change if planners devise a new conception of how the intervention works. My experience, however, is that planners don't change their minds as often as implementers decide to deviate from the original plan. Thus, measuring the integrity of implementation is essential for making causal inferences and for distinguishing between theory failure and implementation failure.

Measuring Outcomes

What good is a "well-oiled" partnership that has good leadership, excellent communication, strong social climate, a high probability of survival, and the ability to deliver (or broker) services on time and according to plan if it cannot make a difference in crime or drug-related outcomes? The most basic, and often overlooked, question is whether the partnership has achieved its outcome goals. Partnerships should not be taken for granted as the only approach or even the most effective approach to achieving crime prevention goals. Estimating partnership impact, and the conditions under which it is effective, remain among the primary reasons for funding evaluation research.

If reliable changes are observed in specific outcome measures (e.g., reductions in violent youth crime or drug use among males aged 17-25), can the observed changes be attributed to the work of the partnership or are they the result of other factors in the partnership's environment? To date, we know very little about the effectiveness of partnerships as a vehicle for preventing or controlling targeted crime, disorder, and drug problems.

Of course, the primary challenge for the evaluator is to design a study that sheds light on the question of whether changes in outcome measures can be attributed to partnership activities or to competing events. (For a comprehensive analysis of design options, see Shadish et al., 2002.) To begin with, I simply want to underscore the distinction between "outcomes" and "effects" as a reminder that program evaluation is funded largely to make causal statements, which is a difficult task. As Granger (1998) notes, "outcomes" are measures of variables that should be affected by interventions, while "effects" are observed outcomes *minus* the estimate of change that would have occurred *without* the intervention. Hence, evaluators typically compute an "effect size" as the mean outcome score for the "treatment" group minus the mean outcome score for the "comparison" group, standardized (Shadish et al., 2002). My point, again, is that researchers should always be looking for ways to measure outcomes for comparison groups to establish good counterfactuals.

Our knowledge of partnerships can be taken to the next level if evaluators take seriously the task of advancing the measurement of partnership outcomes. There are many types and levels of outcome measurement. Using a simple textbook approach, we can distinguish between short-term and long-term outcomes, and if we get specific on the time dimension, we may add intermediate outcomes as well. The first impact question is whether specific partnership activities or events (e.g., designing and starting a media campaign) caused changes in *short-term outcomes* (e.g., increased public awareness of, and positive attitudes about, the importance of parental supervision). The second impact question is whether changes in short-term outcomes will produce changes in *intermediate outcomes* (e.g., improvements in parenting practices). Finally, did these changes in parenting practices produce changes in *long-term outcomes* (e.g., reductions in juvenile delinquency and drug use). In this regard, short-term and intermediate outcomes can be viewed as mediating variables in the theory of change.

Again, we return to the importance of theory specification, whether through inductive or deductive methods.[4] If partnership interventions are complex, we should be prepared for a complex set of outcomes and various paths to achieving these goals. The theory of partnerships outlined earlier suggests that partnerships can seek to influence outcomes through individual, family, small group, organizations, neighborhood, and macro-level causal processes. If the theory of change, as articulated by the partnership, calls for intervention at one or more of these levels, then measurement in those domains should follow.

As one example, the theory of change behind many anti-crime partnerships often alludes to the goal of changing the participating organizations' "way of doing business." If the evaluator decides to take seriously this goal of systemic, organizational reform, then a creative combination of research methods will be needed to look "inside" the participating organizations. Using in-person interviews, employee questionnaires, and existing agency records, the evaluator must determine whether management practices, strategies, and philosophies have changed recently in a manner consistent with the partnership intervention.

At the "street level," I should note that partnerships do not always engage in direct service provision, but rather function as a broker of services. Under these circumstances, the impact questions can be clustered into two groups: (1) did the brokered service make a difference in specific outcomes? and (2) what role did the partnership play in establishing or supporting the service in question?

Community-wide Indicators

For community outcomes, which capture the most common partnership goals, there is the potential to establish comparison (counterfactual) neighborhoods, communities, or cities. For this reason, evaluators have turned to community-wide indicators of social problems with the hope of finding comparable, reliable longitudinal data series. For comprehensive crime prevention initiatives, relevant databases can be found in public safety, physical and mental health, education, social welfare, and the workplace. Because most individual and community-level data are kept in agency records for non-evaluation purposes, the problems with reliability and validity, comparability across sites, efficiency, cost, and program relevance are substantial. There are also political obstacles to full access. Nevertheless, social scientists have managed to mine these data to evaluate comprehensive initiatives. Coulton (1995), for example, identifies a wide range of available community indicators in Cleveland, Ohio, that are useful for estimating the impact of a comprehensive program on children's well-being, including social, economic, health and developmental outcomes. I should note that in the United States, substantial routine information systems and national surveys are available in the public safety arena to capture rates of crime (e.g., UCR, NIBRS, NCVS) and drug use (e.g., ADAM, DAWN, NHSDA, Monitoring the Future).[5]

Coulton also offers a range of census and housing indicators for measuring community context, including socio-economic composition, age and family structure, residential mobility, and environmental stress. Interestingly, environmental stress is defined in terms of the number of vacant and boarded housing, housing code violations, personal crime, and drug arrests. As suggested earlier, evaluators of partnerships should seek to estimate the effects of contextual factors at different stages of the partnership model (Hollister and Hill, 1995). Several key questions can be addressed: (1) Do contextual variables have a direct effect on the composition and functioning of the partnership? (2) Do they have a direct effect on outcome measures, thus serving as plausible rival hypotheses? (3) Do they have indirect effects on outcome measures, thus working through partnership interventions? Unfortunately, many context variables are only measured once every decade as part of the census count, making it difficult to assess change.

I should emphasize that community indicators are not much help without an evaluation design or analysis plan. The interrupted time series design allows the evaluator to test whether the intervention "interrupts" a series of outcome measurement points that extends from pre- to post-implementation. Time series analysis controls for selection bias by having a single site serve as its own control, but it does not control for local historical events that may affect outcome scores. Hence, whenever possible, time series data for non-intervention sites should be collected to control for history. Looking at community indicators over time should help us to understand how complex environments, complex interventions, and multiple outcomes co-vary over time, thus contributing to theory advancement and casual inference.

Call for New Outcome Measures

As we enter the era of public safety characterized by community policing and partnership building, there is a compelling need to develop new measures of agency performance as a prerequisite for conducting a full-scale evaluation of partnerships. To a large extent, coalitions of service-providing agencies are difficult to evaluate when participating agencies use arcane systems to evaluate their own performance. For decades, law enforcement agencies (the lead agencies in most public safety partnerships) have been evaluated by the traditional measures of reported crime rates, total arrests, clearance rates, and response times. These indicators are grossly outdated and out of step with the new community paradigm. In the 21st century, a primary goal is to make government more responsive to neighborhoods and community residents, and to do so by strengthening the relationship between the police and the community (Alpert and Moore, 1993; Rosenbaum et al., 1998). Although effective crime fighting is still important, the community is insisting that policing be fair, just, equitable, responsive to their concerns, and even empowering. The fundamental problem is that we have no system of measurement in place to capture when and where this is happening. The municipal police are simply not accountable on the dimensions of safety that are important to the public.

I am proposing that a system of data collection be established in metropolitan areas capable of providing, on a regular basis, quantitative information about community residents' perceptions, attitudes, and behaviors regarding public safety at the neighborhood level. If New York City (and now dozens of U.S. cities) can use traditional crime statistics to hold police managers accountable for results on a monthly basis, then surely we can develop a similar system of accountability using more relevant outcomes, such as partnership building, community engagement in public safety initiatives, fear reduction, and (of increasing importance) greater public respect, trust, and confidence in the police.

I am pleased to see that consumer-oriented surveys are being used with greater frequency by law enforcement and government agencies. At present, however, their usage can be characterized as infrequent, irregular, unscientific, and narrowly focused. Skogan and his colleagues (e.g., Skogan and Hartnett, 1997) have illustrated the value of random probability samples for community policing evaluations, but these have been annual surveys at the city or neighborhood level. I am calling for police beat or district/precinct level data on a monthly, or at least, quarterly basis. Today the most cost-effective methodology is the telephone survey.[6] But with the rapid growth of information technology, and associated declines in response rates using telephone-based samples, we should begin to explore the utility of the Internet as a low-cost vehicle for Web-based citizen surveys and other public safety functions, such as crime reporting. The Chicago Police Department is embarking on a major technology initiative, which will be documented in a series of studies by Skogan and Hartnett at Northwestern University and by my colleagues and I at the University of Illinois at Chicago. In a few years, we will know much more about the feasibility and impact of new community-oriented data systems.

CONCLUSION

This article attempts to clarify some of the issues involved in the conceptualization and measurement of multi-agency partnerships, with specific application to public safety initiatives. Partnerships have been promoted as a promising vehicle for planning, coordinating, and executing complex, innovative social interventions. Hence, this article gives considerable attention to the measurement of partnership composition, dynamics, and decision making. I have also emphasized the importance of measuring context variables that may shape both partnership process and outcomes, and serve as plausible threats to causal inference.

While inputs, processes, and short-term outcomes are critical components of any evaluation, we cannot lose sight of the fact that partnerships are formed to alleviate specific social problems and are often expected to produce tangible long-term results. Furthermore, partnerships represent only one approach to social intervention (versus, for example, the independent actions of separate agencies). Hence, there is a compelling need to construct rigorous impact evaluations that will tell us whether partnerships play any role in reducing target outcomes, such as violent crime, fear of crime, or other quality-of-life indicators. I have suggested that such evaluations would include a mixture of strong research designs with counterfactuals, a theory (or theories) of change that includes both partnership and contextual variables, a mixture of quantitative and qualitative methods, and a case study framework for understanding the dynamics and external relationships of each partnership. Multisite comparisons will add substantially to our knowledge.

The complexity of inputs, processes, and outcomes associated with multi-agency partnerships should not be used as an excuse to avoid precision in conceptualization and measurement or to argue that "anything goes" when it comes to evaluation. The scientific standards by which we judge the validity of causal inferences have not changed simply because the phenomenon we are studying is more complex.

In the criminal justice field, partnerships have remained relatively simple. Despite the opportunity to create truly comprehensive partnerships, to date law enforcement agencies in the U.S. have not done so. Rather, they continue to focus on what they do best — catching the "bad guy." Public safety partnerships are typically dominated by law enforcement agencies and tend to focus on enforcement and order maintenance strategies, with limited attention to the role of community or other agencies in the prevention of crime. The theory of partnerships I have delineated here — involving multiple agencies

introducing multiple interventions at multiple levels of social influence — has not been tested.[7]

Whether integrated service delivery is a real possibility in public
safety remains to be seen. We have seen blueprints that outline an
array of interventions at different levels, such as the Justice Department's plan for a comprehensive approach to serious juvenile offending (Howell, 1995; Wilson and Howell, 1993). Indeed, several programs that fit within this type of inclusive model outlined here have
been shown to be effective at preventing youth violence under rigorous evaluation standards (see Mihalic et al., 2001). But only a few of
these delinquency prevention programs involve multi-agency partnerships and virtually all of the impact measures are individual-level
outcomes. Hence, we are left with little knowledge about the role of
the partnership itself in producing the observed results or whether
any effects occurred at other levels (e.g., organizations or communities). Documenting effects at other levels is essential for knowing the
probability that these innovations will be institutionalized. I have
suggested the importance of measuring the larger political, economic
and organizational environment in which the partnership operates.
This includes understanding the parent organizations and determining the extent to which their managers, policies, and employee cultures support the idea of multi-agency partnerships

Address correspondence to: Dennis P. Rosenbaum, Professor of Crimi-
nal Justice and Psychology, Department of Criminal Justice (M/C 141),
University of Illinois at Chicago, 1007 W. Harrison St. Chicago, IL 60607.
E-mail: <dennisr@uic.edu>.

REFERENCES

Aldrich, H.E. (1979). *Organizations and Environments.* Englewood Cliffs,
NJ: Prentice Hall.

Alpert, G.P. and M.H. Moore (1993). "Measuring Police Performance in
the New Paradigm of Policing." In: *Performance Measures for the
Criminal Justice System.* Washington, DC: Bureau of Justice Statistics, U.S. Department of Justice. (NCJ-143505.)

Bailey, A. (1986). "More than Good Intentions: Building a Network of Col-
laboratives." *Education and Urban Society* 19:7-23.

Benard, B. (1990). "An Overview of Community-Based Prevention." In: K.H. Rey, C.L. Faegre and P. Lowery (eds.), *Prevention Research Findings 1988*. Washington, DC: Office of Substance Abuse Prevention. (Monograph 3, DHHS Pub. No. [ADM] 89-1615.)

Braga, A.A., D.M. Kennedy and A.M. Piehl (1999). "Problem-Oriented Policing and Youth Violence: An Evaluation of the Boston Gun Project." Final Report submitted to the National Institute of Justice. Cambridge, MA: John F. Kennedy School of Government, Harvard University.

Bronfenbrenner, U. (1988). "Interacting Systems in Human Development: Research Paradigms Present and Future." In: N. Bolger, A. Caspi, G. Downey and M. Moorehouse (eds.), *Persons in Context: Developmental Processes*. New York: Cambridge University Press.

Buerger, M. (1994). "The Limits of Community." In: D.P. Rosenbaum (ed.), *The Challenge of Community Policing: Testing the Promises*. Newbury Park, CA: Sage.

Bursik, R.J. and H.G. Grasmick (1993). *Neighborhoods and Crime: The Dimensions of Effective Community Control*. New York, NY: Lexington.

Butterfoss, F.D., R.M. Goodman and A. Wandersman (1993). "Community Coalitions for Prevention and Health Promotion." *Health Education Research* 8:315-330.

Capowich, G.E. and J.A. Roehl (1994). "Problem-Oriented Policing: Actions and Effectiveness in San Diego." In: D.P. Rosenbaum (ed.), *The Challenge of Community Policing: Testing the Promises*. Thousand Oaks, CA: Sage.

Chavis, D.M., P. Speer, I. Resnick and A. Zippay (1993). "Building Community Capacity to Address Alcohol and Drug Abuse: Getting to the Heart of the Problem." In: R. C. Davis, A.J. Lurigio and D.P. Rosenbaum (eds.), *Drugs and the Community: Involving Community Residents in Combatting the Sale of Illegal Drugs*. Springfield, IL: Charles C Thomas.

—— P. Florin, R. Rich and A. Wandersman (1987). "The Role of Block Associations in Crime Control and Community Development: The Block Booster Project." Report to the Ford Foundation.

Chen, Huey-tsyh (1990). *Theory-Driven Evaluations*. Newbury Park, CA: Sage.

Clarke, R.V. (1995). "Situational Crime Prevention." In: M. Tonry and D.P. Farrington (eds.), *Crime and Justice: An Annual Review of Research* (vol. 19). Chicago, IL: University of Chicago Press.

Coffman, J. (1999). *Learning from Logic Models: An Example of a Family/School Partnership Program*. Cambridge, MA: Harvard Family Research Project (http://hugse1.harvard.edu/~hfrp).

Coldren, J.R., S. Kaminksa Costello, D. Forde, J.A. Roehl and D.P. Rosenbaum (2000). "The National Assessment of the Strategic Approaches to Community Safety Initiative (SACSI), Phase I Interim Report." Chicago, IL: Center for Research in Law and Justice, University of Illinois at Chicago.

Connell, J.P. and A.C. Kubisch (1998). "Applying a Theory of Change Approach to the Evaluation of Comprehensive Community Initiatives: Progress, Prospects, and Problems." In: K. Fulbright-Anderson, A.C. *Kubisch* and J.P. Connell (eds.), *New Approaches to Evaluating Community Initiatives: Theory, Measurement, and Analysis* (vol. 2). Queenstown, MD: The Aspen Institute

—— J.L. Aber and G. Walker (1995). "How Do Urban Communities Affect Youth? Using Social Science Research to Inform the Design and Evaluation of Comprehensive Community Initiatives." In: J.P. Connell, A.C. Kubisch, L.B. Schorr and C.H. Weiss (eds.), *New Approaches to Evaluating Community Initiatives: Concepts, Methods, and Contexts* (vol. 1). Washington, DC: The Aspen Institute.

—— A.C. Kubisch, L.B. Schorr and C.H. Weiss (eds.) (1995). *New Approaches to Evaluating Community Initiatives: Concepts, Methods, and Contexts*. Washington, DC: The Aspen Institute.

Cook, R.F. and J.A. Roehl (1993). "National Evaluation of the Community Partnership Program: Preliminary Findings." In: R.C. Davis, A.J. Lurigio and D.P. Rosenbaum (eds.), *Drugs and the Community: Involving Community Residents in Combatting the Sale of Illegal Drugs*. Springfield, IL: Charles C Thomas.

Cook, T.D. (2000). "The False Choice Between Theory-Based Evaluation and Experimentation." In: P.J. Rogers, T.A. Hacsi, A. Petrosino and T.A. Huebner (eds.), *Program Theory in Evaluation: Challenges and Opportunities*. San Francisco, CA: Jossey-Bass.

Coulton, C.J. (1995). "Using Community-Level Indicators of Children's Well-Being in Comprehensive Community Initiatives." In: J.P. Connell, A.C. Kubisch, L.B. Schorr and C.H. Weiss (eds.), *New Approaches to Evaluating Community Initiatives: Concepts, Methods, and Contexts* (vol. 1). Washington, DC: The Aspen Institute.

Crank, J. and R. Langworthy (1999). "An Institutional Perspective of Policing." Reprinted in: L.K. Gaines and G.W. Cordner (eds.), *Policing Perspectives: An Anthology*. Los Angeles, CA: Roxbury.

Crawford, A. (1997). *The Local Governance of Crime: Appeals to Community and Partnerships*. Oxford, UK: Oxford University Press.

Duffee, D.E., B.C. Renauer, J.D. Scott, S. Chermak and E.F. McGarrell (2001). "Measuring Community Building Involving the Police." (Final report to the National Institute of Justice.) Albany, NY: School of Criminal Justice, University at Albany.

—— R. Fluellen and B.C. Renauer (2000). "Community Variables in Community Policing." *Police Quarterly* 2:5-35.

Dunworth, T., G. Mills, G. Cordner and J. Greene (1999). *National Evaluation of Weed and Seed: Cross-Site Analysis.* Washington, DC: National Institute of Justice, U.S. Department of Justice.

Eck, J. E. and W. Spelman (1987). *Problem Solving: Problem-Oriented Policing in Newport News.* Washington, DC: Police Executive Research Forum.

Ellis, T.M. and S.J. Lenczner (2000). *Lessons from the Field: Community Anti-Drug Coalitions as Catalysts for Change.* Washington, DC: Community Anti-Drug Coalitions of America (info@cadca.org).

Farrington, D.P., R.J. Sampson and P.H. Wikstrom (1993). *Integrating Individual and Ecological Aspects of Crime.* Stockholm, Sweden: National Council for Crime Prevention.

Felson, M. (1998). *Crime and Everyday Life* (2nd ed.). Thousand Oaks, CA: Pine Forge Press.

Florin, P., D. Chavis, A. Wandersman and R. Rich (1992). "A Systems Approach to Understanding and Enhancing Grassroots Organizations: The Block Booster Project." In: H.E. Levine and R.L. Fitzgerald (eds.), *Analysis of Dynamic Psychological Systems.* New York, NY: Plenum Press.

Friedman, W. (1994). "The Community Role in Community Policing." In: D.P. Rosenbaum (ed.), *The Challenge of Community Policing: Testing the Promises.* Newbury Park, CA: Sage.

Fulbright-Anderson, K., A.C. Kubisch and J.P. Connell (eds.), (1998). *New Approaches to Evaluating Community Initiatives: Theory, Measurement, and Analysis* (vol. 2). Queenstown, MD: The Aspen Institute.

Giamartino, G. and A. Wandersman (1983). "Organizational Climate Correlates of Viable Urban Block Organizations." *American Journal of Community Psychology* 11:529-541.

Goldstein, H. (1990). *Problem-Oriented Policing.* New York, NY: McGraw Hill.

Granger, R.C. (1998). "Establishing Causality in Evaluations of Comprehensive Community Initiatives." In: K. Fulbright-Anderson, A.C. Kubisch and J.P. Connell (eds.), *New Approaches to Evaluating Community Initiatives: Theory, Measurement, and Analysis* (vol. 2). Queenstown, MD: The Aspen Institute.

Gray, B. (1985). "Conditions Facilitating Interorganizational Collaboration." *Human Relations* 38:911-936.

Greene, J.R. (2000). "Community Policing in America: Changing the Nature, *Structure*, and Function of the Police." In: J. Horney, J. Martin, D.L. MacKenzie, R. Peterson and D.P. Rosenbaum (eds.), *Policies,*

Processes, and Decisions of the Criminal Justice System. (Vol. 3, *Criminal Justice 2000* series.) Washington, DC: U.S. Department of Justice, National Institute of Justice.

—— W.T. Bergman and E.J. McLaughlin (1994). "Implementing Community *Policing*: Cultural and Structural Change in Police Organizations." In: D.P. Rosenbaum (ed.), *The Challenge of Community Policing: Testing the Promises.* Newbury Park, CA: Sage.

Guba, E.G. and Y.S. Lincoln (1985). *Effective Evaluation: Improving the Usefulness of Evaluation Results Through Responsive and Naturalistic Approaches.* San Francisco, CA: Jossey-Bass.

Hall, R., J. Clark, P. Giordano, P. Johnson and M. Van Roekel (1977). "Patterns of Interorganizational Relationships." *Administrative Science Quarterly* 22:457-473.

Halpern, R. (1994). *Rebuilding the Inner City: A History of Neighborhood Initiatives to Address Poverty in the United States.* New York, NY: Columbia University Press.

Hawkins, D.J., T. Herrenkohl, D.P. Farrington, D. Brewer, R. F. Catalano and T.W. Harachi (1998). "A Review of Predictors of Youth Violence." In: R. Loeber and D.P. Farrington (eds.), *Serious and Violent Juvenile Offending: Risk Factors and Successful Interventions.* Thousand Oaks, CA: Sage.

—— R.F. Catalano and J.Y. Miller (1992a). "Risk and Protective Factors for Alcohol and Other Drug Problems in Adolescence and Early Adulthood: Implications for Substance Abuse Prevention." *Psychological Bulletin* 112:64-105.

R.F. Catalano and Associates (1992b). *Communities that Care: Action for Drug Abuse Prevention.* San Francisco, CA: Jossey-Bass.

Heinz, J.P. and P.M. Manikas (1992). "Networks Among Elites in a Criminal Justice System." *Law and Society Review* 26:831-861.

Hollister, R.G. and J. Hill (1995). "Problems in the Evaluation of Community-Wide Initiatives." In: J.P. Connell, A.C. Kubisch, L.B. Schorr and C.H. Weiss (eds.), *New Approaches to Evaluating Community Initiatives: Concepts, Methods, and Contexts.* Washington, DC: The Aspen Institute.

Hope, T. (1995). "Community Crime Prevention." In: M. Tonry and D.P. Farrington (eds.), *Crime and Justice: A Review of Research* (vol. 19). Chicago, IL: University of Chicago Press.

—— (1994). "Problem-oriented Policing and Drug Market Locations: Three Case Studies." In: R.V. Clarke (ed.), *Crime Prevention Studies* (vol. 2). Monsey, NY: Criminal Justice Press.

Hopkins, R.H., A.L. Mauss, K.A. Kearney and R.A. Weisheit (1988). "Comprehensive Evaluation of a Model Alcohol Education Curriculum." *Journal of Studies on Alcohol* 49:38-50.

Hough, M. and N. Tilley (1998). *Auditing Crime and Disorder: Guidance for Local* Partnerships. (Crime Detection and Prevention Series Paper 91.) London, UK: Home Office.

Howell, J.C (ed.), (1995). *Guide for Implementing the Comprehensive Strategy for Serious, Violent, and Chronic Juvenile Offenders.* Washington, DC: Office of Juvenile Justice and Delinquency Prevention, U.S. Department of Justice.

ISA Associates (1993). *CSAP National Evaluation of the Community Partnership Demonstration Program: Third Annual Report.* Washington, DC: Center for Substance Abuse Prevention, U.S. Department of Health and Human Services.

Jencks, C. and S. Mayers (1990). "The Social Consequences of Growing Up in a Poor Neighborhood." In: L.E. Lynn and M.F.H. McGeary (eds.), *Inner-City Poverty in the United States.* Washington, DC: National Academy Press.

Jessor, R. and S.L. Jessor (1977). *Problem Behavior and Psychosocial Development: A Longitudinal Study of Youth.* New York, NY: Academic Press.

Johnson, C.A., M.A. Pentz, M.D. Weber, J.H. Dwyer, N.A. Baer, D.P. MacKinnon, W.B. Hansen and B.R. Flay (1990). "Relative Effectiveness of Comprehensive Community Programming for Drug Abuse Prevention with High-Risk and Low-Risk Adolescents." *Journal of Consulting and Clinical Psychology* 58:447-456.

Kandel, D., R. Kessler and R. Margulies (1978). "Antecedents of Adolescent Initiation into Stages of Drug Use: A Developmental Analysis." *Journal of Youth and Adolescence* 7:13-39.

Katz, D. and R.L. Kahn (1978). *The Social Psychology of Organizations.* New York, NY: John Wiley and Sons.

Kelling, G.L., M.R. Hochberg, S.L. Kaminska, A.M. Rocheleau, D.P. Rosenbaum, J.A. Roth and W.G. Skogan (1998). "The Bureau of Justice Assistance Comprehensive Communities Program: A Preliminary Report." Washington, DC: National Institute of Justice, U.S. Department of Justice.

—— A.M. Rocheleau, D.P. Rosenbaum, J.A. Roth, W.G. Skogan and N. Walsh (1997). "Preliminary Cross-Site Analysis of the Bureau of Justice Assistance Comprehensive Communities Program. Final report to the National Institute of Justice." Cambridge, MA: BOTEC Analysis Corporation.

Kim, S., C. Crutchfield, C. Williams and N. Hepler (1994). "An Innovative and Unconventional Approach to Program Evaluation in the Field of Substance Abuse Prevention: A Threshold-Gating Approach Using Single System Evaluation Designs." *Journal of Community Psychol-*

ogy (Center for Substance Abuse Prevention [CSAP] Special Issue):61-78.

Klitzner, M. (1992). Personal communication. Meeting of the Technical Assistance Committee to the National Evaluation of the Community Partnership Program, ISA Associates, February 27, 1992, San Diego.

—— (1993). "A Public/Dynamic Systems Approach to Community-wide Alcohol and Other Drug Initiatives." In: R.C. Davis, A.J. Lurigio and D.P. Rosenbaum (eds.), *Drugs and the Community: Involving Community Residents in Combatting the Sale of Illegal Drugs*. Springfield, IL: Charles C Thomas.

Kubisch, A.C., C.H. Weiss, L.B. Schorr and J.P. Connell (1995). "Introduction." In: J.P. Connell, A.C. Kubisch, L.B. Schorr and C.H. Weiss (eds.), *New Approaches to Evaluating Community Initiatives: Concepts, Methods, and Contexts*. Washington, DC: The Aspen Institute.

Lavrakas, P.J. (1985). "Citizen Self-Help and Neighborhood Crime Prevention Policy." In: L.A. Curtis (ed.), *American Violence and Public Policy*. New Haven, CT: Yale University Press.

Leventhal, T. and J. Brooks-Gunn (2000). "The Neighborhoods They Live In: The Effects of Neighborhood Residence on Child and Adolescent Outcomes." *Psychology Bulletin* 126:309-337.

Loeber, R. and M. LeBlanc (1990). "Toward a Developmental Criminology." In: M. Tonry and N. Morris (eds.), *Crime and Justice: A Review of Research* (vol. 12). Chicago, IL: University of Chicago Press.

Lurigio, A.J. and D.P. Rosenbaum (1986). "Evaluation Research in Community Crime Prevention: A Critical Look at the Field." In: D.P. Rosenbaum (ed.), *Community Crime Prevention: Does it Work?* Beverly Hills, CA: Sage.

Lyons, D. (1995). "Responsiveness and Reciprocity: Community Policing in Southeast Seattle." Paper presented at the 1995 Annual Meetings of the Law and Society Association, Toronto, Canada, June 1-4. Seattle, WA: University of Washington Department of Political Science.

Marris, P. and M. Rein (1967). *Dilemmas of Social Reform: Poverty and Community Action in the United States*. New York, NY: Atherton Press.

Maxfield, M.G. and E. Babbie (2001). *Research Methods for Criminal Justice and Criminology*. Belmont, CA: Wadsworth.

Mazerolle, L.G., J. Roehl and C. Kadleck (1998). "Controlling Social Disorder Using *Civil* Remedies: Results From a Randomized Field Experiment in Oakland, California." *Crime Prevention Studies* 9:141-159.

McElroy, J.E., C.A. Cosgrove and S. Sadd (1993). *Community Policing: The CPOP in New York*. Newbury Park, CA: Sage.

Mihalic, S., K. Irwin, D. Elliott, A. Fagan and D. Hansen (2001). *Blueprints for Violence Prevention.* (Juvenile Justice Bulletin [July].) Washington, DC: Office of Juvenile Justice and Delinquency Prevention, U.S. Department of Justice.

Miller, W.B. (1962). "The Impact of a 'Total Community' Delinquency Control Project." Social *Problems* 10:168-191.

Mizrahi, T. and B. Rosenthal (1993). "Managing Dynamic Tensions in Social Change Coalitions." In: T. Mizrahi and J.D. Morrison (eds.), *Community Organization and Social Administration: Advances, Trends, and Emerging Principles.* Binghamton, NY: Haworth Press.

Murray, D.M. and C.L. Perry (1986). "The Prevention of Adolescent Drug Abuse: Implications of Etiological, Developmental, and Environmental Models." In: C.L. Jones and R.J. Battjes (eds.), *Etiology of Drug Abuse: Implications for Prevention.* Washington, DC: U.S. Government Printing Office. (National Institute on Drug Abuse Research Monograph 56. DHHS Pub. No. [ADM] 86-1335.)

O'Conner, A. (1995). "Evaluating Comprehensive Community Initiatives: A View from History." In: J.P. Connell, A.C. Kubisch, L.B. Schorr and C.H. Weiss (eds.), *New Approaches to Evaluating Community Initiatives: Concepts, Methods, and Contexts.* Washington, DC: The Aspen Institute.

O'Sullivan, E. (1977). "Interorganizational Cooperation: How Effective for Grassroots Organizations?" *Group and Organizational Studies* 2:347-357.

Pawson, R. and N. Tilley (1997). *Realistic Evaluation.* Thousand Oaks, CA: Sage.

Pentz, M.A., J.H. Dwyer, D.P. MacKinnon, B.R. Flay, W.B. Hansen, E.Y. Wang and C.A. Johnson (1989). "A Multicommunity Trial for Primary Prevention of Adolescent Drug Abuse." *Journal of the American Medical Association* 261:3259-3266.

Prestby, J.E., A. Wandersman, P. Florin, R. Rich and D. Chavis (1990). "Benefits, Costs, Incentive Management and Participation in Voluntary Organizations: A Means to Understanding and Promoting Empowerment." *American Journal of Community Psychology* 18:117-149.

—— and A. Wandersman (1985). "An Empirical Exploration of a Framework of Organizational Viability: Maintaining Block Organizations." *Journal of Applied Behavior Science* 21:287-305.

Radosevich, M., L. Lanza-Kaduce, R. Akers and M. Krohn (1980). "The Sociology of Adolescent Drug and Drinking Behavior: A Review of the State of the Field." *Deviant Behavior* 1:145-169.

Ramirez, D., J. McDevitt and A. Farrell (2000). *A Resource Guide on Racial* Profiling *Data Collection Systems.* Washington, DC: U.S. Department of Justice.

Robinson, K.L. and S.J. Elliott (2000). "The Practice of Community Development Approaches in Heart Health Promotion." *Health Education Research* 15:219-231.

Roehl, J.A., R. Huitt, M.A. Wycoff, A.M. Pate, D.J. Rebovich and K.R. Coyle (1996). National *Process Evaluation of the Weed and Seed Initiative.* (Research in Brief series.) Washington, DC: National Institute of Justice, U.S. Department of Justice.

Rogers, P.J., T.A. Hacsi, A. Petrosino, T.A. Huebner (eds.) (2000). *Program Theory in Evaluation: Challenges and Opportunities.* San Francisco, CA: Jossey-Bass.

Rosenbaum, D.P. (2002). "Neighborhood Watch Programs." In: D. Levinson (ed.), *Encyclopedia of Crime and Punishment.* Thousand Oaks, CA: Sage.

—— (1998a). "The Use of Network Analysis for Understanding Citywide Anti-Crime Coalitions." Paper presented at the annual meeting of the American Society of Criminology, Washington, DC, November.

—— (1998b) "The Changing Role of the Police in North America: Assessing the Current Transition to Community Policing." In: J.P. Brodeur (ed.), *How to Recognize Good Policing: Problems and Issues.* Newbury Park, CA: Sage.

—— (ed.), (1994). *The Challenge of Community Policing: Testing the Promises.* Newbury Park, CA: Sage.

—— (1988). "Community *Crime* Prevention: A Review and Synthesis of the Literature." *Justice Quarterly* 5:323-395.

—— (1987). "The Theory and Research Beyond Neighborhood Watch: Is it a Sound *Fear* and Crime Reduction Strategy?" *Crime & Delinquency* 33:103-134.

—— (ed.) (1986). *Community Crime Prevention: Does it Work?* Beverly Hills, CA: Sage.

—— (forthcoming). "Drug Abuse Resistance Education (D.A.R.E.)." In: *Encyclopedia of Juvenile Justice.* Thousand Oaks, CA: Sage.

—— E. Hernandez and S. Jr. Daughtry (1991). "Crime Prevention, Fear Reduction, and the Community." In: W.A. Geller (ed.), *Local Government Police Management* (Golden Anniversary ed.). Washington, DC: International City Management Association.

—— S. Bennett, B. Lindsay and D.L. Wilkinson (1994). *Community Responses to Drug Abuse: A Program Evaluation.* Washington, DC: National Institute of Justice, U.S. Department of Justice.

—— and P.J. Lavrakas (1995). "Self-Reports about Place: The Application of Survey and Interview Methods to the Study of Small Areas." *Crime Prevention Studies* 4:285-314.

—— and S.J. Kaminska-Costello (1997). *Salt Lake City's Comprehensive Communities Program: A Case Study.* Cambridge, MA: BOTEC Analysis Corporation.

—— and G.S. Hanson (1998). "Assessing the Effects of School-based Drug Education: A Six-Year Multi-Level Analysis of Project D.A.R.E." *Journal of Research in Crime and Delinquency* 35:381-412.

—— A.J. Lurigio and R.C. Davis (1998). *The Prevention of Crime: Social and Situational Strategies.* Belmont, CA: Wadsworth.

Roth, J.A., J.F. Ryan, S.J. Gaffigan, C.S. Koper, M.H. Moore, J.A. Roehl, C.C. Johnson, G.E. Moore, R.M. White, M.E. Buerger, E.A. Langston and D. Thacher. (2000). *National Evaluation of the COPS Program: Title I of the 1994 Crime Act.* Washington, DC: National Institute of Justice, U.S. Department of Justice.

Sadd, S. and R. Grinc (1994). "Innovative Neighborhood Oriented Policing: An Evaluation of Community Policing Programs in Eight Cities." In: D.P. Rosenbaum (ed.), *The Challenge of Community Policing: Testing the Promises.* Newbury Park, CA: Sage.

Sampson, R.J. (1997). "Collective Regulation of Adolescent Misbehavior: Validation Results from Eighty Chicago Neighborhoods." *Journal of Adolescent Research* 12(2):227-244.

Schermerhorn, J., Jr. (1981). "Open Questions Limiting the Practice of Interorganizational Development." *Group and Organization Studies* 6:83-95.

Schuck, A.M. (2001). "Understanding the Role of Neighborhood in the Long-Term Criminal Consequences of Childhood Maltreatment." Dissertation prospectus submitted to the School of Criminal Justice, University at Albany.

—— and D.P. Rosenbaum (in press). *Promoting Safe and Healthy Neighborhoods: What Research Tells Us About Intervention.* (Prepared for the Aspen Institute Roundtable on Comprehensive Community Initiatives.) Washington, DC: The Aspen Institute.

—— and C.S. Widom (in press). "Childhood Victimization and Alcohol Symptoms in *Females*: Causal Inferences and Hypothesized Mediators." *Child Abuse and Neglect.*

Shadish, W.R., T.D. Cook and D.T. Campbell (2002). *Experimental and Quasi-Experimental Designs for Generalized Causal Inference.* Boston, MA: Houghton Mifflin.

Shaw, C.R. and H.D. McKay (1942). *Juvenile Delinquency and Urban Areas.* Chicago, IL: University of Chicago Press.

Sherman, L.W., D. Gottfredson., D. MacKenzie, J. Eck, P. Reuter and S. Bushway (1997). *Preventing Crime: What Works, What Doesn't, What's Promising.* Washington, DC: National Institute of Justice, U.S. Department of Justice.

Skogan, W.G. and S.M. Hartnett (1997). *Community Policing, Chicago Style.* New York, NY: Oxford University Press.

Spergel, I.A. (1990). "Youth Gangs: Continuity and Change." In: N. Morris and M. Tonry (eds.), *Crime and Justice: A Review of Research* (vol. 12). Chicago, IL: University of Chicago Press.

Thornberry, T.B., M.D. Krohn, A.J. Lizotte and D. Chard-Wierschem (1993). "The Role of Juvenile Gangs in Facilitating Delinquent Behavior." *Journal of Research in Crime and Delinquency* 30(1):55-87.

Tilley, N. (2000). "Problems, Policing, and Communities." Paper presented at the international conference on community policing research, Northwestern University, Chicago, Illinois, October, 2000.

U.S. Bureau of Justice Assistance (2001). *Comprehensive Communities Program: Program Account.* Washington, DC: U.S. Department of Justice. (NCJ 184955.)

—— (1996). *Comprehensive Communities Program: Update.* Washington, DC: U.S. Department of Justice. February 15.

U.S. President's Commission on Law Enforcement and Administration of Justice (1967). *The Challenge of Crime in a Free Society.* Washington, DC: U.S. Government Printing Office.

Wandersman, A., P. Florin, R. Friedmann and R. Meier (1987). "Who Participates, Who Does Not, and Why? An Analysis of Voluntary Neighborhood Associations in the United States and Israel." *Sociological Forum* 2:534-555.

Warren, R.L., S.M. Rose and A.F. Bergunder (1974). *The Structure of Urban Reform.* Lexington, MA: D.C. Heath.

Wasserman, S. and J. Galaskiewicz (eds.), (1994). *Advances in Social Network Analysis.* Newbury Park, CA: Sage.

—— and J. Galaskiewicz (eds.), (1993). "Advances in Sociology from Network Analysis." *Sociological Methods and Research* (Special Issue): 22(1).

Weiss, C.H. (1995). "Nothing as Practical as Good Theory: Exploring Theory-Based Evaluation for Comprehensive Community Initiatives for *Children* and Families." In: J.P. Connell, A.C. Kubisch, L.B. Schorr and C.H. Weiss (eds.), *New Approaches to Evaluating Community Initiatives: Concepts, Methods, and Contexts.* Washington, DC: The Aspen Institute.

—— (1972). *Evaluation Research: Methods for Assessing Program Effectiveness.* Englewood Cliffs, NJ: Prentice-Hall.

Whetten, D. (1981). "Interorganizational Relations: A Review of the Field." *Journal of Higher Education* 52:1-27.

Wilkinson, D. and D.P. Rosenbaum (1994). "The Effects of Organizational Structure on Community Policing: A Comparison of Two *Cities.*" In: D.P. Rosenbaum (ed.), *The Challenge of Community Policing: Testing the Promises.* Newbury Park, CA: Sage.

Wilson, J.J. and J.C. Howell (1993). *A Comprehensive Strategy for Serious, Violent, and Chronic Juvenile Offenders.* Washington, DC: Office of Juvenile Justice and Delinquency Prevention, U.S. Department of Justice.

Wilson, J.Q. and R.J. Herrnstein (1985). *Crime and Human Nature.* New York, NY: Simon and Schuster.

Yin, R.K. (1989). *Case Study Research: Design and Methods.* Newbury Park, CA: Sage.

NOTES

1. These changes should be interpreted with caution because law enforcement respondents were aware that the survey was funded by the COPS office, which provided funding for their community policing programs.

2. The conclusions are based on both qualitative field data and quantitative data from pre-post resident surveys and police crime data. However, no comparison group data were collected.

3. See Shadish, Cook and Campbell (2002, pp.9-12) for a discussion of the distinction between molar and molecular causation in the context of experimentation.

4. In partnership settings, researchers should bring a knowledge of the literature, but should ultimately respect the theory of action implicit or explicit in the action plan, however the members arrive at it. If their thinking is unclear about theory, the evaluator will need to facilitate the explication. Otherwise, the measurement plan will not correspond to the actual interventions.

5. Uniform Crime Reports (UCR); National Incident Based Reporting System (NIBRS); National Crime Victimization Survey (NCVS); Arrestee Drug Abuse Monitoring (ADAM); National Household Survey on Drug Abuse (NHSDA); Drug Abuse Warning Network (DAWN). See Maxfield and Babbie (2001) for an overview of these data bases.

6. I have previously argued that surveys are valuable for understanding the social ecology of crime prevention perceptions and behaviors in small

geographic areas (see Rosenbaum and Lavrakas (1995), and that surveys are essential for evaluating agency and program performance (Rosenbaum et al., 1991).

7. My comments about the absence of full-scale partnership evaluations should not deter researchers from studying various "pieces of the pie." Documenting the dynamics among partnership members, for example, or estimating the effects of a single partnership intervention are very worthy research objectives and should help to build a larger body of knowledge in this area.